Field Archaeology in Britain

Field Archaeology in Britain

JOHN COLES

METHUEN & CO LTD LONDON

First published 1972
by Methuen & Co Ltd
11 New Fetter Lane
London EC4P 4EE
Reprinted twice
Reprinted 1979

© 1972 John M. Coles

Printed in Great Britain at the
University Press, Cambridge

ISBN 0 416 76540 8

Contents

vi *Contents*

Preface

This small book has emerged as a result of a belief on my part that the student of archaeology should possess a guide to some of the techniques of observation and recording of the material remains of man's past, to the processes of their recovery and conservation, and to the aims and methods of archaeologists in treating the evidence. The growth of archaeology as a subject for study in Universities, in national and regional societies, in Extra-Mural and Adult Education courses, allied to the increasing number of excavations in this country, clearly indicates a growing interest in the past; it is the purpose of this book to provide some information, selective though it may be, for people who are sufficiently concerned about this aspect of human history actively to participate in the recovery and consideration of the evidence.

The book is not aimed at the professional archaeologist, who will direct and supervise the recovery of evidence through fieldwork or excavation, but at those who may wish to understand the techniques of archaeology, and the reasons behind them, who will on occasion assist in small- or large-scale excavations and field projects, or who will sometimes undertake their own fieldwork in the discovery and explanation of ancient features.

The book has six main sections. In the first, archaeology is described as a technique for the recovery of evidence, and the roles of archaeologists, amateur and professional, are briefly discussed. The second section considers the ways by which archaeological sites are discovered, through fieldwork, aerial photography and detection devices. There follows a section on the types and uses of maps in this country, and on the variety of simple surveying procedures which have been found useful in the recording of sites and field surveys; these procedures are presented in some detail as they are basic to the accurate recording of all kinds of evidence. A fourth section deals with excavation, and tries to describe the methods of digging, recording, sampling and conserving on a site; other chapters in this section discuss the differing ways in which sites are examined today, the organization of an excavation and the questions of labour relations and safety. The fifth, short, section outlines some of the ways by which archaeologists manipulate their evidence, to obtain the maximum amount of information from it. A final section briefly indicates how prehistoric archaeology is organized in Britain, and the kind of jobs that are likely to be available to students; the vital role of the amateur archaeologist in rescuing evidence of man's past behaviour in these islands is stressed.

The techniques that are described are applicable to most types of archaeological site in any area of human activity, but the illustrations have been restricted to prehistoric sites from England, Wales and Scotland. A list of some of these sites, chosen as examples of the application of the techniques described here, is given at the end of the book, following a general list of books that deal with archaeological approaches and procedures.

I am grateful to the following archaeologists who have given permission to reproduce illustrations from their reports: Mr L. Alcock and the Camelot Research Committee (fig. 12), Mr P. Ashbee (fig. 58), Miss M. Cra'ster (fig. 57), Miss E. Dowman (fig. 75), Mr P. Fowler (fig. 78), Miss A. Henshall (fig. 68), Professor S. Piggott (fig. 13, 59), Dr J. K. S. St Joseph (plates 1–4), Mr D. Simpson (fig. 4, 13, 59), Dr I. Stead (fig. 64), Dr M. Stewart (fig. 1), Dr G. Wainwright (fig. 62 and plate 6), the Society of Antiquaries of London (fig. 12, 62). All of the other drawings and photographs are the author's, sometimes redrawn from sources acknowledged in the captions.

Parts of the text have been read by a number of archaeologists and others, all of whom have made valuable comments and suggestions. I am grateful for this interest and assistance from

John Alexander, M.A., Ph.D., F.S.A., Department of Extra-Mural Studies, London University; Richard Atkinson, M.A., F.S.A., Department of Archaeology, University College, Cardiff; Elizabeth A. Dowman, B.A., London; Dick Feachem, M.A., M.Sc., F.S.A., Ordnance Survey, Southampton; E. T. Hall, D.Sc., Littlemore Scientific Engineering Company, Oxford; Hugh McKerrell, B.Sc., Ph.D., A.R.I.C., Research Laboratory, National Museum of Antiquities of Scotland, Edinburgh; L. P. Morley, Photographic Department, University Museum of Archaeology and Ethnology, Cambridge; Janice Price, B.A., Methuen; J. K. S. St Joseph, O.B.E., M.A., Ph.D., F.S.A., Committee for Aerial Photography, Cambridge; R. R. Shiach, C.Eng., F.I.C.E., Survey and Development Services, Edinburgh; Geoff Wainwright, B.A., Ph.D., F.S.A., Inspectorate of Ancient Monuments, Department of the Environment, London; Sister Pauline Willcox, S.R.N., O.N.C., Millfield School, Somerset. The whole text has been read by Bryony Orme, B.A., Department of History, University of Exeter, who has suggested various improvements, and to whom I extend my thanks. I also thank my wife Mona for her assistance during the preparation of the book, and for help in compiling the index.

I Prehistoric archaeology

1 Archaeology as a technique

Archaeology means different things to different people. To some it conjures up delicious thoughts of treasure, to others a more controlled but equally satisfying feeling of excitement as the past is revealed. To some who have experience of digging on extremely large sites it may recall tedious work as a very small cog in a very big machine, to others who have led or worked on small-scale projects it may bring painful memories of evidence misunderstood or destroyed through lack of experience or other circumstances.

Archaeology has existed as a subject of serious study for over a century, yet there still remain many definitions of the term, even if it is restricted to the field of prehistory. Prehistoric archaeology may be said to deal with extinct non-literate societies, but this is not to say that archaeologists are therefore entirely restricted in the type of evidence they can use; literary evidence may have survived from contemporary and adjacent societies which can illuminate prehistoric groups (for example, Iron Age communities recorded by classical writers), and ethnographic observations from the recent past can be used to explain aspects of ancient behaviour (for example, hunting methods of African non-agriculturists).

Even so, prehistoric archaeology suffers from the difficulties imposed by its very definition, that the societies with which it is concerned *are* extinct and have left an incomplete record of their organization and activities. It is one of the tasks of archaeology to recreate so far as is possible the events of the past, through the systematic accumulation of data and through the application of interpretive techniques.

Whether or not the aim of archaeology should be to project a simple backwards extension of history is debatable. Grahame Clark has said, 'It is often, and I think rightly, held that archaeology should not be counted as a separate field of study so much as a method of reconstructing the past from the surviving traces of former societies' (1957).[1] If so, it can be nothing more than a technique, and the archaeologist has been described as a technician who applies a set of established procedures to the surviving evidence both in the earth and above it. To this view there are several opponents, for whom Sir Mortimer Wheeler may speak, 'He is primarily a fact-finder, but his facts are the material records of human achievement; he is also, by that token, a humanist, and his secondary task is that of revivifying or humanizing his materials with a controlled imagination that inevitably partakes of the qualities of art and even of philosophy' (1956, 228). The lines are not, on reflection, all that divergent, and one might be said to carry on from the other.

Prehistoric archaeology is not prehistory, but exists as a scientific discipline, recovering and manipulating data that can yield information about human behaviour in the past. Beyond this, attempts can be made towards the ultimate 'revivification' of the data through the prehistorian's imagination, and here the scientific mantle of archaeology often falls away. The statement, 'But let us now ignore the "facts" which only tend to blur the truth and see if imagery can tell us more'[2] may be a somewhat uncontrolled exercise of the imagination, but it is legitimate, and necessary, to attempt to humanize the data, to bring them to life, wherever possible.

To do this, however, archaeologists should be equipped to study systematically to gain the evidence necessary for their objectives, and this must involve a set of procedures, learned, adaptive, and transmitted to all working on the problem. This need not mean that archaeologists are robots, methodically

[1] References thus quoted appear in the lists of books and articles at the end of this book.
[2] A. Davidson, Silbury Hill, in M. Williams (ed) *Britain. A Study in Patterns.* Research into Lost Knowledge Organization, London, 1971.

extracting information to be organized into behavioural patterns, but it does mean that they must be aware of the potential data to be gained through excavation and the application of interpretative methods. It is not good enough to recover evidence, however fragmentary, and not to ask questions of it; it is wrong to gather material for the sake of it alone, and not to seek to explain the reasons for its presence.

The achievement of prehistoric archaeology is that it provides a perspective for our own history and for our own behaviour. Its results may not be entirely pleasing to any ideas of the unique, possibly divine, character of man on earth, it may emphasize the less 'civilized' aspects of man, but it will also show up in bold relief the mainstream developments in the emergence of human culture as a thoughtful, adaptive and communicable state of existence. At a lower level, it can provide evidence about pre-historic communities that is more factual than historical docu-ments produced by contemporary or near-contemporary alien groups. 'The spade is indifferent to the opinions or prejudices which lay behind the objects it digs up' (de Paor 1967, 106). In the same vein, it can produce data about historically-documented societies whose records reflect major political, religious and economic events and completely ignore the human achievements of ordinary people. At any level and at any time, prehistoric archaeology can amplify our meagre knowledge of an ancient society by a single stroke, by a unique discovery, whether it be a great treasure or a single grain of wheat, that casts entirely new light upon the achievements of a community.

The limitations of prehistoric archaeology are not to be under-emphasized. The differing degrees of preservation of material remains may produce a distorted picture of human behaviour in the past; as an example, the non-survival or non-recogni-tion of vegetable materials on many archaeological sites, coupled with the excellent preservation of animal bones, may lead to false impressions about major food supplies and economic activities in prehistoric times. As another, the absence through decay of wooden remains from most sites in Britain inevitably tends to diminish the importance of wood and wood-working in the mind of the prehistorian. Equally, the archaeologist may not be equipped, materially or mentally, to recover all that *has* survived, or may not interpret correctly that which has been found (p. 233). Here sampling procedures (p. 217) are a start towards adequate recovery of potential evidence, and there is much to be said for leaving sites to the improved excavation techniques of posterity.

Finally, prehistoric archaeology recovers evidence of anonymous people, people with no names, either personal or tribal. No record survives of their language or their music, little of their leisure activities, less of their religion. No evidence of the relationship between selected individuals will survive except in unusual circumstances, and prehistoric archaeologists can rarely single out a particular person who made something of note, or who received special treatment, while alive, from his contemporaries. These limitations emphasize again the need for general vigilance on the part of archaeologists in recognizing and preserving evidence of all kinds.

In the past ten years the practice of archaeology, as a technique for recovery, has become more and more exacting, with ever greater precision in the application of procedures for dating and identification, with increasing sophistication of interpretive procedures and with an augmented sense of responsibility towards the evidence in the ground.[1] The days of nondescript and random excavation in barrows or on other visible prehistoric sites are happily drawing to an end, although some of the excavations of this character still in progress are disguised by the term 'rescue'. With the increase in technical know-how, and with the rapid rise of the explanatory approach to prehistoric remains, any participant in an archaeological operation must be fully aware not only of the potentialities of the site but also of his or her own capabilities; the latter is one of the subjects to be discussed under the heading of 'conscience' (p. 230).

Archaeologists need to be trained not only as technicians, but also as humanists, to understand and to explain the processes of behaviour that resulted in the deposition of the material remains undergoing examination. The technical procedures can be outlined, and experience will enhance the performance of these methods, by an *archaeologist*, but the other aspect cannot be neglected, and its acquisition is basic to a *prehistorian*.

[1] The historical development of archaeology, and its firm base on pioneering work done in the decades before 1960, are outside the scope of this book.

2 Roles in archaeology: the amateur and the professional

The roles of the amateur archaeologist and the professional archaeologist are not difficult to distinguish in Britain, if we can avoid the unpleasant and untrue connotations of amateur = inexperienced, professional = expert. Both should be expert in their own fields of participation, and the fact that one may make his or her living from the practice should not detract from the value of the other's contribution.

The organization and conduct of a competent field project in archaeology generally requires a variety of talents, a leader, specialists in various disciplines, supervisors who have experience in the field of study, and assistants who are generally called volunteers or, simply, workers, to distinguish them from the others. The relationship between these different groups of people on an archaeological site may be complex, and some aspects of this are considered later in addition to the following notes.

In a relatively large project, the workers' role is simple, to follow the instructions of their supervisor, to learn any necessary techniques from him or her, to gain an insight into the particular problems of the site through work, observation and thought. This holds true for both excavation and field studies where consistent walking and observation may be more important than the routine surveying or other procedures underway. But in both excavation and in field studies, the amateur will not generally be as efficient in workload as the professional who has all the help of his particular training and experience behind him. Where the amateur archaeologist cannot be touched for value is in his or her own geographical area. Only those people who live in or otherwise know a region intimately can be relied upon for consistent and accurate information about potential sites where inconsistencies in the geographical structure of the landscape may not be immediately apparent, or where traditional local activities may take place, or where local landowners may reveal data of importance to people known to them. Few professional archaeologists can possess such unrivalled knowledge about a particular area. For an amateur, starting fresh, such knowledge can be most easily obtained at a preliminary level through local societies and museums, but there is no substitute for *consistent* fieldwork. And there can be no doubt that the value of such work is in direct proportion to the qualities of observation and recording that the amateur may possess through training and experience.

The importance of such detailed area knowledge and systematic fieldwork can be emphasized by an assessment of the proportion of sites discovered in recent years in France, where it is estimated that 25 per cent of known archaeological sites have been discovered by accident, over 70 per cent by systematic search, and less than 5 per cent by the sophisticated techniques of aerial and magnetic surveys. For Britain, a personal estimate of these three avenues of discovery would greatly increase the percentage found both by aerial photography and by accident, but nevertheless there would remain a sizeable proportion of finds made through the exercise of good judgment and consistent presence in the field on the part of amateur archaeologists. Doubtless the advent of motorway archaeology (p. 251) will add to the achievements of systematic search in this country, and the burden of this task is borne almost solely by local amateur societies.

Another field in which the amateur can contribute substantially is in small research projects that may not be considered important enough for large-scale operations or any financial aid. This work generally consists of area surveys for particular types of site, such as this survey of circular enclosures (hut-circles) in east Perthshire (fig. 1), or a geographical study of selected and known material such as pots or stone axes; the purely typological studies of artefacts, of great value to archaeology, are of course open to both professionals and amateurs, and there are notable contributions made by the latter in British prehistory; but these are outside the scope of this book.

What the amateur should *not* undertake on his own is clear enough. No project should be initiated if there is little or no chance that it will be completed, or if it seems likely that the problems, whatever form they take, will be beyond comprehension and solution. The problem of the non-completion of archaeological work in this country is extremely large, although not as large as in France, and refers mainly to excavations rather than other field projects where destruction is not initiated by the spade (p. 210). Some excavations in Britain are physically not completed, either

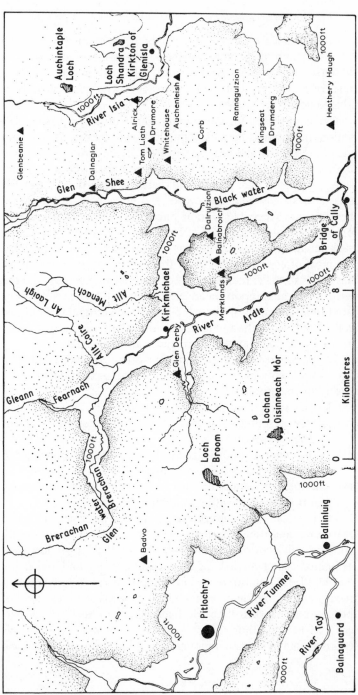

Fig. 1 Distribution map of circular enclosures (triangles) in eastern Perthshire; part of field survey 1957–60 to show the density and positioning of such enclosures in areas now of restricted agricultural value (after Stewart 1962).

because finance or, more usual, labour, dries up (through an excess of rainfall or cold weather), and some of this work is initiated by amateurs who do not acknowledge the potential interest and support of the local societies who might have been able to help finish the work.

The main reason for the preponderance of uncompleted excavations in Britain is the lack of publication of the results, and here again amateurs must bear some of the blame. Many sites have been excavated by professional archaeologists who steadfastly refuse to publish their results, and there can be no justification for this; at best, however, the records and finds, hopefully comprehensible, are accessible in some public institution, be it museum or university department. The amateur, however, may not have such inbuilt protection, and privately held notebooks and finds are most often irretrievably lost through the passage of time. It has been estimated that the study of material and records, and the writing of a final report on an excavation, will take about two or three times as long as the actual digging; such estimates should be considered before the amateur, who after all presumably earns his or her living doing another job, undertakes any excavation.

The possibility of a purely amateur-organized and -conducted excavation being successfully concluded can be considered under the following headings:
(1) are adequate funds and labour available?
(2) are the techniques for the recovery and conservation of the evidence adequate?
(3) is there enough knowledge available to allow the evidence to be interpreted in the field and afterwards?
(4) will there be sufficient time and energy left to study and report on the excavation in publishable form?

The prospect of treasure, however, is not to be dispelled by such reasoning, and doubtless many secretive excavations and tomb-robbing will continue in this country. In Belgium it has been estimated that over half of all excavations are undertaken by 'unqualified dilettanti, or by surreptitious excavators who often have no other aim than to enrich their collections with a sherd of pottery or a worked flint' (de Laet 1957, 79). Such a high percentage of unauthorized excavations does not exist in this country, but a certain amount does, and conscientious local amateur archaeologists are likely to be the only people who have a chance of discovering the extent of the damage and halting it through local society or museum action; this may not be considered to be one of the more pleasant tasks of an amateur archaeologist.

A field of prehistoric archaeology in which amateurs and professionals tend to part company abruptly is that sometimes described as 'dotty archaeology' or 'the lunatic fringe'. In a country so abundant with prehistoric monuments, barrows and cairns, stone circles and standing stones, impressive forts and embanked enclosures, there has accumulated a body of opinion that concerns itself with alignments and positions of stones or trackways or field boundaries, themselves entirely legitimate areas for research; sometimes, however, these are considered as evidence for extraordinary, almost supernatural, events, involving not only migrations of unlikely tribes but also mystic and cavernistic presences such as are completely and utterly unrecorded by any scientifically observable evidence. The definition of archaeology as 'the unwarrantable deduced from the unverifiable' seems appropriate here, and one can only regret that so many imaginative processes are expended in this field.

Perhaps the greatest achievement of amateur archaeologists in Britain is the enthusiasm and interest they bring to a subject that may tend to be difficult, dry and tedious at times. Most fieldwork is physically hard, and a professional or amateur can expend much energy in directing or assisting on an excavation. Similarly, in studying the remains and writing the report, there is a large quantity of detailed information to be assessed, and in some cases the volume of this is quite beyond comprehension; individual examination of 20 000 potsherds or flints may serve as an example, and not an excessive one.

'There *is* a romance in digging, but for all that it is a trade wherein long periods of steady work are only occasionally broken by a sensational discovery, and even then the real success of the season depends, as a rule, not on the rare "find" that loomed so large for the moment, but on the information drawn with time and patience out of a mass of petty detail which the days' routine little by little brought to light and set in due perspective.'[1]

[1] C. L. Woolley, *Dead Towns and Living Men*. Cape, London, 1932.

To this the amateur archaeologist can bring dedication, interest and enthusiasm, and these will be a constant source of encouragement to the professional who is concerned with problems of approach, technique and adaptive procedures as the work progresses. There is no reason why both amateur and professional should not share in the momentary thrill of discovery, but it is essential that they do share in the *real* romance of archaeology, which is found in piecing together the past, in the excitement of following the processes of recovery and intepretation through to the writing of prehistory and the explanation of human behaviour.

II Discovery of the evidence

1 Discovery of sites by fieldwork

It is difficult to generalize about the methods used in the discovery of archaeological sites. Sites vary in their physical characteristics, their state of preservation and in their environmental setting, and where one site may be readily apparent to all, another of the same type may be entirely disguised through decay or cloaked by vegetation.

The first requirement for any archaeologist who sets out actually to discover ancient sites is an understanding of the geographical features of the area. A person who is familiar with a region in different seasons and at different times will soon learn what is entirely natural to the area, the line of the hills, the angle of growth of the trees and shrubs, the sources of water, the spread of low vegetation. There is only one way by which this familiarity with an area can be achieved, and this is by walking over the ground, where irregularities on surface features can be noted and questioned.

The archaeologist must train himself to search for the unusual elements in this landscape. Differential growth of vegetation may not be apparent at all times of the year, but observation will soon tell if such a feature appears in times of drought or flood. An unusual contour on a hill, a slight hump or depression on a slope, may also become apparent through consistent observation over time and in different lights; a low sun, for instance, may suddenly throw up in highlight or shadow the existence of a physical feature not otherwise recognizable to the eye. Shallow floodwaters or light snow will do the same. Slight changes in soil colours are also a guide to the former alteration of the land, and may only be apparent at certain seasons and in certain conditions, where different rates of crop growth may also be apparent from the ground as well as from the air. Such unusual features as these are a first hint to the archaeologist that something is not natural to the scene, and further investigation can then take place.

One of the primary sources for the discovery of sites is natural or artificial erosion of deposits, through river or stream action, or through human interference. Running waters erode and deposit material, and constantly expose and mask other geological features. Consistent search is the only appropriate way by which an archaeologist can utilize such agencies, as a single ancient feature such as a pit may only be revealed for an extremely short time before being completely removed by continuing erosion. Features such as ditches will not disappear as rapidly, but delay again will lose potentially valuable evidence.

Of far greater significance to the archaeologist in particular, and to prehistory in general, is human interference with the landscape. Excavations in towns and cities for buildings and car parks destroy archaeological evidence incredibly fast, and the use of heavy earth-moving machinery on roads and motorways, in bridge-building, in pipe-laying and in gravel extraction processes, also lead to once-only, unique, opportunities to record features almost as they vanish (p. 251). Nonetheless, such chances to observe and record, sometimes to excavate, should not be missed by the archaeologist. The illustration (fig. 2) shows part of a Bronze Age cemetery and Neolithic settlement at Grantully, Perthshire; pipe-laying operations in 1965 produced a trench that was inspected just before it was filled in, and this inspection led to the discovery of the site subsequently excavated (see plate 7).

In any form of fieldwork involving the search for ancient sites, library and museum studies should feature at an early stage. Maps of the area should be consulted for the location of remains recorded by the Ordnance Survey (p. 52), and museum records and notes in the local society's journal should also be incorporated in the gradual build-up of knowledge about the area. Local land-owners and occupiers should be consulted about possible sites and areas that seem worth particular attention; ploughmen and especially shepherds are the best sources of information about unusual features. At the same time as this personal contact is made with landowners and tenants, permission must be obtained for access to the land. Most farmers and others readily give permission for a search, subject to the usual commonsense rules about crops and gates, and it is essential that archaeologists should respect the land and its occupants. The goodwill that

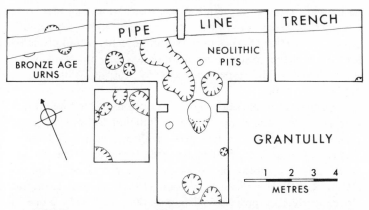

Fig. 2 Exploratory excavation of area around pipe-line trench at Grantully, Perthshire, 1966; Bronze Age urns discovered in trench sides, 1965. For area excavation of this site, 1967, see plate 7.

tends to build up over a period of time between landowners and archaeologists, leading often to the receipt of interesting data on both sides, can be dissolved by a single stroke of carelessness, a trampled crop, an escaped animal, a pile of litter. The effect is not limited to the person responsible, and future prospective archaeologists and naturalists may be surprised by their welcome.

Through the observation of geological features and processes, through adequate search of the records, through local information, the archaeologist can start his search for ancient sites with a good body of evidence already to hand, and in this country it is unlikely that from all these sources he would begin work with absolutely no clue as to the possible location of remains. The next logical step would be to gain an acquaintance, however nodding, with the sort of material likely to be encountered. This is not only the structural features on the ground, but also the small artefacts, the implements and other equipment, that may be exposed on the ground through erosion or the activities of animals and plants. At this stage we should distinguish between the general search for ancient remains of all periods and types, and the particular search for traces of activity of certain groups. There is a difference, for example, between the likely positions of farmsteads and hunters' camps; the former would tend to be larger in size, and sited near or on arable land, the latter would be smaller, less permanent, types of structure placed near water supplies or in passages between hills where game might move. Systematic search for particular types of burial monuments would probably lead the archaeologist into local topographical situations where monuments of this type were already known to have been deliberately built.

A number of publications give descriptions of the major types of prehistoric sites in this country, with illustrations of actual surviving monuments in relatively intact and in decayed states. Such descriptions are nowhere consistently gathered together, but useful surveys appear in works by Corcoran (1966), Thomas (1960), Feachem (1963) and Wood (1963), as well as in the Ordnance Survey professional papers (No. 13, 1963). None of these have over-abundant illustrations, and in any case there can be no substitute for the actual inspection of known monuments as a guide to the recognition of ancient features. The principal surviving prehistoric monuments in England have been listed and briefly described in Thomas' book (1960), and those for Scotland by Feachem (1963), and the amateur archaeologist should be familiar with the material in his own area.

The recognition of the debris of occupation or other activity should also be a part of the archaeologist's preparation. From the geographical features noted above, likely areas of activity may be singled out, and then inspection for other remains can be carried out. Small fragments of pottery or stone are the most likely to have survived the processes of decay, and the archaeologist should be aware of the types of small artefacts, for recognition and collection at first, and for study and comparison afterwards. Potsherds from the Neolithic, Bronze and Iron Ages in Britain may not be immediately recognizable as anything of real value, as they may be black or brown, rough and friable, crumbling with frost or rain; on the other hand, other pieces may be extremely well-preserved and at once attractive to the collector. Familiarity with previous finds from the area, available in the local museum, is essential for the recognition of such material, and for the awareness that not all potsherds are necessarily prehistoric if they have been collected from the earth. A glance at the 'midden' at the bottom of the garden, or in a farmer's yard or manured field, will soon disabuse anyone of the belief that modern material is not abundantly represented almost anywhere. It is a useful if unnerving exercise to inspect and excavate one's own 'dump' after a period of accumulation of non-flammable rubbish. And after centuries of carting manure out from a village and spreading it upon the neighbouring fields, the surface finds made are likely to represent a jumble of interests and periods of activity, with no doubt potsherds of all ages including the ubiquitous 'willow pattern'.

Stone fragments are the other type of debris that may be represented in some quantity on ancient sites. Chips of various stones, including flint, may be a guide to the presence of ancient activity, but some study is required on the part of the archaeologist before he accepts these as of human production. Many areas of Britain possess enormous natural deposits of flints, quantities of which are chipped by water or frost action and the archaeologist should be aware of the possibility of finding naturally deposited flint or other stone on his suspected sites. He should also be conversant with the types of fracture that occur on flint, and be able to separate thermal from mechanical fracture; useful guides to this appear in Oakley (1952) and Watson (1950), and the archaeologist will not only save himself time but also embarrassment if he can competently sort his material before landing it upon an overworked museum curator. He should also be aware that the ordinary flint-knapping site is likely to yield proportions of waste chips to finished implements in the order of 200 : 1 or thereabouts, if in fact the implements were left on the site.

Other types of stone fragments that may be significant include fire-crackled or burnt pieces which, if visible in quantity, may indicate the presence of ancient cooking-places or sites of other activities involving the heating of stones; a search for potsherds should be carried out here with particular care.

In fieldwork involving a systematic search for stone or other small artefacts, the weather plays a large part. Freshly ploughed soil tends to cling to material and disguise its presence, but rain will often provide the right conditions for recognition of pottery and flints glistening in the light.

A prerequisite to any fieldwork of this character is the provision of adequate maps (p. 52) and the facilities for recording sites and other finds on them (p. 117). The proper use of maps will generally impose some sense of order on even the most absent-minded archaeologist, in the delimiting of areas for search and in the even coverage of the ground. All areas should be inspected, even the most uninviting, as sites are quite as liable to repose within a wood or beneath a piggery as standing proud on an open field. It should not be necessary to emphasize that the work should be done on foot, or at worst (or best?) on horseback, and not from a car or other mechanically propelled vehicle. Distribution maps of sites that run conveniently along road systems should always be suspect in this country, at least until they have been checked by fieldwork in the peripheral areas, and it is an interesting exercise on a winter's night to overlay a road network on a linear or spider-like distribution of ancient sites.

Grid and system walking
The area, then, must be covered completely, and to do this it is probably useful to operate a grid and system walk procedure. By this, the area to be covered is divided into sectors on the map, using visible boundaries such as fences, ditches and woodland as convenient divisions (e.g. fig. 3). Each sector then is systematically searched, either by a single archaeologist operating on a strictly controlled series of lines (a miniature grid within the sector), or, better, by a small group moving at a uniform pace over the sector so that no areas are missed; the boundaries should be inspected on all occasions they are used as sector edges. Only in this way can some assurance be gained that all the area has been searched, that all the plough furrows or molehills have been looked at, that all the visible and recognized features have been noted. Another advantage of this sytem is that where time is a problem, the

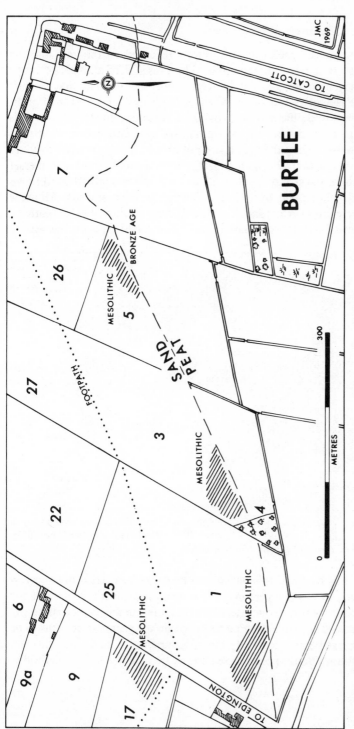

Fig. 3 Map of fields on sand and peat at Burtle, Somerset. Grid and system walk procedure, 1969–70, yielded four Mesolithic settlements on edge of sand island, and other finds.

sectors searched can be carefully recorded on the map and the others left for another time. The presence of animals or crops may hold up the search over certain sectors. The line of least resistance is too often taken in fieldwork, and well-trod paths employed; the system provides a reminder not to fall into this habit. Of course, the best-organized grid and system walk is of no use if the participants are not able to recognize what they are looking for. The map (fig. 3) shows a small area in Somerset where a grid and system walk in 1969 revealed hitherto-unknown Mesolithic and Bronze Age sites on the edge of a fen. All areas were numbered, and large fields were divided by footpath or fen-sand borders into more easily controlled areas for the search.

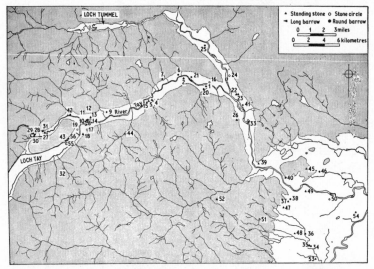

Fig. 4 Distribution map of Neolithic and Early Bronze Age monuments in Strathtay, Perthshire; field survey 1964. Stipple indicates land over 500 ft O.D. (from Coles and Simpson 1965).

Fieldwork of this nature can probably be carried out successfully by a single person, but for many reasons it is preferable for a team of two to operate. More than this number can occasionally cause disorganization not only within the group, over areas to be covered and recorded, but also upon the land, and farmers without doubt prefer to see one or two archaeologists methodically working over the land rather than a horde of people moving apparently at random. Another disadvantage in a large team is the inevitable multiplied delay when one or another member makes a 'find' and stops to record it. It is better to form independent teams of two from a larger group for most fieldwork. The result of a season of such an organized search for field monuments appears in fig. 4; many of the sites shown on this map of Strathtay in Perthshire were already known, but a proportion were new discoveries. The linear nature of the distribution is admitted, but the preference for river terraces for the building of these structures seems assured.

Equipment

The equipment necessary for fieldwork of the sort described above is relatively simple, and is dependent upon the requirements of the survey which might be divided as follows:

(1) Accurate recording of sites upon the map (p. 120)
>   maps and aerial photographs
>   60 metre tape
>   prismatic compass
>   ruler and protractor

(2) Record of the features of the site (p. 117)
>   10 metre tape (optional), or 60 metre as above
>   3 metre spring tape
>   hand level
>   metric grid paper (1 mm squares), board and pins
>   camera, exposure meter, scale

(3) Collection of geological and other samples (p. 217)
>   stout plastic bags
>   wire closures
>   metal labels and stylo or pencil (H)
>   trowel

(4) Collection of prehistoric or other material exposed (p. 45)
>   medium-weight plastic bags
>   wire closures
>   metal labels and stylo or pencil

(5) General equipment
>   pencils, eraser, knife, first-aid kit
>   notebook for all observations and measurements

2 knapsacks, one for equipment, one for samples
(food should be kept apart from the samples, in case of
reciprocal contamination).

In addition to this equipment, it has been found useful in certain
situations to prepare a record card upon which all relevant features
can be entered; the advantage of such a card is that it reminds the
archaeologist of questions that he might later wish to ask and
answer. A multiple-entry card of this nature might look as follows,
but could be altered to suit local requirements:

1. Site name (convenient identifiable name)
2. Location (National Grid Reference to 8 places)
    (Parish or other local designation, and county)
3. Elevation (approximate, from contours on map)
4. Landowner   Address
    Occupier   Address
    Former owner/occupier   Address
    Attitude (towards archaeology)
5. Description of site (with sketch)
    Dimensions (including height, depth)
6. Local environment
    Outlook (if on slope)
    Vegetation (immediate and adjacent)
    Water supplies (type and distance)
    Soils (superficial and subsurface)
    Adjacent features (other sites, quarries, etc.)
7. Disturbance (present condition of site)
    Threatened
8. Special features (local record of finds, peculiar structural
    features, etc.)
9. Small finds on surface   Position
    from eroded areas   Position
10. Samples taken, and reason for them Position
                                        Position
11. Photographs (details of direction)

12. Publications
13. Date of record
14. Recorded by

2 Discovery of sites by aerial photography

Aerial photography has without question made the greatest
contribution of any method yet devised to the discovery of
archaeological sites in Britain. A large proportion of these sites
are of the historic period, but hundreds and hundreds of sites of
pre-Roman times have also been shown to exist through aerial
reconnaissance and photography.

Aerial photographs of archaeological sites were taken in the
first decades of this century, at a time when the potentialities of
the distant viewpoint provided by an aircraft were already being
realized through the use of photographs for geographical
research. Careful study of aerial photographs taken during the
1914–1918 War provided an opportunity to interpret features not
only of enemy activity but also of more ancient origin, and from
this point the theory of aerial photography as a source for the
discovery of archaeological sites emerged.

The technique depends upon the character of the remains.
Features in relief such as banks and ditches, mounds and walls,
are visible on the ground, but an observer is unlikely to pick out
minute depressions or elevations from a vantage point which may
be either too close to the feature to see it in perspective or too far
from the feature to recognize its existence. The aerial camera with
ordinary film will be unlikely to disclose sites invisible to the
naked eye, as in all, or almost all, cases, features picked out from a
distant overhead viewpoint will be observable on the ground
once the site is known to exist; the last is the crucial element.

It should be pointed out here that it is not the photographs that
disclose the sites, but the acute eye of an observer. The photographs merely record the sites after they have been found by an
observer who has the knowledge and experience to recognize
them from the aircraft. The aerial photographs that are published

tend to be of very clearly defined sites, but many sites are barely recognizable even under good conditions. And many sites that have been discovered from the air have not been photographed due to bad conditions of one sort or another.

Shadow sites

Sites that survive as low banks or mounds, or shallow depressions, are recognized from the air through a careful choice of the conditions for photography, in times of the season and of the day when the sun will cast lengthened shadows from extremely slight elevations of the ground, or will shade a shallow depressed area; oblique sunlight, available in early morning or late evening, and at different times of the year, emphasizes relief (plate 1). Once a hint is obtained that a feature thus revealed may be important, the build-up of a set of aerial photographs using different angles of light and viewpoint may allow an accurate assessment of the nature and scale of the feature. Such sites are called 'shadow sites'. A useful example of this is provided by the ancient field systems that still survive, although in a much reduced state, in parts of southern England; careful selection of the angle of lighting and the viewpoint of the observer can reveal fields separated by low banks, sometimes with associated partly sunken trackways leading to embanked farmsteads or other enclosures.

It is not only shadow that reveals the existence of these sites, but also light reflected towards the observer by the angle of the feature such as a sloped ditch or mound side. A light fall of snow, slightly drifted, may also accentuate the relief of low banks or ditches, not only to an observer in the air, at relatively low altitude, but also on the ground where he may be acting as ground control. Water will also help to emphasize the depressed features of a site, and many a ploughed-out barrow has been recognized or clarified by this. Frost is a particularly useful phenomenon for providing contrasts between elevated and depressed areas of a site both through differential frost thickness and through unequal rates of melting on disturbed and undisturbed ground. All of these aspects are available for observation and recording at appropriate times, but the archaeologist must be there to take advantage. The theory is clear, the practice takes organization and effort.

Soil sites

Even more sites have been discovered in Britain by the recognition of soil differences. Modern agricultural procedures with the deep ploughing of arable land, and the clearance of less favourable areas for the introduction of cultivation, tend in time to reduce ancient earthworks to a uniform level, so that no features remain to cast shadows. Other sites of great antiquity may already have been levelled in any number of ways, so that no elevations, however minute, remain to guide the searcher.

The levelling of such features will not, however, result in uniformity of the soil either upon or beneath the surface, where the plough or bulldozer has neither penetrated through nor entirely removed or mixed the archaeological deposits. Patterns in the bare soil or in the vegetation will remain or develop as a result of the continued existence of such contrasting deposits as anciently disturbed or altered earth and unaltered virgin soil around the site (plate 2). Several examples may be noted here, taken mainly from the chalklands of southern England where freshly ploughed land provides extremely good conditions for the recognition of 'soil sites'. A ploughed-out barrow, for instance, may appear as a circular area of white chalk representing (the lower part of) the body of the mound, ringed by a darker circle produced through the earthen fill of the original quarry ditch; of course the ploughing away of the mound will have spread the chalk around the area so that the contrast may be reduced. In the siltlands of East Anglia, the same contrast will be available to the observer, the light-coloured silts of the mound being distinctly unlike the peaty fill of the ditch.

Different and perhaps more interesting types of site are the small plots of arable ground worked in the Bronze and pre-Roman Iron Ages. These low banks of chalk dividing small fields have mostly now been destroyed, but are still recognizable by the contrast between the spread of chalk from the field-banks and the ordinary soils; the distant vantage point provided by aerial photography is of course essential here.

Crop sites

Such soil differences are revealed by ploughing, and thereafter these will be masked by the growing vegetation, and it is here that aerial observation has made its greatest number of discoveries. Vegetation is dependent to a great extent upon soil, and differences in the character of the latter will affect the growth of the former. Increased depth of soils with greater organic content (p. 183), such as occur in silted-up ditches, pits, scoops and hollows, will encourage the growth of certain crops, including grasses; in contrast the adjacent shallower less-disturbed soils will support less dense and shorter vegetation (plate 3).

The reverse effect is also present, where ancient stony deposits, the remains of paved areas within and around houses, metalled roadways, the lower courses of stone walls, or internal packed clay floors, will generally prove to be impenetrable by roots, or will not hold as much moisture for the crop. The result is less dense and shorter, relatively stunted growth when compared with the neighbouring crop, whether this be upon unaltered ground, or, more spectacularly, upon deeper organic soils.

The effects of increased or decreased depth and character of the supporting soil are complex, and the above notes should be considered only as a general statement of the theoretical basis for the use of such 'crop sites' as sources of discovery. Different types of soil will yield somewhat different results, mostly in measure rather than character, in its effect upon crops growing in the situations noted above. The type of vegetation under observation is also crucial. Long-rooted cereals such as oats, barley and wheat, are particularly suitable; root crops such as turnip or sugar-beet are, logically, not affected to anything like the degree of the cereals (plate 4), but can yield on occasion interesting results. Grasses for grazing or haying are disappointing in normal growing conditions in this country, and do not often have significant and observable differential growth patterns.

Of the greatest importance is the weather, for a dry season will yield results far greater in quantity than would normally be imagined. An example is given below, but it is certainly worth noting here that a period of drought, accompanied by relatively high temperatures, may well produce information in quantity and in quality of precision that could never be achieved in a long run of normal years. The latter half of the growing season in Britain, generally between late May and early July, is the period where weather conditions are likely to be at their best for crop observations, and if a dry phase develops, the conditions are likely to be adequate and possibly exceptional. What is required here is a consistent observation pattern, to see the crops develop until the optimum condition is reached when the darker and taller growth of vegetation over buried ditches and depressions is most apparent; shadow sites may emerge from this. Later in the growing season, such local dark effects may persist as the adjacent crop ripens and turns yellow.

The essential point that must be made here, and accepted by archaeologists who wish to utilize such tremendous opportunities as are offered through aerial observation, is that of repeated reconnaissance. Agricultural rotation may, over a period of years, bring suitable crops into most fields within a given group, and by building-up a series of observations through photography the archaeologist may be able to complete his jigsaw and interpret the individual pieces of evidence available at different times.

The major contribution to archaeological aerial photography in the past twenty years has been made by Dr J. K. S. St Joseph, Director in Aerial Photography in the University of Cambridge. One of the best examples of the value of consistent air coverage, and also of the rapid advance in knowledge through a single exceptional season, is provided by Dr St Joseph's work on round barrows in a small area of north-east Essex and east Suffolk. Up to 1959, about 50 such barrows had been recorded on Ordnance Survey maps, producing an extremely localized distribution pattern (fig. 5); in the drought of 1959, and in subsequent seasons' work, aerial reconnaissance revealed the existence of an additional 200 barrows, an increase of 400 per cent, with an accompanying alteration in distribution pattern (fig. 5) which needs no comment here. The flying-time involved was no more than a few hours in total, but the work was done at the right times over several years.

Of course, certain areas cannot be searched from the air by ordinary methods. Towns and villages overlie ancient remains whose existence cannot be discovered in this way, and woodland and farmsteads also obscure potential areas. One estimate of the quantity of land in England thereby made unavailable for aerial search is as high as 25 per cent, and for these areas there is no substitute for fieldwork.

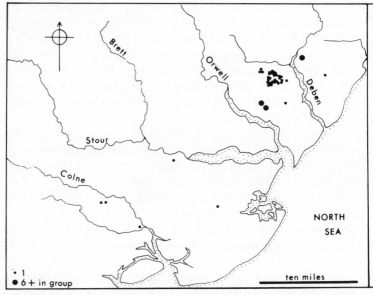

Fig. 5 Distribution map of barrows in north-east Essex and east Suffolk. Left, as known in spring 1959. Right, as known in 1965. The increase in

Equally, not all visible marks on an aerial photograph need represent ancient disturbances or activities. Fungus rings may look like ploughed-out barrow ditches; wartime manœuvres and constructions, temporary motorcycle racetracks, dismantled hen-houses, and so on, may leave marks resembling ancient features and many of these have misled archaeologists of all degrees of experience. What is required in these suspected or uncertain cases is firm ground control, field observation and recording, local information of likely events, continued aerial surveillance. It is extremely difficult for a specialist in aerial reconnaissance to attempt to recognize and comment upon photographs of shadow, soil or crop 'sites' submitted at random by archaeologists and others; the local worker, who knows the area, its position, soil, crop, weather, and likelihood of particular remains, is better able to inspect such photographs and carry out the fieldwork necessary to confirm or deny the presence of ancient sites. If the local worker cannot see any features on the photo-

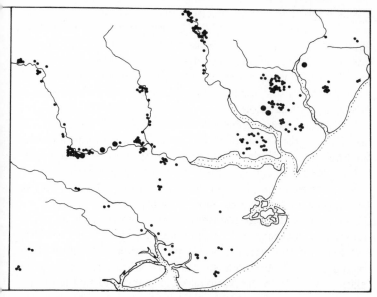

*numbers and the change in distribution is mainly the result of aerial recon-
naissance in drought conditions of 1959 (after St Joseph 1966).*

graph, and could not from the air, it is highly improbable that
the specialist will be able to conjure anything from the picture
submitted.

Sources

The sources of supply for aerial cover of an area are varied.
Generally the archaeologist will find that the local flying club will
include individuals who either take photographs themselves or
are prepared to fly interested parties around their region. Rates
for the latter operation are not only unofficial but subject to a
great range; perhaps £10 per hour should be considered as a
going rate for purposes of budgeting. A large expanse of ground
can be covered in an hour's flying, but the archaeologist must be
prepared to take his own photographs with an easily manipulated
camera, and a trial run will almost certainly be found to be
necessary to gauge camera settings and exposure meter readings.
The advantage of using such informal assistance is that the

archaeologist can obtain precisely the sort of approach to the site or area that he requires, both in angle and height (subject to flight regulations), and, if adequate time has been spent in considering the potentialities, the angle of light and the correct crop or soil cover. It is, of course, essential that the observer be trained in map-reading and identification of landmarks so little time is wasted over orientation.

Official air photographic cover, the province of the R.A.F., is now held by the Department of the Environment, and inquiries for England and Wales should be made to the Air Photography Officer, Room II/4, Department of the Environment, Whitehall, S.W.1. For Scotland, it is the Air Photographs Officer, Scottish Development Department, York Buildings, Queen Street, Edinburgh 2. The requests for photographs should give the sheet number of the relevant 1-inch map, and the National Grid Reference of the area for which photographs are required. A tracing at the 1-inch scale should also be supplied for ease in relating the area to the National Grid maps held by the photographic unit. For England and Wales some information about the type of feature suspected to exist should be provided, so that the relevant photograph, with due regard to height of camera, vegetation and season, can be supplied. Air photographs cannot normally be inspected for selection, except in Scotland where a search of possible useful photographs is permitted, and photographs can be borrowed on occasion.

Many of these photographs are 'verticals', at a scale of 1/10 000 or smaller, and are not particularly useful for recognition of crop marks, as the scale is too small. But overlapping photographs can be viewed stereoscopically and this may yield valuable results from sites with features in relief, such as Iron Age hill-forts.

Other vertical photographs, taken at much lower heights, can sometimes be obtained through libraries or planning officers, and these are a fruitful source for the archaeologist.

The main body of photographic material of particular relevance to archaeology is that held by the Committee for Aerial Photography in the University of Cambridge, and assembled since 1945 under the directorship of Dr J. K. S. St Joseph. Many of these photographs are low-level oblique views, taken from heights of between 1200 and 1500 ft, at carefully chosen times of the year.

Another source of more general archaeological interest is that provided by Aerofilms Limited, 4 Albemarle Street, London, W.1., a member of the Hunting Group of Companies. Many photographs of known archaeological features are available from Aerofilms; these are obliques, and vertical cover is provided by another member of the Hunting Group, Hunting Surveys Limited. Prints of Aerofilm photographs are available in sizes from about 15 by 15 cm to over 1.50 by 1.00 m, and a catalogue with a selection of the photographs can be obtained. The complete Library of Aerial Photographs is available in the London office. Special photographs can be taken of any site in Britain, prices on application.

Oblique photographs are generally more suitable for archaeological interpretation than are vertical photographs, and are somewhat less demanding of the photographer than strictly controlled verticals. However, oblique photographs in pairs can seldom be viewed stereoscopically, and difficulty may arise in plotting any archaeological features on to a plan (such as large-scale map).

Map-making

For map-making, vertical photographs are essential, and the advances in this field are truly extraordinary. Ground surveying requires an enormous number of observations, and in difficult terrain such as mountainous areas, or marshlands, the progress can be extremely slow. In contrast, the use of photographs and plotting procedures can reduce the total mapping time by a very large factor. Few archaeologists, if any, will be trained sufficiently to carry out cartographic work from the air, but the advantages of photogrammetry as a survey method are so great that some idea of the principles and procedures used might be considered essential. Air survey carried out with adequate ground control not only allows the construction of detailed maps, and an un-biased, because unselected, record of features, but also yields data about the dimensions of height that are more detailed than that appearing on any Ordnance Survey map. Regular methods of air survey allow ground contours to be drawn at 10 ft intervals without any difficulty, and methods noted below add further precision to this.

The basic requirement of photogrammetry is that all of the

ground is covered by overlapping runs of photographs taken from the same height with something like 60 per cent overlap both fore and aft. The lateral overlap between strips need not be great. The problem of verticality is now removed by standard procedures. Photogrammetric methods with stereo-plotting machines then can reproduce in minute scale the precise conditions under which successive photographic pairs were taken. These are placed at a scaled distance apart, and are viewed and positioned stereoscopically so that the relative tilts of the photographs can be reproduced. The resultant picture is in three dimensions, a model, and can be measured, reduced or enlarged, and thereby related to ground control points which have been precisely determined. After this has been done, the instrument can draw contours and produce the scaled map to a very high degree of accuracy; as an example, from photographs taken at 10 000 ft, the heights on the map should be accurate to within about 2 ft, and can be much better than this.

The archaeologist should be aware of the potential speed and accuracy of photogrammatric methods for mapping of areas in detail. Various facilities for such work exist in Britain at the moment, and University Departments of Geography are a useful source to consider, as well as commercial firms such as Huntings. The advantage of enlisting the aid of a research-orientated department lies in the potential free assistance the archaeologist may receive if his project appeals sufficiently, and is broad enough to allow full participation of specialists in other areas of interest (p. 218).

3 Discovery of sites by detection devices

There are a variety of methods by which reasonably accurate ideas can be gained of the structural features of a site before excavation. The methods range from the comparatively unsophisticated dowsing, probing, augering, and 'bosing' procedures which depend to a very great extent upon the experience and touch of the operator, to highly technical geophysical techniques which can be carried out by slave labour in the field.

The simple methods are more or less self-explanatory.

Dowsing

Dowsing is a well-known phenomenon, generally associated with the discovery of sources of water, and many dowsers appear also to be able to detect the presence of metals, and differences in superficial geological deposits. The equipment needed is basic, consisting of a Y-shaped piece of wood, often of willow, or two thin metal wires held together by a tie near an end. The two ends of the apparatus are held in the hands, the short stem of the Y pointing forward. Precise positions of the hands and the shape of the wood or wire are the individual dowser's own province or secret. Traverses of a site can be carried out on a miniature grid and system walk procedure, and the behaviour of the sticks, generally a strong dipping movement, will reveal to the dowser the presence of the features he has set himself out to recover. There is no doubt that buried ditches can be indicated by this method, the explanation for which has yet to be discovered. It is a perfectly valid procedure to employ, but perhaps more than other detection devices needs excavation to confirm its findings.

At Pitnacree in Perthshire, dowsing suggested that a barrow was not encircled by a ditch, and that the barrow had been placed upon a low gravel bank in an otherwise sandy terrace of the Tay; the edges of the gravel were detected by dowsing. Both suggestions were confirmed by excavation.

Probing

The use of the probe in investigating sites may also be valuable before excavation. The probe consists of a metal rod, of steel or less heavy alloy such as Duralumin, about 2 cm in diameter, perhaps a metre or more in length, and with a T-handle firmly bolted to its top. The tip of the probe may be sharply pointed, or faceted to a spade-like end; if the latter, it must be evenly faceted on two sides to prevent deflection. Such a probe can be readily home-made, but others can be purchased ready for use; a Duralium probe can be made for about £5, and commercial products will cost upwards of £10.

The probe is pressed into the ground, generally with considerable force, until it is halted by the unyielding bedrock. Minor obstacles such as stones will generally be pushed aside or crushed, but a large series of probes is needed which yield a consistent pattern before firm conclusions can be drawn about the presence or absence of subterranean features. A string grid is the most convenient way to obtain such a pattern, the intervals between probes dependent on the area to be covered and the degree of detail required. A marked peg should be put in to record the depth of the probe's penetration on each point on the grid, or measurements can be put on to squared paper. It will be found useful to mark a series of divisions on the probe for easy estimation of depth. The metal can be grooved in various ways, e.g. a single groove for 25 cm from the tip, double for 50 cm, triple for 75 cm; further divisions may be confusing. The marks are best seen if the grooves are filled with Araldite mixed with a colour.

Problems with the probe are of several kinds. The differences between soil and subsoil in sandy or clayey areas may be too slight to be felt by the user, and the physical difficulties of pushing the probe into stiff and wet material can be great; the work is extremely strenuous. There is also a risk that archaeological material such as pottery or stone tools may be struck if the area is probed at very small intervals. However, accurate plans of ditches and, sometimes, pits, have been obtained from the method, and often it will aid the archaeologist in setting out suitable areas for excavation. The positions of the filled-in inner ditch of the Iron Age fort at Wandlebury, Cambridgeshire, on a chalk ridge, can be accurately located by probing (see fig. 57).

Augering

The auger is a similar type of implement to the probe, but is of greater value in that it will penetrate to greater depths with less physical force required. It consists of a large corkscrew attached to a straight metal shaft, surmounted by a T-handle. The screw can be detached from the shaft so that additional straight lengths of shaft can be added. The whole affair is twisted into the earth, and by bringing it up at regular depths the soil held by the screw-coils can be examined. The same result can be achieved by a post-holer auger, which has a single flapped disc at its end, inclined slightly to act as a screw; this requires rather more downward pressure to keep it driving into the earth, but has been found successful on occasion in determining subsurface features in advance of excavation. The disc diameter of this tool should be

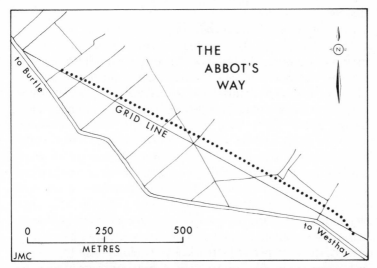

Fig. 6 Map of part of the Abbot's Way, a timber road of circa 2000 B.C. in Somerset, as revealed by restricted excavation and by augering, 1966–7; each dot represents about ten auger holes.

about 10 cm, and additional lengths of shaft can be attached. The use of an auger, and a probe, has revealed the lines of several ancient wooden roadways in Somerset, now covered by 1–1.5 m of peat; excavations have confirmed the results. The auger was found to be particularly valuable in tracing the Abbot's Way, a timber road of *circa* 2000 B.C., for over one kilometre (fig. 6).

The sampling-type of auger or borer, such as is used by palaeobotanists for collecting very accurate quantities of peat and clay, is not suitable for anything other than these substances, and even sand will eventually cause damage to the instrument. The Hiller borer is perhaps the best-known of such tools; it allows penetration through a series of extension poles to very great depths, well over 20 m, and through a chamber it can bring up a complete vertical section of material as the boring progresses. It is expensive to purchase, and can be easily distorted and therefore ruined by over-excessive use in particularly stiff deposits. Occasionally, hefty versions of these augering devices can be power-driven by Land-Rovers and other sources, but these are not likely to be the concern of archaeologists alone.

'*Bosing*'

This is another method depending upon the personal sensitivities of the archaeologist. The method is simple enough, and can be used on sites where the bedrock or compact subsoil lies near the surface, and where ancient features such as ditches or pits are likely to have been cut into these. A heavy wooden mallet can be used, or a metal container filled with lead and mounted on a handle about 1·5 m long. The implement is thudded-down on to the earth, and the resulting sound recorded. Over undisturbed ground the sound will be dull; over a ditch or pit cut into a hard surface and filled with softer material the sound will be more resonant, and may be doubled. Careful repetition of the procedure, aided by a listener stationed about 3 m away, may yield suggestions about the positions of underground features. Again, a grid system should be used, and observations, or rather recordings, noted on paper or by marked pegs. Equipment for precise 'echo sounding' might also be useful if the features are likely to be very deep, but the application of this to archaeological sites is not widespread.

There are three methods for the detection of buried features which are based upon geophysical principles. The first of these, resistivity survey, has been in use since 1946; magnetic methods were introduced in 1957 and electro-magnetic procedures in 1962.

Resistivity

Measurement of the electrical resistivity of the soil was first developed for geological purposes, and civil engineers were among the first to employ instruments designed for the purpose. The principles of the method are simple enough, and relate to the fact that rocks and soils conduct electricity mainly through the presence of moisture containing mineral salts in solution, in the interstices of the mass. Differences in structural features beneath the surface may support unequal variations in the water-content of the ground and these variations can be detected by measuring the resistance of the ground to a flow of electricity. The resistance mainly depends on the dampness of the earth, and therefore buried ditches and hollows will produce readings of low resistance, and stone walls and floors will be indicated by readings of high resistance. A basic soil resistivity meter would consist of two metal probes inserted, say, 10 cm into the ground and 30–50 cm apart. These would be connected to a battery and the ratio of the voltage to the current flowing between the probes could be measured. The current penetrates in different directions, and does not only flow directly between the probes; without this deep penetration, the method would not be a reasonable proposition. A basic difficulty, of probe contact resistance (variable between insertions and often of greater impact than the resistance of the soil between the probes), is removed by the use of four probes set in a line or in a square; square-wave DC current flows between the outer probes, and the resulting voltage difference between the inner detecting probes is measured. The presence of features which are of a resistance unlike that of the normal soil causes the current pattern to be distorted, and the continuous linear readings taken will indicate the presence of an anomaly (fig. 7).

The most suitable soils for the resistivity method are those resting upon a well-drained subsoil like gravel or chalk; in these conditions, ditches and pits will be easily detected. The first

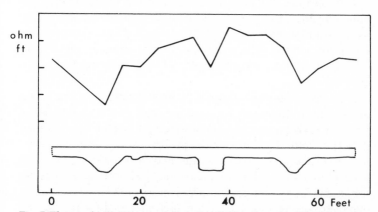

Fig. 7 Electrical resistivity survey across a Beaker burial site at Dorchester, Oxford. Above, *the curve of the traverse, with probes set four feet apart.* Below, *schematic section across the site, showing outer ditches and central burial pit (after Atkinson 1963, 24).*

application of the method, in 1946, was on henge monuments in Oxfordshire under these ideal conditions, and the results were extremely successful (Atkinson 1963). Clays are less amenable, as the soil and subsoil tend to be too closely comparable in the presence of salts and acids in water solution. Sandy soils and stony soils are often unsuitable, due to lack of solubles, variable contact conditions and soil inhomogeneity. Recently ploughed soils are often too aerated and loose in texture for easy results, unless the probes are inserted to the level of the furrows, or the soil is well trampled. Rainfall before a survey may improve the potential results, but heavier rain will tend to mask anomalies such as small ditches; drought will also cause problems through masking of resistivity contrasts. The difficulties of resistivity survey are not restricted to choice of soils and conditions, as the interpretation of the anomalies can also be puzzling. The general rule of stone walls = high resistivity, silted ditches = low resistivity, can be reversed or at least upset by such occurrences as stone packing or infilling of a ditch, or robbing of walls.

The procedure for setting out a resistivity survey of a site is relatively simple. A string with regular intervals marked on it by coloured ties or a plastic tape, is laid on the ground so that it cuts across the suspected feature. The probes of the five-probe system (see below) are put into the earth at pre-determined intervals along the line and the readings are noted and plotted as a graph, with resistance as abscissa and distance as ordinate. A grid can be set up for an area survey, and the traverse readings, when combined, will produce a contour plan of equal resistances over the area.

A decision about the distance between the probes is important in any linear traverse. The ordinary rule is that the distance between each pair of probes will roughly equal the depth of detection limit. Therefore, if the probes are very close together, say 40 cm, features deeper than this may be missed; however, too wide an interval, well over a metre, may yield imprecise locations for anomalies and reduce the effectiveness of the traverse. About one metre seems to be a generally useful interval for the probes, particularly if the site has been chosen on the basis of a good aerial photograph. The auger or probe can often quickly establish the best position for a first traverse.

There are a variety of resistivity survey instruments available, costing from about £50 to £200. The Megger Earth Tester (about £150) is generally mounted on a tripod; the operator generates the working voltage by cranking the machine. The switching system operates with five probes of which four work at one time, while the fifth is moved along the traverse line; this allows consecutive readings to be made without excessive loss of time. A change-over switching system must be supplied by the user of this and the following two instruments, the Tellohm (£150) and the Gossen Geohm (£30).

The Martin-Clark Meter (£65) has been specially devised for archaeological work, and is extremely compact. The operator can hold it in one hand, and therefore follow the probes as they are moved; the usual long probe-leads are unnecessary. In addition, a change-over switch holds the five probe-leads and can be rotated so that the unused probe is easily moved to its new position at the head of the line to become the leading probe of the next group of four (fig. 8). The illustration shows the probe (5) already in place,

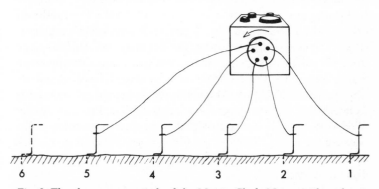

Fig. 8 The change-over switch of the Martin-Clark Meter, with probes in place (after Aitken 1969, 699).

and when the switch is turned once more, probe (1) is eliminated and can be moved to position (6) ready for the next reading. The probes and leads are colour-coded to avoid confusion over plugs, and the design of the probe, of 1 cm diameter steel, allows a horizontal handle for carrying and extraction, and a step for insertion to a uniform depth using the foot.

Resistivity survey is an established method for detection of buried features on gravel and other suitable subsoils, and further experimental work is being carried out on chalk and other soil types to ascertain the wider potential value of the technique.

Magnetic

The magnetic location of archaeological features is a development from geological prospecting techniques. The categories of buried remains that can be detected through magnetic survey, other than iron objects, include fired clay structures such as kilns and hearths, and pits and ditches filled with soil or domestic rubbish. The magnetic disturbance caused by these buried features are much weaker than those produced by iron, and they depend on various magnetic effects produced by fire and high humus-content. The principle behind the method is the existence of thermo-remanent magnetism. A mass of clay heated to about 700 °C (a dull red heat) acquires a weak but permanent magnetism on cooling; soil and stone will also be affected in the same way if iron oxides are present. In unbaked material the magnetic 'domains' within the grains of haematite in the iron oxides are randomly orientated and therefore tend to eliminate each other's magnetic effect. Upon heating, however, the domains will tend to align upon the earth's magnetic field at this time, and this alignment will be retained as the material cools. The magnetic effect will not now be self-eliminating. Magnetite reacts somewhat differently to haematite, but the magnetic effect is similar. Pits and ditches filled with organic material will also produce a magnetic effect because the susceptibility of the filling is greater than that of the subsoil in which the features were made; the effect is a magnetic discontinuity.

The thermo-remanent magnetism of fired clay or susceptible soils in a pit distorts the magnetic field of the earth from its norm in the immediate vicinity of the feature. The measurement is made of the deviation of the magnetic intensity from that expected under normal conditions.

The instruments that are currently in use in Britain for magnetic location of archaeological features are the proton magnetometer, the proton gradiometer, and the differential fluxgate gradiometer. The first of these is probably the machine most commonly encountered in archaeological prospecting, although it is expensive (£1000 or more). The detector is a small bottle of water or alcohol enclosed in an electrical coil, and the magnetic intensity is determined from the behaviour of the protons in the hydrogen atoms in the liquid. The instrument itself amplifies and meters the weak signal in the coil, allowing a plot to be produced. The proton gradiometer employs two detector bottles, one near each end of a staff, 1.5–3.0 m long, which is held upright. A simple version of this instrument does not record absolute values but emits a sound which the operator can interpret in terms of anomalous features in the ground; this version costs about £150. The fluxgate gradiometer operates on a somewhat different principle, but uses two detectors held in a vertical plane; differences in magnetic intensities are indicated on a meter. This instrument is as expensive as the proton magnetometer, and is not yet widely available for archaeological work.

The procedure for carrying out magnetic location work is straightforward, and area surveys rather than single linear traverses are generally employed. The area is marked out by wooden pegs set 15 m (or 50 ft) apart, and each square thus formed is, in turn, covered by a string grid so that marks occur on the lines at intervals of 1.5 m (or 5 ft). The string used should be non-shrinking. The detector bottle is moved along the grid in lines, and with very little experience the assistant will learn exactly when he can move so that the instrument readings can be made as rapidly as is consonant with accuracy. Each square will consist of 121 measurements, but the examination of a series of adjacent squares will reduce this to 100; each square should take about 10–15 minutes to complete the first series, after which abnormal readings are investigated by more closely spaced measurements to determine the strength and location of anomalies.

In good conditions this procedure is to a great extent a mechanical operation of a somewhat boring nature for the bottle-holder, and the operator too must be prepared for little other than the rapid accurate reading and recording of the measurements on squared paper. The subsequent investigation of abnormalities is naturally of greater immediate interest to both.

Many sites, however, are not entirely suitable for this work, if trees, bushes, or long grass impede the string grid or the cable linking the bottle and the instrument. The sensitivity of the proton-type instruments to iron causes difficulties with wire fences, iron fenceposts or other agricultural debris such as bits of machinery, bolts and nails that may clutter the soil. The proton magnetometer should operate successfully if kept at least ten metres from wire fences, and thirty metres from electricity cables (buried or overhead), water and gas mains, or steel-framed buildings. Electric trains or trams on DC power within 8 km will also create problems for magnetometer. Igneous rocks have a basic thermo-remanent magnetism that is likely to completely disguise archaeological features. The gradiometers are unaffected by DC power, diurnal changes and magnetic storms, and might

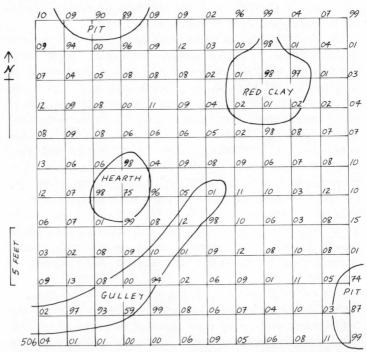

Fig. 9 *Readings obtained by a proton-magnetometer at the Rainsborough hill-fort, Northants, with features identified by subsequent excavation (after Aitken 1969, 688).*

therefore be considered to be more suitable instruments for magnetic location work, but all have made or are likely to make very considerable contributions to archaeological prospecting.

These contributions include the discovery of many pottery kilns and baked clay hearths, as well as pits and ditches filled with domestic and other debris. Visually blank interiors of Iron Age camps have been very successfully explored, and storage and rubbish pits identified and proved by excavation, on a number of occasions. One example of the method in operation can be seen in fig. 9, which represents the readings obtained by a proton magnetometer at the Rainsborough Iron Age hill-fort. The area covered in detail is 25 ft square, and the readings shown are only the final two digits from the most sensitive of the meters; the change from 00 to 99 is only a change of 1 unit, the increase of the magnetic intensity by one gamma. The subsequent identification of the anomalies was made by excavation.

Electromagnetic

Electromagnetic instruments are the most recent development in the field of archaeological detection. They were first designed to discover metals, employing principles used in mine detectors, but through experiment and elaboration it has been found that they are also useful in detecting magnetic soil anomalies of rather shallow character. There are two main types of instrument, the Pulse Induction Meter and the Soil Conductivity Meter. The first of these is particularly sensitive to metal objects, so that it would be of value in preliminary surveys of areas known to contain graves with possible grave goods, or rooms of houses with likely pottery or metal objects; it will also detect bolts and nails and other stray metals lying at random in the ground. The instrument applies pulses of magnetic field to the ground from a transmitter coil, and the resultant currents and magnetic fields from metal and certain soils are detected by a receiver coil. Varying coil sizes can be used, the largest about 50 cm square, the smallest about 7 cm square; the largest is for rapid coverage of a large area, and provides the greatest depth penetration. Detailed search is thereafter carried out with smaller coils. Readings can be taken over a nylon string grid, the coil being placed on the intersections of the string grid, at intervals of as little as 15 cm. The instrument operator records the meter readings on squared paper so that anomalies can be noted that are significantly higher or lower than the average or background reading of the soil or other overall deposit. The illustration (fig. 10) shows the readings taken over part of a floor of a small room on the island of Delos, and indicates the amplitude of the anomalies, and the nature of the late second century B.C. finds. Particularly sensitive detectors of the Pulse Induction type cost about £120 (e.g. Geo-Electronics

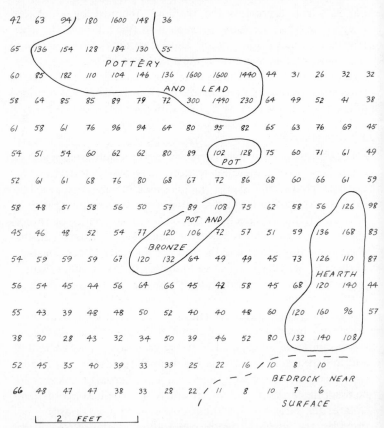

Fig. 10 Readings obtained by a Pulse Induction Meter in a house on Delos, showing the anomalies produced by subsequently discovered pottery, lead and bronze objects, as well as a hearth and shallow bedrock (after Archaeometry 11, 1969, 168).

C400) and are much superior to the detectors based on 'beat frequency' or 'induction balance' principles. These inferior detectors use one or more high frequency oscillators, and often suffer from false readings due to soil conductivity of electricity and other non-metallic features; they cost from £15 upwards, and are popular and perfectly legitimate toys so long as they are not used on protected sites (p. 247) or without the permission of the landowner or occupier. The question of ownership of any finds made is not in doubt (p. 46). Known archaeological sites should not be searched with such detectors unless on an organized archaeological basis, with the full knowledge and co-operation of the local society and museum.

The Soil Conductivity Meter consists of a radio transmitter and receiver in continuous operation and the detection of subsoil features is achieved by the measurement of the distortion of the transmitted field by changes in the conductivity of the soil under the instrument. The transmitter and receiver coils are set at right-angles to one another at opposed ends of a 1 m bar which is carried horizontally by means of a strap. The instrument (about £100), weighing about 8 lb, is set to a mid-scale reading over 'neutral' ground and a traverse is then made. Anomalies are detected by the deflection of the meter needle (fig. 11). Pits produce slightly positive conductivity anomalies, with downward needle deflection, and metals produce strongly positive anomalies, with upward needle deflection. Objects of ferrous and non-ferrous

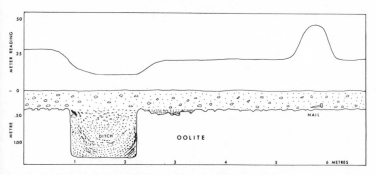

Fig. 11 Soil conductivity survey. Above, *the curve of the traverse with needle set at mid-scale reading.* Below, *the archaeological features recorded (after Soil Conductivity Meter manual).*

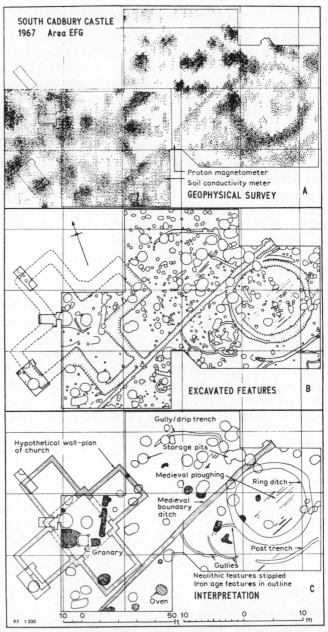

Fig. 12 Geophysical survey of area at South Cadbury Castle, Somerset, using a proton-magnetometer and a soil conductivity meter, for comparison with the features as subsequently excavated and interpreted (from Alcock 1968; copyright Camelot Research Committee).

metals can be located at considerable depths, and depths themselves can be estimated from the needle deflections. Pits as small as 30 cm diameter and 10 cm deep have been detected. In use it is important to carry the instrument horizontally and without excessive jiggling; long grass and other low obstructions may pose problems. However, movements by the operator at a slow walking pace will in fact cover a large area in a relatively short time; an assistant is generally required to put in stakes or pegs where anomalies are noted.

The exact position of an isolated metal object can be determined by a sideways motion of the instrument until a maximum needle deflection is recorded, then a sideways pass on a line at right-angles to the original line will fix the point of the find, beneath the meter itself, when the needle is again deflected to a maximum. A soil anomaly will be indicated by a maximum needle movement as the instrument passes over the boundary between undisturbed and disturbed soil.

This instrument has been extensively used at South Cadbury in Somerset in conjunction with a proton magnetometer and other detection devices. The recordings were converted into dot density patterns (fig. 12), in which dots were scattered at random around the point of reading; the magnetometer dots show the strength of the anomaly, and the soil conductivity dots represent divergences from a normal undisturbed area of the site. The plots from both instruments agreed closely, and excavation indicated the degrees of accuracy achieved.

4 Collecting and collections

The field archaeologist may be concerned with the discovery of sites, or the plotting of sites over an area of ancient exploitation, but at various stages in his work he will encounter the problem of the collection of stray or single finds, or from surface sampling, and he will have to face up to the accumulation of actual objects obtained from these several sources.

Landowners and, more particularly, landusers, have generally gathered material from their land through agricultural or other activities, and there are few farmers in Britain who do not possess, or did not possess, prehistoric artefacts of stone, metal or pottery. Often these will have been thrown aside, as of no interest and no value, and there are recent examples of precious metals being disposed of in this way, only to be rediscovered later. The find-spots of such discarded objects are clearly of restricted value to the archaeologist. More to the point, however, is the fact that such objects may be turned over to the first interested person who happens along. The question of true ownership first arises, then the problem of disposal.

Ownership of finds

In England, the general rule is that all objects of any material except gold and silver are the property of the owner of the land upon which the objects were found. This is clear enough, and the archaeologist must therefore assign any finds, other than of gold or silver, to the owner of the land. The fact that a tenant-farmer has gladly given the objects he has found to a field archaeologist is of no moment, as they did not belong to him. The archaeologist who comes into possession of finds in this way, or if he collects them himself from the ground, must inform the landowner of their existence, and be prepared to hand them over. A carefully prepared statement of the significance of the objects, in terms of additions to knowledge rather than monetary value, may be presented to the owner with a recommendation that they should go to the local museum, but it is for the owner to decide. A clear and honest appraisal of this situation should be put before the landowner when the first finds are made or recognized to have been made, and generally a reasonable solution about their care can be worked out. There is no entirely adequate solution without the local museum's involvement (see below).

Treasure trove

An object of gold or silver, or with gold or silver parts, is subject to different treatment upon discovery. In England and Wales, any such object must be reported at once to the local coroner, who then holds an inquest to decide if the objects are Treasure Trove. The objects will be held by the coroner until the inquest achieves a decision.

The evidence to be given will relate to the particular circumstances under which the objects were found, as well as details of the character and age of the objects.

If it is determined that the objects were deliberately hidden (in the earth or in any other place), that there was an intention to recover them, and that the owner cannot now be traced, then the objects are Treasure Trove and belong to the Crown by virtue of royal prerogative. In this case, the national museum collections may claim the objects and hold them on behalf of the Crown. The value of the finds will be determined on the basis of expert advice by museum specialists, a full antiquarian value rather than merely that of the weight of precious metal, and this can be paid, and usually is paid, to the *finder* if he has been prompt in reporting the objects to the police and through them the coroner.

Non-disclosure of the finds is a criminal offence, and the finder may not only lose part or all of his compensation, but be subject to possible fine or imprisonment.

If the keepers of the national or local museum collections do not require the objects, if for instance they are duplicated already or badly damaged, then they will be returned to the *finder* who may dispose of them as he wishes.

The inquest may determine that the objects were not deliberately hidden with a view to eventual recovery; they then are not Treasure Trove and will be returned by the coroner to the *landowner* who can dispose of them. Stray single objects of precious metal may have been accidentally dropped and lost, and are therefore not Treasure Trove. Other objects may have been deliberately buried but without the intention to recover them, e.g. grave goods with a burial and again these are not Treasure Trove. If there is an anomaly in the law, it is that between landowner and finder, each of whom may gain possession of the objects (or their value) depending on the Treasure Trove decision. The reward to the finder is not statutory but is a general practice and the ownership of stray finds of precious metal need not necessarily descend upon the landowner; the court can award it to the finder if it so wishes, and has done so on occasion. There is one certain thing in all this, and that is that concealment of finds is not only a criminal offence but is also not an economically viable proposition for the finder. A private sale will not yield the sum that would be awarded by the Crown if the object was Treasure Trove and taken for a collection; the antiquarian value of an object is greatly increased through its provenance and details of discovery being known. And there would be, or should be, few landowners who would not reward the finder of a precious object if the court decided it was the property of the owner of the land.

The law of Treasure Trove in Scotland is somewhat different, as *all* objects found in the earth are Treasure Trove. They do not have to be of gold or silver, nor do they have to have been hidden with intent to recover. Important finds are generally taken by the National Museum of Antiquities of Scotland, but others may be returned to the finder, and payment as in England may be made.

Surface sampling

In addition to the acquisition of stray material from landusers and by finds made by the field archaeologist, there are occasions when a site, newly discovered, can be seen to have a large quantity of material on its surface. The problem facing the archaeologist here is how much, and how, to collect. The most common answer is to collect everything, and on the majority of prehistoric sites in Britain this is not likely to result in a tremendous accumulation of material. The technique used, however, should not be the collection and lumping together of everything from the area; this would effectively destroy any surface evidence that the site had several periods of occupation, or that different activities had been carried out in different parts of the site.

A solution is to grid the area (p. 110), using grid divisions as small as is convenient (e.g. 5 m on a 100 m grid), and collect everything from each square. The material from each square is kept separate from other material. Subsequent examination may indicate areas of concentration of activities, may indicate a horizontal movement of the occupation over time, or may point to the existence of areas where specialized activities had taken place. The details of the examination of material from the squares are plotted directly upon the grid plan.

If the site is large, and the quantity of surface material is great, some form of 'random sampling' could be employed. A grid is used, and all material from certain squares is collected, either every other square, or any other consistent scheme. It is unlikely that British prehistoric sites will yield such quantities of surface material as to require 'random sampling' techniques.

There is no certainty, in any case, that the total or 'random' surface collection from a site will reveal its contents. Both natural and human agencies that might bring material to the surface are so varied that there can be no guarantee that the material is an accurate reflection of that beneath the ground. The only way to see if it is, is to dig the site.

Private collections

There can be little justification for the existence of private collections in Britain today. In every way, national or local museums are better equipped to accept, treat, record and save material than are individuals. Objects that have been recovered by field archaeologists from the ground or from landusers should be passed on to the local or other museum as soon as is conveniently possible. Here they can be cleaned, decay arrested, and a full record of their find-spot and description made. The archaeologist handling in such material should furnish all the relevant details in an orderly fashion. These details should include a brief description of the objects, the location where they were found (with National Grid Reference), name and address of finder, name and address of owner; there should also be a full description of the conditions under which the find took place, so that an assessment can be made of the possible significance of the find. Such a description may indicate the presence of a hoard of objects, or a single burial, or a cemetery, or a settlement.

The above refers to material that actually comes into the hands of the archaeologist, either through his own discoveries or through donations to him by others. There will still remain, however, a large number of finds in private collections, whether a few stray objects on a landuser's mantel or kitchen shelf, or a quantity of miscellaneous material accumulated by a collector who searches for objects or buys them from local people.

In the first example, a few stray items held by the finder, the archaeologist should attempt to record all the details of the finds, writing descriptions, making sketches, wherever possible. These details can then be passed on to the local museum for permanent record and mapping. Occasionally the interest shown in the finds will result in their donation to the museum, but it is better not to press for this too strongly at first. In recording details of find-spot and association, the archaeologist should be extremely careful about giving unqualified acceptance to this in his notes. There is a difference between a vague comment about an area of a farm, or even a particular field, and being taken to a place and shown where the discovery was made. There may not be any difference in the lack of documentary evidence, but the degree of conviction of the finder, and an assessment of his memory, can usually be calculated. If only a vague area can be indicated, then this must be recorded without influencing the finder to supply more precise and cheering data. A National Grid Reference (p. 58) is essential, even if it covers a wide area. Far better this than a find-spot recorded, and published (actually), as 'the field with the eight haystacks'.

In the second example, where the archaeologist encounters a serious private collector, with an accumulation of purchased material, even more care needs to be exercised. The establishment of good relations is vital, and the archaeologist should indicate his willingness and ability to provide information about the objects. The material in a collection of this sort is the most prone to dispersal and disappearance in time, as there is no guarantee that the heir to the collection will wish to save it; many examples are known of the disposal of such material by destruction or neglect.

The objects should be described, drawn or sketched, and photographed if at all possible. Note of provenances should be made although extreme caution must be placed upon this data. The passing-on of objects from finder to go-between to collector almost always results in loss of accurate provenance, and gain in provenance designed to increase interest and/or value. The notes taken by the archaeologist could be duplicated and a set presented to the collector as well as to the museum. Attempts should be made to interest the collector in presenting his material to the museum, or to allow its proper publication in the local journal, but again extreme caution in approach is desirable. Some collectors are only too willing and generous in allowing access to their material, but others are not. It is precisely the same situation as with landowners and landusers (p. 13), where a build-up of goodwill can be destroyed by a single careless mistake.

A criticism of local museums that is sometimes made is that they do not show interest in local finds, do not display them, and give scant acknowledgment to the finders. It is disheartening to have a find swallowed up by museum, put into a box in a store, and not recorded in print with the finder's name. Archaeologists must be aware of this problem, and can attempt to explain the value of a permanent place for objects where they can be studied in the future. The keepers of museums are bound by their circumstances, and the lack of display space in many small museums is generally the result of years of neglect by public authorities. If the situation appears intolerable to the owner of a collection, the best procedure is to record fully the objects, make full-size drawings, take photographs, and thereby reduce the potential loss if the collection never enters a museum.

Fakes

The private collector is the most susceptible person to forgeries and fakes. Being without the knowledge of the museum expert, he falls prey to the most blatant fakes and 'plants', and it is not a happy occasion when he is told, as he must be, that doubt must exist about certain of his precious objects. The museum authorities are in the best position to determine the authenticity of finds, through knowledge of the great range of material that comes on the market from time to time. In Central Scotland, for instance, the date of accession of certain bronze objects in many local museums generally leads the expert to yet another forgery, turned out in quantity in 1890 and distinguishable by several characteristics of the metal and its casting. The archaeologist should be aware of the various ways by which commonly available objects were made, and should have knowledge of the local forgeries in his museum (generally not on display), as preparation for any inspection of local collections. He should also be extremely cautious in his diagnosis and in his expression of doubts.

III Recording of sites

1 Maps

The first essential in any site recording, whether in notebook form or as a publication, is the accurate geographical positioning of the site upon suitable maps. Most published reports of archaeological excavations or fieldwork begin with a verbal description of the site in terms of its proximity to better-known landmarks, such as towns. Sites published in national journals also often have a small-scale map included, so that the reader who may be entirely unfamiliar with the region can identify the general area in which the site appears. In British archaeology a standard practice has developed for putting this introductory data into a convenient and economical form for publication, and an example appears in fig. 13. This consists of three maps, the first consisting of a small-scale map of a very large area, large enough for its outline to be instantly recognizable by almost anyone who has heard of the country. Within this map appears a block marking the position of the second map on the page, which is generally at county or area level of scale, and often with some geological information shown; other sites of interest and towns can also be indicated. Again, a small block marks the position of the third map, which places the actual site under report in its immediate setting in relation to fields, roads and houses. Scales of the last pair of maps should be shown, and the three maps are orientated in the same plane.

These maps lead the reader from a general location of the area

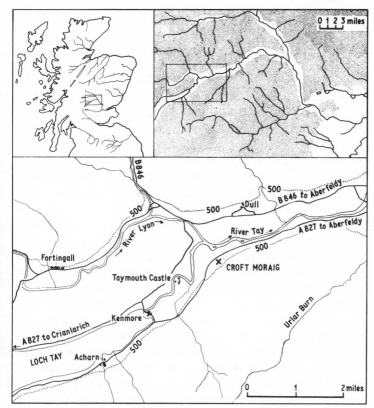

Fig. 13 Location maps of site at Croft Moraig, Perthshire (see fig. 4 for sites within area of second map) (from Piggott and Simpson 1970).

to a precise position of the site in relation to present geographical features. All necessary maps are available in Britain through the quite exceptional service rendered by the Ordnance Survey, and the archaeologist's choice is extremely large. Other, private, organizations also produce excellent maps suitable for fieldwork over wide areas, and some of these are also noted below.

No serious archaeological work can be completed without maps, and an understanding of the types available and their particular usefulness to archaeology is essential, as is experience in working with maps. The occasions where large-scale maps have to be produced by the archaeologist are many (p. 60), but sometimes large-scale Ordnance Survey maps can be adapted for direct archaeological use.

One-inch maps (1/63 360)

The smallest-scale map that is generally applicable to detailed archaeological work is the 1-inch map (1 inch to 1 mile), which covers Great Britain in 189 sheets at the scale of 1/63 360. Each map covers an area of about 700 square miles, and shows almost all roads, towns and villages, rivers and larger streams, and wooded areas. Contours of the land are marked at vertical intervals of 50 ft above mean sea level. Other topographical detail, such as marsh and pasture, parks and quarries, is also provided. Landmarks such as churches and castles, pubs and post offices, and antiquities, are often represented on these maps but, of course, not all of the last can be shown, and only the prominently visible ancient monuments are consistently shown. The maps of this 1-inch series are also marked with the National Grid (see below). The maps at this scale are suitable for a variety of archaeological needs, beginning with the preliminary planning of an area survey based upon geographical boundaries of hills and rivers (e.g. fig. 4). Known sites and other finds can be plotted upon the maps, which are at a sufficiently small scale to enable the user to plot finds of imprecise provenance (e.g. with village or farm name only) with a large circle or special symbol. In the field, the 1-inch map can be used for general plotting of sites but in most cases the scale is too small for precision, and other maps should be employed. Some archaeological fieldwork, however, is combined with hiking and other recreational pursuits, and the 1-inch map is perhaps the best scale for this, covering enough ground in enough detail to serve both purposes.

These maps are being replaced by maps at 1/50 000 (about $1\frac{1}{4}$ inches to the mile), and the sheets for southern Britain, up to Lancs and Yorks, should be completed by 1974, the northern part of Britain by 1976. These maps will eventually allow more detail to be presented, but the first series will be simply 20 per cent expansions of the old 1-inch maps.

Another series of maps suitable for the planning of fieldwork over a wide area, in conjunction perhaps with other activities, is the ½-inch maps published by John Bartholomew & Son, Ltd, Edinburgh. The scale of these (1/126 720) is extremely small, but the use of colours in vertical contouring (at 100 ft intervals) allows a reasonably accurate impression to be gained of the terrain over the area of each map, about 60 by 30 miles. The maps do not have National Grid lines. They cost 44p each.

2½-inch maps (1/25 000)

A much better map for the sort of detailed area surveys that will generally be carried out is the relatively recent 2½-inch map (2½ inches to 1 mile) produced by the Ordnance Survey; the scale is actually 1/25 000. Many of the Second Series of these maps cover an area 20 km east–west and 10 km north–south (about 12½ by 6¼ miles), which is twice the area of the First Series; together, these Series cover almost all of Britain except the western islands of Scotland. All roads and most tracks are indicated, as well as footpaths, field boundaries and smaller features such as individual buildings. Altitudes are shown by contours at 25 ft intervals, and spot heights appear along some roads. For detailed area surveys, this scale is extremely useful as sites or finds can be located on the map reasonably accurately within individual fields or other small areas. The maps are aligned upon the National Grid, and can be identified by reference to the 1-inch series and its National Grid marking (p. 58). They cost from 38 to 49p each.

Six-inch maps (1/10 560 and 1/10 000)

The map most commonly employed by field archaeologists in Britain is the 6-inch map (6 inches to 1 mile), which can show every footpath, field boundary and small building that existed when the survey was made. Maps at this scale of 1/10 560 cover all of Britain, and most of these are now available with National Grid lines; parts of Scotland still have the earlier series without this. The area covered by each map is exactly 25 sq. km. Contours are shown at 50 ft vertical intervals, and Bench Marks (p. 97) as well as spot heights are indicated. This series is being replaced by 1/10 000 scale maps with contours at 5 m intervals, 10 m in mountainous areas, but it will be some time before the replacement is complete. Archaeologists should make sure that the scaled ruler they employ is the correct one of either 1/10 560 or 1/10 000 for the particular map they are using. This scale of map is extremely valuable for the detailed plotting of sites and other finds, and is often used by local and county museums for complete coverage of a restricted area. The scale is large enough for individual fields to be marked with landowners' names and other potentially valuable data. It is not, however, suitable for use as a base map in plotting linear earthworks or multiple features whose precise physical relationship to each other is important, as the scale is too small; an HB pencil line can range in width from 0.15 mm (sharp) through 0.30 mm ('average') to 0.80 mm (slightly blunt), and these represent 1.5, 3 and 8 m on the ground. A similar difficulty arises if the map is to be used for accurate plotting of sites and finds within a small area such as a 10-acre field which might cover an area on the map of 2 cm square; measurements by tape can be made from field corners or other features recorded on the map, but the position of the pencil on the map may not be strictly proportional to the datum for measurement on the ground, and errors of a magnitude of 3 to 5 m can be incorporated in the plotting. When used for general area survey work, however, the 1/10 000 map is invaluable, if the Ordnance Survey has been able to maintain its policy of constant revision; it is wise not to rely upon ancient versions of 6-inch maps if more recent editions are available at 82p.

25-inch maps (1/2500)

For more precise recording upon the actual map, the 25-inch series (25 inches to 1 mile) are a useful source, and these are the largest-scale maps at present available for all of Britain except a few mountainous and moorland areas. A series of 50-inch maps exists for many urban areas. The 25-inch maps, at a scale of 1/2500, are currently being produced with National Grid lines, but many areas will only be covered by an older series for some time to come. The maps show Bench Marks and spot heights as well as contours at vertical intervals of 50 ft; the new metric series now becoming available will show heights of Bench Marks to two decimal places of a metre, and spot heights to one place. The detail shown on the 25-inch series is exactly that of the 6-inch series, with the addition of field numbers, arranged by parishes, and field areas in acres or hectares. The field numbering system has been particularly useful for the recording of sites and finds, and is currently being reconsidered by the Ordnance Survey. The use of the National Grid Reference system is not to be disregarded even if field numbers are used. The advantage of 25-inch maps is of course that sites can be reasonably accurately plotted on to the map (e.g. fig. 3); a fine pencil dot or line will represent about 0.3 of a metre on the ground, so measurements with a tape can be rounded off to the nearest half metre. The area represented by one of these maps is covered by $\frac{1}{16}$ of a map at 1/10 000 (6-inch map), and for a general area survey the 1/2500 series is too bulky, and expensive as well. For two purposes, however, this scale is extremely useful. Linear earthworks can generally be plotted direct on to the map without much loss of accuracy, using simple measurements by tape. And the map, cut if needed to fit, can be used direct as the base for a plane-table survey of earthworks or other multiple-measurement features (p. 84). These maps cost from £1.10 to £1.65.

The Ordnance Survey also publishes Bench Mark lists arranged by one 1-km squares of the National Grid (see below), identified by the National Grid Reference of the south-west corner of the square. The lists provide a description of the Bench Mark and its location, with National Grid Reference to within 10 m, the altitude of the mark in metres and in feet to two decimal places, and the year in which the mark was levelled. Bench Mark lists are obtainable from the Ordnance Survey, Southampton.

If the information on these or on any other Ordnance Survey maps is to be used in publications, either as direct copy or redrawn, permission should be sought, for copyright reasons, from the Director-General, Ordnance Survey, Romsey Road, Maybush, Southampton SO9 4DH. Data from maps published more than fifty years ago may be reproduced without such permission.

Specialized maps
There are other maps, published by the Ordnance Survey, which the archaeologist will find particularly useful in considering surveys over larger areas, or in carrying out work on distributions generally. These are maps published at a scale of

1/625 000 (about $\frac{1}{10}$ inch to 1 mile), and cover Britain in two sheets, North and South. Together they form a single map 1 by 1.6 m (42 by 64 inches). One of these maps (Physical) shows land formations by relief and drainage patterns, another (Solid Geology) indicates the stratigraphical geological formations of the country, and there are also Rainfall maps and a Vegetation map for northern Britain. These maps can be used in conjunction with the relevant British Regional Geology series, published by the National Environment Research Council through its Institute of Geological Sciences. Nearly twenty of these Regional Geologies are available, at about 30p each.

The Ordnance Survey also publishes archaeological and historical maps. Since its early years, the Survey has devoted much of its energies to the recording of visible antiquities, and a number of maps with accompanying explanatory text have been produced. The Ancient Britain map shows over one thousand sites of prehistoric and early historic times overprinted on a base map with National Grid lines. Another map, Southern Britain in the Iron Age, shows late pre-Roman sites and finds on a physical base map. Other maps cover Roman sites, the Roman Walls, Dark Age and Monastic Britain.

The archaeologist should avail himself of the excellent types of map described above for his preliminaries to fieldwork, his actual time in the field, and his further consideration and publication of results. A part-set of 1-inch maps will always be useful, for walking, driving and general recording of archaeological features. Many archaeologists make a habit of buying the relevant 1-inch map of any area in which they happen to find themselves, and the library thus established is generally put to good use in time.

National Grid
All modern Ordnance Survey maps now bear the National Grid. This is, in essence, a series of squares the sides of which are parallel to, or at right-angles to, the line representing the central meridian of Ordnance Survey mapping. The main grid lines used for reference are 100 km apart, and each 100-km square has a two-letter symbol, beginning in southern Britain with the letter S or T, in northern Britain with N, and with H in the

Orkneys and Shetlands. The 100-km squares are divided into 10- and into 1-km squares on the 1-inch and 2½-inch maps. Using these, and further subdivisions that appear on the margins of the 2½-inch and 6-inch maps, each point can be given a unique map reference relating to its position first eastwards and then northwards of an arbitrary point to the south-west of the Isles of Scilly. This reference remains the same whatever the scale of map, but its precision varies according to the scale. Thus, the position of Stonehenge can be quoted as SU 123422 (fig. 14). This means that the 100-km square in which the site lies is SU, and that within this square the site is 12.3 km to the east (the

Fig. 14 Ordnance Survey map showing position of Stonehenge at National Grid Reference 123422, accurate to within 100 m; at eight places, the reference is accurate to within 10 m, 12274219. (Crown Copyright reserved.)

easting reference), and 42.2 km to the north (the *northing* reference) of the south-west corner of the SU square. On the 1-inch map for this area, the 1-km squares are marked by lines, and the 0.3 easting and 0.2 northing in the reference are estimations. On the $2\frac{1}{2}$-inch and 6-inch map, the grid lines also represent the same 1-km intervals, but along the margins of the map, each of these kilometres is divided into 10 parts representing 100 m on the ground; this allows for an actual measurement of the third place in the easting and northing reference, and can be used for an estimation of a fourth place in the reference system. This would then be accurate to within 10 m on the ground. It is absolutely essential to remember that eastings are recorded before northings. For a series or collection of National Grid References (N.G.R.) of sites within a small area lying entirely within one 100-km square, the two-letter prefix is sometimes omitted, but really it is better to give the full reference each time.

2 Elementary surveying practices

One of the first requisites of an archaeological site survey or excavation is an accurate plan of the area and the site contained therein. Sometimes the area around a site can be mapped by photogrammetry (p. 29) and this is particularly useful in difficult terrain or if the relevant area is extremely large. The huge expanse of ground covered by the ancient city of Teotihuacan in Mexico was mapped from aerial photographs, and in this country the intelligent use of vertical photographs has been valuable for mapping sites in their setting on small islands of western Scotland. On other occasions, the Ordnance Survey maps can be used directly as base maps for archaeological site or area survey reports (p. 57). However, archaeological sites themselves, such as camps, barrows, middens, standing stones, and their immediate environment, must be measured and plotted anew by the archaeologist or another competent person. No great experience is necessary for this, but there is a set of procedures to follow that have been found to be useful for the rather simple archaeological surveying that is generally considered to be adequate for site reports. In addition, there is now available a wide range of equipment, some of it inexpensive, that can help the archaeologist in the sometimes tiresome business of producing an essentially accurate plan of his site.

Scales of precision and reproduction
The words 'essentially accurate' are important. Most site plans that are published appear at very small scales, generally covering no more than the average page size of the journal (about 20 by 15 cm), occasionally produced as 'pull-outs' covering two or four times this area. Even so, for a big site such as a fort or camp, or large henge monument, the plan is reproduced at something of the order of 1/1000 or even 1/2000; for a barrow of ordinary size, the scale will be larger, 1/200. At these scales, the width of a pencilled line may represent a large area on the ground, from 6 cm to 60 cm. In planning a site, therefore, the archaeologist should decide at what level of accuracy his measurements should be in view of their eventual reduction on paper either in the field or in terms of possible publication. Generally the archaeologist should take this question into consideration for his site plans made in the field, but there is something to be said for due concern being given to publication reductions of the site plans. The table below gives some approximate limits to the degree of accuracy required for field plans at specified scales, made with firm 'sharp' HB pencil lines of 0.2 mm.

Scale	Accuracy of measurement required	
1/5	to nearest	2 mm
1/10		5 mm
1/25		1 cm
1/50		2 cm
1/100		5 cm
1/250		10 cm
1/500		20 cm
1/1000		50 cm

The archaeologist who is required to carry out his own surveying, either as leader of an excavation team, or as a volunteer helper, should be aware not only of the above degrees of accuracy, but also of the range of instruments available and the procedures likely to be required for field plans. Several principles are basic to surveying in any archaeological situation, and these are:

(1) the survey should progress from the whole to the part, from the framework to the detail;
(2) independent checks must be made of measurements;
(3) maps and plans are two-dimensional representations of three-dimensional features, and represent not the distance separating two points on the ground but the distance between the points if they were at exactly the same level.

Horizontal measurement

Pacing

For the archaeologist engaged in field reconnaissance, in carrying out necessarily rapid surveys of sites, in general sketch work not involving precision in measurements, the use of pacing can be of considerable value. One of the best examples of this in Britain is the 'Grinsell pace' as a standard of measurement for the description of round barrows of the Bronze Age. L. V. Grinsell's particular pace, used for measuring the diameters of many hundreds of barrows in southern England, and checked several times each year, is 0.914 m (1 yard); the author's, not as regularly checked, is 0.99 m (1 yard, 3 inches).

The field archaeologist willing to rely upon his own pace as a means of measurement must work at this to obtain a standard. It is better to walk naturally, and, with experience, to convert the number of paces to metres, rather than to try to walk at a metric unit which is even more elongated than a yard. To determine the pacing unit, about twenty lengths of a measured 100 m on even ground should be paced, and this will give an average unit. Thereafter, measured pacing should be carried out on rough pasture, up and down shallow slopes and along a metalled road or path. Each of these will yield its own pacing unit which should be noted and remembered by the archaeologist. It is not possible for any suitable degree of accuracy to be achieved by pacing on extremely rough ground such as ploughland, or up or down steep slopes. Practised pacing can be accurate to perhaps 5 per cent or even better, and the archaeolo-

gist will find this a useful aid not only in carrying out the work
noted above, but in using the technique as a preliminary to
setting out a measured survey; the question of scale can often
be resolved by a few minutes' pacing around a site.

Chain surveying

This is the simplest form of surveying, but requires much walking,
a small team, and the plan is not produced on the site. Chain
surveying is well adapted for small surveys on open ground, and
will produce very accurate plans. The field party should consist
of the surveyor and two chainmen, but often the surveyor will
have to make do with only one helper. The equipment necessary
for the survey consists of a chain (20 or 30 m long), ten surveying
arrows, six ranging rods or poles, a linen or metallic tape, and
(all optional) cross staff, optical square or box sextant, clinometer and offset rod.

Equipment   The chain most suitable for archaeological work is
the Engineer's Chain or Land Chain, 20 or 30 m long, and about
£10. Many archaeologists prefer to use metallic or linen measuring tapes, and these are accurate enough for most purposes, but
the chain is extremely hardy, of steel wire, is easy to use in the
field, and will stand up to any amount of pulling and tugging
that will stretch a tape or perhaps pull off its looped end or its
case. The chain will also not flap in the wind as will a light tape,
and this is probably its main advantage over a tape. The chain
links consist of straight wires with looped ends, and each link
is joined to the next by three wire rings (fig. 15). Each end of the
chain has a brass swivel handgrip which is included in the
measurement. The illustration shows that each straight wire,
plus its rings, totals 0.2 m. Every metre along the chain is fitted
with a plastic yellow tally, and there are red numbered tallies
at every 5 m; these numbered tallies run from each end to the
centre, to allow the chain to be used from either end. The
readings are made by observing the nearest marker and then
adding or subtracting the additional distance to obtain the
absolute value; estimations can be made of these distances or
can be made with a spring tape, if such a degree of accuracy is
necessary.

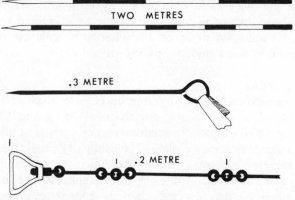

Fig. 15 Ranging rods or poles with divisions of 0.5 m and 0.2 m; surveyor's pins or arrows with red tab; land chain (part) with each straight wire plus its rings totalling 0.2 m, the handgrip being included in the first 0.2 m.

Surveying arrows are made of cast steel wire 40 to 45 cm long, pointed at the lower end for fixing in the ground and looped at the top for carrying; red tabs are generally attached so that they are less easily lost in the field (fig. 15). Arrows should not be put down flat on the ground at any time as they are practically invisible in rough grass. They are used in chain survey to mark the ends of chain lengths when a line is being chained or ranged, and to mark temporarily any other point of the survey. Arrows cost £2 for 10, and a field archaeologist can rarely have too many.

Ranging rods or poles are of seasoned timber or metal alloy, either 6 ft or 2 m long and painted alternate red and white or black and white in bands of one foot, 0.5 or 0.2 m (fig. 15). One end is generally shod with a metal point for driving into the ground. Rods are used in chaining to mark conspicuous points. They cost about £2 to £4, but suitable substitutes can be home-made from broomstick handles; garden bamboos are not really suitable for sighting accurately.

Linen or metallic tapes are used for making all short measurements in a chain survey. These consist either of an all-linen tape or one in which fine copper wires are woven for strength. Plastic coatings on both allow the tapes to be cleaned and preserve the markings. They come in a variety of lengths in a plastic, metallic or leather case with a flush-fitting wind-up handle; useful lengths for archaeological work are 20 and 30 m, but occasionally the 60 m tape will be found useful. Entirely metal tapes can also be obtained, and these will be more accurate than the linen variety, but are heavier; a 10-metre metal tape is likely to be useful during excavations. Most of these tapes have a ring handle at the end, and the outside edge of this should be included in the measurement, i.e. the edge should be held against the post or other beginning point. Such tapes should never be allowed to get excessively wet or dirty, or, if this happens, they should be dried and cleaned as soon as possible. Mud can often be removed during rewinding by allowing the tape to enter the case between two fingers which scrape off the dirt. If the tape is wet, it should be dried in a loose coil before rewinding, otherwise it will swell and probably jam in the case. Tapes should not be constantly dragged along the ground, and when reeling in, it is better to walk towards its end. Prices of tapes vary, but as a rough guide, a 30 m metallic tape will cost £5.

Other equipment which may be found useful in a chain survey includes the cross staff, optical square and box sextant. All of these are designed to allow lines to be laid out accurately at certain fixed or movable angles to the main line (p. 76).

Ranging a line The actual chain survey will have terminal points called stations (fig. 17, A, B, etc.). If these are a considerable distance apart, it will be necessary to put in intermediate points between the stations; this operation is called ranging the line. In archaeological fieldwork it is often necessary to set out a line of considerable length, from which offsets to details are dropped, and the accurate establishment of the line is essential. In ranging the line, the surveyor stands behind one of the station poles or ranging rods and sights the distant pole, at the same time directing his assistant to move to the right or left to locate a third (intermediate) pole in its proper place on the line. The correct order of ranging a line this way is shown in fig. 16, so that the first intermediate is put in at the greatest distance from the surveyor. If the reverse is carried out, i.e. if 3 is put in first, then it will obscure the sighting of 2. The assistant must position the pole by obeying the signals of the surveyor, generally right or left arm held out to indicate movement to left or right of the pole, and both arms up to show that the position is accurate. The poles must be put in vertically. The surveyor may find that the best position for sighting is about one metre behind the station pole, and rapid alternative viewing by right or left eye will indicate errors of intermediate positions quickly.

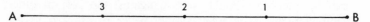

Fig. 16 Ranging a line between A and B; the poles are positioned in the numerical order shown for sighting.

Chain survey   In a chain survey of an area, the area is always divided up into a series of triangles, linked to each other by common sides; all the sides are measured by chaining, and this provides the basic framework for the area (fig. 17). The sides of the triangles should run as close to the boundaries of the area, or to other features, as possible, so that offsets can be easily measured (p. 73). The sides of the triangles are all ranged lines, and must be accurately measured, so that the triangles will fit together in drawing the plan of the area. Checklines across the triangles should be ranged and chained to prove the accuracy of the fieldwork (fig. 17, line AE, CE).

The basic procedures to follow for a chain survey in the field are:
(1) walk over the site, note its shape and surface features, boundaries and suitable positions for stations and survey lines;
(2) select main positions for the main stations. The care with which these are chosen will determine the ease and accuracy of the subsequent work. The survey lines should be as few as are consistent with obtaining a rigid scheme. One long line should run through the area, to form a base upon which the survey lines are built (fig. 17, AB). All triangles to be measured should have angles between 30° and 120° if possible. Lines should be on easily worked ground free from obstacles (p. 78), and as many as possible should be working lines, i.e. for offsets (fig. 17, AD, etc.). Sufficient checklines should be provided (fig. 17, AE, CE);

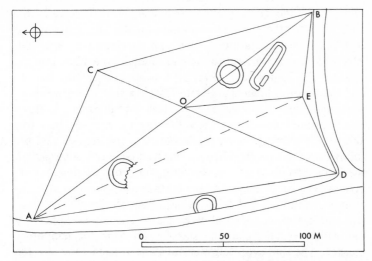

Fig. 17 Chain lines across a site at Dalnaglar, Perthshire, to show positions of triangles to be chained, and major features (circular enclosures and long house) to be planned. Compare this method with plane-table surveys of the same site, figs 41–3. Based on comparative surveys made by the author in 1960.

(3) mark the survey stations (fig. 17, A, B, etc.) with poles or ranging rods;
(4) chain the main lines, and locate and measure the offsets simultaneously, the surveyor booking all measurements (p. 70);
(5) chain all subsidiary lines (OC, OD) and checklines (AE, CE).

Chaining a line The team required should ideally be three people, the surveyor who directs operations and books the measurements, and two assistants, one the leader who takes the outer end of the chain and the ten arrows, one the follower who should be the more experienced of the two. If only two people are available, then the surveyor will act as the follower.

The follower holds the end of the chain at the station point, and the leader stretches the chain out in the direction of the line under measurement. He should pace out an approximate chain length, to avoid a sudden jerk of the chain as it reaches its limit. The leader then stands to one side and is directed by the follower until the chain is accurately on the line. An arrow is then put in the ground on the line, and the chain is pulled tight. The arrow is then moved to the end of chain and stuck into the ground. The leader then moves off towards the sighting station, and the follower again sights him from the first arrow position. A second arrow is put in by the leader, and after this is firmly and accurately positioned, the follower picks up the first arrow and keeps it. In this way, the leader fixes the arrows, and the follower collects them. When the tenth chain length is measured, the leader proceeds to the eleventh point, but he now has no arrows. The follower goes to the tenth arrow, puts in a *different* temporary marker, and removes the arrow. He should now have ten, and if not, they start all over again. The ten are handed to the leader, and the chaining starts again from the temporary marker. The surveyor–follower must note each time the ten chain lengths have been measured.

Several points should be made here about chaining. Careful note of arrows must be made, as they can easily be lost. The use of arrows in long grass is unsuitable, as the follower may not be able to find the arrow left by the leader as he moves to another length. The chain itself is dragged along, and should be wiped clean after use, and folded so that it can be either unfolded easily or thrown out into an open position next time.

In all surveys, linear measurements are always *horizontal* distance between two points. When the ground between is sloping, some method of obtaining a true horizontal distance between must be obtained. This is particularly relevant for the accurate planning of barrows, forts and so on. There are two methods of doing this, by stepping and plumbing, and by measuring along the slope and calculating the true horizontal distance.

Stepping and plumbing   This is a downhill operation generally. The follower holds the chain handle on the ground while the leader holds out a reasonable length of chain, 10 m or so, to prevent undue sag. The leader stands to one side as before, to allow sighting, then he holds the chain level and plumbs down with a plumb-bob to the ground where he fixes an arrow (fig. 18).

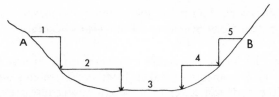

Fig. 18 Stepping and plumbing across a small valley or wide ditch; five stages from A to B.

A plumbing arrow, fitted with a lead weight near its point, can be used in place of the plumb-bob. It is best to work downhill if at all possible, in regular steps of 10 or 20 m, depending on the angle of slope and the need to keep the chain horizontal. The chain can be laid on the ground for the line direction, and a steel tape or metallic tape used for the stepping and plumbing. The surveyor–follower can ascertain if the tape or chain is horizontal by visually checking that its angle to the plumb line is 90°.

Measuring along a slope   If the slope is uniform or with only a couple of changes, measurements can be made directly along the surface of the ground and their true horizontal distances calculated by means of an Abney level (p. 109). The angle of slope can be determined with this level; if AB = slope distance (fig. 19), AC = horizontal distance, and α = angle of slope, then $\dfrac{AC}{AB} = \cos \alpha$, therefore AC = AB $\cos \alpha$. The true horizontal distance is therefore calculated, but only if the slope is uniform.

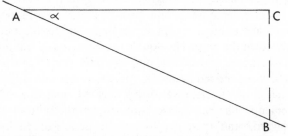

Fig. 19 Measuring a horizontal distance along a uniform slope, using the angle of depression.

For archaeological purposes, the stepping and plumbing method is probably more convenient and sufficiently accurate.

Offsets　To locate the actual boundaries of a survey, perpendicular measurements are taken from suitable points along the chain line, and these are called offsets (for procedures, see p. 73). They are necessary only at the points which will determine any change in boundary line, i.e. any boundary if straight can be accurately located by an offset at each end, and intermediate offsets, other than several as a check, are a waste of time. In offsetting any irregular or curvilinear boundary, the practice is to treat it as a series of straight lengths, the ends of each of which need to be measured (e.g. fig. 20, road to west of line AD measured by offsets to nine positions). The care with which the eventual plotting is done, and its scale, will determine the degree of precision required in the spacing and reading of offsets (p. 61).

Other offsets will of course allow the archaeological features of the area to be plotted. The central points of features can be measured and subsequent subsidiary measurements taken, or the ends or sides of the structure can be measured and incorporated in the plan. If the edges of the triangles have been chosen carefully, most features will be easily plotted by offsets, but in the case of isolated features well away from a line, the use of an optical square or cross staff may be required, or the measurement can be made by triangulation from three points on the line, two to provide an intersection, the third as a check.

Booking the chain survey　Field books are generally about 20 by 12 cm, opening lengthwise, and must fit the surveyor's pocket. The pages are unlined except for a single or double red line vertically down the page. The double line helps to prevent mixing of chain distances and offsets, and all chain measurements are entered between the red lines. The space to either side is reserved for sketches of the features being located, and the offsets' measurements. The entries are booked from the bottom of the page upwards and therefore follow the path worked by the surveyor. The notes must be clearly expressed and written. The sketches should be exaggerated sideways to provide space for

clear figures, but should be clearly expressed in their relation
to the chain line (fig. 20). The surveyor should always face in
the direction in which the line is being chained to avoid errors
of booking on the wrong side. The first pages of the book should
carry sketches of the layout of the main survey lines, with

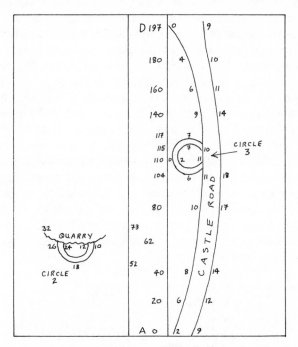

Fig. 20 Booking a chain survey of line AD, Dalnaglar (fig. 17).
Entries in metres.

stations identified by letters, and with arrows to show the
direction of chaining. There should also be sketches of the main
station points which will be 'tied' to adjacent permanent points,
in field ditches or fences, gate posts, road centres, large trees or
rock faces, etc.; the direction of the various chain lines should
also be noted in these sketches (see fig. 53). Further detail about
the nature of the ground under survey, such as wooded areas,
marshy patches, and the direction of flow of streams and drains,
should be recorded in the book. The sketches, notes and bookings

must be sufficiently clear to allow another person to plot the survey accurately, and this is the ultimate test.

Plotting the survey This work is generally not done in the field, but it is desirable for it to be carried out as soon as possible after the fieldwork is completed. The first essential is the determination of the scale, already considered by the surveyor in the degree of accuracy to which he has worked (p. 61). The maximum dimensions of the plan should be noted, and allowance made for a margin around the edge. The north bearing should if possible lie at the top of the plan, and space should be left for a scale at the base, and title, if required, at the top. Some regard should be paid at this moment to the question of the publication of the plan, so that its alignment on the paper can be suited to the appropriate journal. A useful procedure is to plot roughly the outline of the survey on tracing paper so that its size and shape can be visualized upon the final drawing paper. The scale to be used is then fixed, and the base line, or longest line, is laid down, followed by the end stations and intermediates. The main triangles attached to the base line are laid down by striking intersecting arcs with a beam compass (fig. 17).

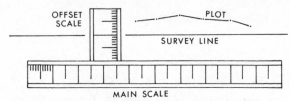

Fig. 21 Offset scale for plotting details from a chain survey or levelling operation.

The checklines come next, to verify the triangles. The remainder of the triangles and survey lines are then laid down, and the detail is ready to plot. The accuracy of the entire plan depends on the rigid triangular system, and it is therefore essential to draw these with fine pencil lines, H or 2H, on fairly hard paper.

The *detail* of the survey can be plotted at two different levels. The most accurate, and tedious, is to scale off on the lines the chainages at which offsets were taken, and then to use a set square to draw perpendiculars upon which the offset lengths are scaled. The other method is to employ an offset-scale (fig. 21). An ordinary scale is held parallel to the survey line so that the zeros coincide. The chainages are observed along the edge of this main scale, and upon it is moved the small offset-scale which is about 5 cm long with a central transverse zero line, to run on the chained line. Offset measurements can be scaled off on either side of the zero line, and detail drawn in as the offsets are plotted. After the plan is completed, the topographical features are inked in, the triangles erased; the stations are generally also inked in as circles or circled dots. The title, north bearing (p. 115) and scale can then be added to complete the plan.

Offset procedures   The purpose of the chain survey is to obtain an accurate scaled representation of the area, and the boundaries of this area are all obtained by offsets, perpendicular measurements taken from the line to a boundary point, or from a boundary point to the line. There are various ways by which this is achieved using the tape, and on occasion the optical square or cross staff can be used, but if the main lines of the survey are well positioned, the problems of offsets by tape alone can easily be overcome.

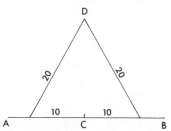

Fig. 22 Erecting a perpendicular to line AB from a point C upon the line.

To erect a perpendicular to the chain line at a point *upon* it, two methods can be used, if the optical square or cross staff is not available or suitable. In the first, AB is the chain line and C is the point from which a perpendicular is to be erected (fig. 22). Equal distances are measured along the chain, say, 10 m, and arrows are put in. The end ring of the tape is attached by one arrow and the 40 m mark on the tape is held or fixed to the other arrow. The surveyor then holds the 20 m mark on the tape, and moves away from C until the tape is taut. An arrow put in marks the point D, and DC is perpendicular to AB. In the second method, the 3–4–5 principle is used (fig. 23). From C, on AB, a distance of a multiple of 4 m (which need be no greater than 16 m but should be not less than 4 m) is measured and an arrow is put in (D). The tape end is then pinned to C and the mark on

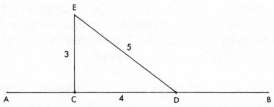

Fig. 23 Erecting a perpendicular to line AB from a point C upon the line.

the tape representing twice the distance already measured (CD) is fixed or held at D. The surveyor then takes the mark on the tape representing 3 m or its multiple, as chosen, and walks from C until the tape is taut. An arrow here marks the point E and CE is perpendicular to AB. This method is very commonly employed in setting out areas for excavation, and the positioning of the tape only on two sides of the triangle will save some confusion over multiples.

To drop a perpendicular to the chain line from a point outside it, two methods can be used. In the first, the tape is fixed to the point C and uniform arcs are cut on the line AB (fig. 24). The distance between these two points is then bisected by direct reading of the chain on AB, and D is thus found and arrowed. CD is perpendicular to AB. In the second, the 20 m mark on

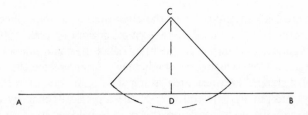

Fig. 24 Dropping a perpendicular to line AB from a point C off the line.

the tape is fixed at the point C, and the tape is stretched so that its zero end can be fixed by an arrow on the line AB at E (fig. 25). A second arrow is put on the tape at the 10 m mark, and the 20 m mark is then released to swing down on to line AB at D, which is arrowed. CD is perpendicular to AB.

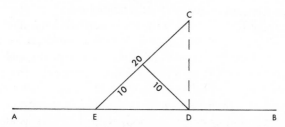

Fig. 25 Dropping a perpendicular to line AB from a point C off the line.

For short offsets from a chain line near boundaries or other features, estimates by eye of the perpendicularity of the tape to the line can be sufficient for some archaeological surveying at small scales; a limit of about 3 m should be adhered to, beyond which other methods should be used. Another rather rough method is that of swinging the tape. The end is pinned to the ground at the point off the line, and the taut tape is swung over the line on the principle that the shortest distance from the point to the line will be at right-angles to the line. This method is often sufficient for offsets of short lengths, perhaps up to 6 or 7 m, but beyond this the tape may sag, and the method is unsuitable for rough grass areas where the tape will not swing freely.

If the feature lies far from the line, it is often more convenient to triangulate it than to attempt to drop a perpendicular. To triangulate a point, tapes are fixed by arrows to two suitable positions on the line, well away from, and one one each side of, the estimated perpendicular intersection. The measurements are then made by stretching the tapes, or one in turn, to the feature. The position is later plotted by compass intersection on the plan.

Offsets can also be located accurately by optical instruments and for long offsets, the use of these is recommended. The simplest form is the cross staff which can be home-made for an outlay of next to nothing. A small board, 15 cm square, has a nail driven partway into the wood near each corner (fig. 26). The board is mounted on a pole at a height convenient to the viewer, about 1.5 m high. By aligning two diagonal nails on the main line, and fixing or holding the pole on the ground at this position, the viewer can move around and direct the positioning of a ranging rod into line with the other nails; the line of the cross staff pole and the rod will then be at right-angles to the main line. A proper cross staff is an equal-armed metal cross, mounted horizontally on a socket fitting over a pole; the ends of the arms form vertical sighting slits. These can sometimes be obtained with a compass mounted in the middle. A more compact type has a round or octagonal body with sighting-slits allowing angles to be set up at 90° and at 45°. All of these cross staffs must be set up with the pole vertical, and two small spirit levels clamped to the sides of the pole will allow this to be done easily.

Fig. 26 Cross staff for sighting positions at a right-angle to a line; can be in two pieces, the board fitting on to a pole of about 1.5 m length.

The optical square is an extremely compact instrument about 6 cm in diameter and 2.5 cm high. It is a reflecting type, which depends for its working on the principle that if a ray of light be incident on a mirror the angle of incidence is equal to the angle of reflection. In use the observer holds the instrument, a plan of which is in fig. 27, in his hand, or preferably on a mounting pole or tripod, and peers through the pinhole aperture at A. Through the top half (clear glass portion) of mirror D he sees the sighting pole at B. The reflection of another pole at C, movable by a helper, strikes the mirror E which is wholly silvered and is reflected to the lower (silvered) part of mirror D and thence to the observer's eye. The observer can thus see both pole B and C at the same time, and when these appear in mirror D as a straight line, then pole B is at right-angles to pole C, both taken through the observation point.

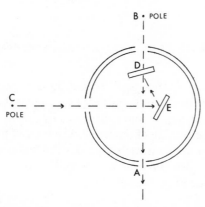

Fig. 27 Sketch plan of an optical square to show how pole C can be aligned at a right-angle to line AB.

The optical square is particularly useful in a chain survey as it can indicate to the observer the exact point on a chain line where a perpendicular, dropped from a point well outside the line (such as a field corner, or centre point of an archaeological feature), will land. This is achieved by the observer walking along the chain line keeping the pole at the end of the chain line in the centre of the clear position of mirror D until he sees the reflection of the other pole (at C) coinciding with D on the mirror. When these coincide, the observer is at the point where the perpendicular falls. To set out a perpendicular on the right of the chain line, the instrument is turned upside down, or the observer turns to face the opposite direction. The optical square costs about £11.

The box sextant operates on the same principle as the optical square, but the mirror E is movable, and can measure angles of 1 minute of arc. To observe the value of an angle, the operator stands at A (fig. 28), sights pole B in the clear part of the mirror,

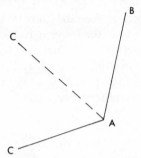

Fig. 28 Field positions in using a box sextant to determine the angle of position C relative to A on line AB.

then turns a milled screw until the reflection of pole C appears and coincides with B on the mirror. The angle is then read on a graduated arc on top of the instrument by means of a vernier moving with the turning of the screw. The limit of the arc is 120° or 135°, and for angles greater than this the best procedure is to split them into two portions and record each separately. Box sextants are expensive, at about £25.

Obstacles in chaining (for measurement of length) By the use of plumb-bobs, obstacles such as walls or hedges can be overcome (fig. 29). By erecting and dropping perpendiculars, build-

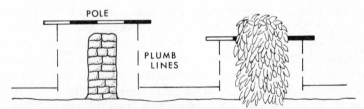

Fig. 29 Obstacles in chaining a line. The pole provides a horizontal measurement over a wall or through a hedge; the pole positions are plumbed on to the chain or tape.

ings that block the line can be by-passed, but it is better to set out lines to avoid such obstacles at the beginning of a chain survey. For a wide flat obstacle such as a lake or marsh, two methods can be adopted. For the first, select any convenient point C and from AC drop a perpendicular to the chain line

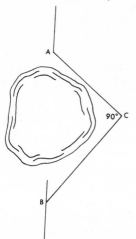

Fig. 30 Obstacles in chaining a line overcome by erecting a perpendicular.

to cut it at B (fig. 30). Then AB (the required length) = $\sqrt{AC^2 + CB^2}$. For the second, select any point C, project the line AC so that AC = CE (fig. 31). Project the line BC so that BC = CD. Then AB (required length) = DE. Sometimes a point on a line will be inaccessible to its direct measurement by

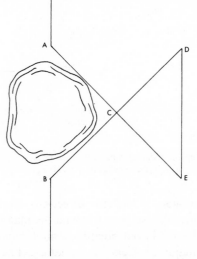

Fig. 31 Obstacles in chaining a line overcome by projecting lines.

chaining, for example, when it is across a river (fig. 32). To measure AB, erect a perpendicular BC from B on the line. Bisect BC at D. At C erect a perpendicular CE to BC, E being located on this line and on a line ranged through A and D. AB (the required length) = CE. If the line approaches the river

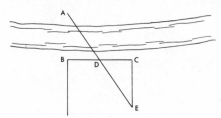

Fig. 32 Obstacles in chaining a line.
The measurement required (AB) equals CE.

at an acute angle, a subsidiary line BC can be set out parallel to the river bank (fig. 33). On this line, drop a perpendicular from A to meet the line at C. Measure BC and project the line, so that BC = BD. At D erect a perpendicular to CD that cuts the chain line at E. As the triangles are equal, then AB (the required length) = EB.

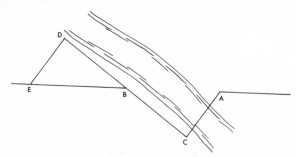

Fig. 33 Obstacles in chaining a line.
The measurement required (AB) equals EB.

Obstacles in ranging a line (for direction) A good surveyor will try to fix his main stations to avoid the major obstacles that might hinder his work, but often he cannot avoid them all, and hills are the major problem. In ranging a line over such an obstacle, both ends of the line may be visible from intermediate points, or they may *not* be so visible, and different procedures apply. If both ends can be seen from a central point, the cross staff can be employed. Set up the cross staff and sight one of the stations A through one pair of vanes. Without moving the instrument, moving around and sight back through the same vanes to find the other station B. If this is not cut by the sights, move the cross staff until B is seen, then carry out the same procedure of reversed sighting to A, until gradually the required position is found. This method can be carried out by one person, and is generally similar to the Gradually Approximating Method or Reciprocal Ranging Method using ranging rods and two persons (fig. 34). In this, the end poles A and B are very carefully

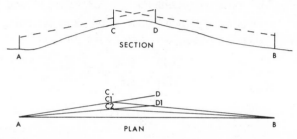

Fig. 34 Obstacles in ranging a line. The gradually approximating method to complete a straight line between two points (A and B) visible from two positions (C and D).

plumbed vertical, and the surveyor goes to pole position D, his assistant to C; from D, poles C and A are visible, and from C, poles D and B can be sighted. The surveyor at D sights A and ranges C to C_1, the assistant at C_1 sights B and ranges D to D_1. D_1 sights A and ranges C_1 to C_2, and so on until the amount of error is gradually reduced and all four poles are in a straight line. This method is suitable for setting out a base line across an elevated site such as a hill-fort, or large barrow. In the former case, however, and for a line over a long hill, the size of the area may be such that a large number of poles are required; exactly the same procedure can be carried out, as long as A can sight B and C, B can sight C and D, C can sight D and E, etc. A ranges B in line with C, B ranges C in line with D, and so on, repeating until the whole line is ranged correctly (fig. 35).

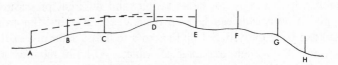

Fig. 35 Obstacles in ranging a line. The same method as in fig. 34 but using more poles on a larger site such as a hill-fort.

If both ends are not visible from intermediate points, such as in the case of a camp on a rocky cliff undergoing erosion, a 'random line' can be run clear of the cliff (fig. 36). Establish a line from A to avoid the obstacle, and on to this line drop a perpendicular from B to cut the line at B_1. Measure AB_1 and BB_1. $AB = \sqrt{AB_1^2 + BB_1^2}$. To range the line AB, locate D (and other points) by erecting a perpendicular at D_1, and extending it to D, the distance D_1D being achieved by the formula

$$\frac{D_1D}{AD_1} = \frac{B_1B}{AB_1}$$

then
$$D_1D = \frac{B_1B}{AB_1} \times AD_1.$$

To lay off a line parallel to the chain line, if a grid line is impossible to prolong due to obstacles, two points A and B are

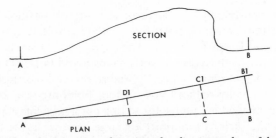

Fig. 36 Obstacles in ranging a line. A random line is run clear of the cliff, and perpendiculars are dropped from this line to establish positions D and C on the AB line required.

set up on the chain line, and perpendiculars are erected AC and BD (fig. 37). These are measured and made equal, to whatever

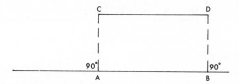

Fig. 37 Laying-off a line parallel to line AB by erecting perpendiculars (figs 24–5).

length is required, and CD is therefore parallel to AB. The original line can be recovered by reversing the procedure beyond the obstacle. To lay off a line parallel to the chain line from a point A outside the line, a suitable tape length AB is selected to arc on to the line at B and C (fig. 38). Along the line, D and E are chosen so that DE = BC by direct measurement. The tape is placed at D, and a second tape at E, and where they meet at

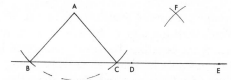

Fig. 38 Laying-off a line parallel to line BC from a point A off the line.

a distance DF and EF, each equalling AB and AC, the point F is arrowed. AF is parallel to BCDE. This method again is useful where a new grid line is to be started at a more convenient point, and the grid lines are to be parallel. Another way of achieving this is by selecting any convenient point (B) on the line and bisecting the distance between A and B by direct reading (fig. 39). An arrow is put here at C. Another arbitrary point on the line is

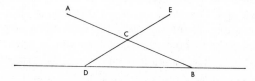

Fig. 39 Laying-off a line parallel to line DB from a point A off the line.

selected (D) and the line DC is projected to E so that DC = CE. AE is parallel to DB.

Plane table surveying

This method of surveying is not now employed to any great extent for engineering work because it is not sufficiently accurate. However, for *archaeological* surveys of small areas, the principle of the technique is a good one, because (1) the degree of accuracy of a proper plane table survey is generally adequate, (2) the procedures can be carried out by one or two persons, and (3) the resulting plan is developed on the site as the work progresses, and not after leaving the area.

Equipment   The equipment necessary for plane table surveys is a plane table with tripod, an alidade or sight rule, a spirit level, a trough compass, a plumb-bob and supply of paper and pencils.

The *plane table* consists of a mahogany board, 46 cm square or 61 by 46 cm, with aluminium battens beneath and a racer ring for attaching the board to the tripod. The tripod is generally of teak with adjustable legs and aluminium fittings. With an essential canvas case to protect the board, the whole outfit can cost about £60, but much cheaper versions exist, with a softwood board, fixed hardwood tripod and single bolt attachment, and this with case might cost less than £30. Second-hand outfits are often available, and ex-Army plane tables are sometimes extremely cheap if incredibly heavy. In setting up, the table must be levelled, and this is most easily achieved by the use of an additional piece of equipment, an adjustable head, which fits between the tripod and the board; this can cost from £16 to £30 new.

The *alidade* at its simplest is a plastic or boxwood ruler, 40 or 50 cm long on which are mounted two perpendicular sights, one at each end. One vane has a narrow vertical slit, the other vane has a wider slit through which is stretched a vertical wire. The line of sight through the slit to the wire is parallel to the edge of the rule. The simplest form costs *c.* £4. More elaborate alidades exist, with a movable parallel arm and a small spirit level attached. Telescopic alidades are also available, and are essential for surveys over large areas; these generally have provision for measurement of slopes and distances (p. 88).

As noted, the plane table survey is not as accurate a method as others, and it is essential that further potential sources of error should be avoided. The principles described below are of paramount importance, but other minor sources of trouble also exist. The paper to be used should be hard and of a quality, and expense, to avoid distortion by damp. It should be mounted on the board by paste, tape or pins; if the latter, these should be put in at the sides or undersurface of the board, as nothing should project above the level of the upper surface. The paper *must* be taut and immovable on the board.

In setting up the survey, three conditions must be satisfied:
(1) the table must be centred over a chosen station or point on the ground, by the use of the plumb-bob suspended from the top of the tripod;
(2) the table must be levelled, by placing the spirit level on the table in two positions at right-angles, until the board is level; an adjustable head on the tripod will be useful here, otherwise the tripod legs can be raised or lowered;
(3) the table must be orientated, and is so described when it is placed so that all the lines of the paper are parallel to the corresponding lines on the ground.

Orientating the table (fig. 40)   The table has been positioned over point A on the ground and levelled. A line ab has been drawn on the paper towards the station B on the ground at a scale appropriate to the size of the table. The table is now moved to station B, centred over B and levelled. To orientate the table, the alidade is placed along ba and the table is rotated (gently, by loosening the screw holding the board to the tripod) until station A is sighted through the alidade. When this is achieved, ba is parallel to BA, and the table is clamped in this position by tightening the screw. The table is now ready for further sighting (to C).

Another way of orientating the table is by the use of the trough compass, a compass needle in a long slender metallic or wooden box. At station A, the compass is placed on the table and moved about until the needle floats centrally, and a fine pencil line (2H or 3H) is drawn along the side of the box. At B or any other station the table can be orientated by placing the compass against the line, and swinging the table until the needle floats centrally. This method of orientating is not as accurate as the other, because local metals may attract the compass, but it can be useful in finding a rapid approximate position for the table prior to the final adjustment by sighting.

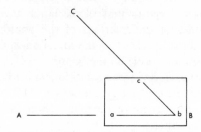

Fig. 40 Plane-table surveying. Orientating the table.

The technique of plane tabling involves positioning the alidade accurately on the paper. The ruling edge of the alidade must be in contact with the actual point on the paper to which, or from which, the line is being drawn. If the alidade has a parallel movable arm, this is the part that is brought across to the point. In sighting through the alidade, the instrument should be pivoted about a finger tip or the blunt point of a (cleaned) match, not a pencil point and not a pin stuck into the point. The perforation of the paper in these ways will almost always lead to an enlargement of the hole, and the precise point on the paper will be lost. The use of an alidade with a movable arm is desirable if not absolutely essential. In drawing rays from the station point, for radiation or intersection (see below), the lines should actually appear on the paper only at or near their presumed destination, i.e. at their approximate length or intersection; preliminary pacing and arranging of the survey is essential (see below). The prolongation of the drawn rays will only confuse the detail and obscure the station point on the paper. When sighting a station, do not lean on the board, and keep all movements that affect the board, i.e. positioning the alidade and drawing rays, to the lightest possible touch. The centring, levelling and orientation of the board must not be upset.

Fieldwork The fieldwork to be done before the survey commences is simple, but careful consideration of the problem and the approach to it will save time and trouble. The area to be included on the plan should be paced so that an approximate size and shape is determined. This, and the size of the plane table, will determine the scale of the plan and the positioning of the survey and sight stations on the table. The choice of sight stations is also made now, and poles or ranging rods put in and plumbed vertical. The main or survey stations are marked by pegs driven into the ground, so that the plane table can straddle them. The principle for choosing main stations is the same as for a chain survey; that the stations can bring in as much of the site detail as possible. The sight stations will be selected as marking positions where change in boundary alignment occurs, or any other important visible features exist. As in any survey, the framework should be fixed first, and the detail later; in plane tabling, this should mean that rays are only drawn to locate the main features of the area, which is thereby plotted on the plan, and, subsequent to this, rays can be drawn to plot detail by reoccupation of the survey stations. It is possible that the best method for plotting the framework is not the best for detail; *intersection* is a useful method for the former, *radiation* and direct measurement for the latter.

The methods used in plane table survey are radiation, traversing, intersection and resection, and three of these are suitable for archaeological work. The choice of a particular method depends upon the shape of the site, the assistance available, and in some cases the preference of the individual surveyor.

Radiation This method is limited in its application, because each sight station must be visible from the chosen main or radiating station (fig. 41). If, however, the boundaries of the area chosen are clearly visible from a vantage point, e.g. over the centre of a barrow, then radiation is a useful and accurate method to employ. Two people are required. The sight stations are marked by poles, and the main station (o) is selected. The table is centred, levelled and clamped. The trough compass is positioned and a line drawn to indicate the orientation. A point o is selected on the paper to represent the main station O. The alidade is placed so that its arm touches o, and a ray is drawn towards sight station A; the alidade is then moved, its arm always touching o, and rays are drawn to all the other site stations B, C, D, E, F and G. Measurements are then made from O to A, B, and so on, and these are scaled off on the rays oa, ob, and so on. The various points are then joined, and the plan is then

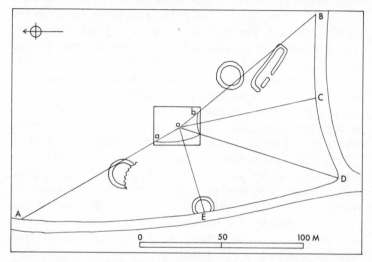

Fig. 41 Plane-table surveying by radiation of a site at Dalnaglar, Perthshire, to show the positions of the sight stations from the central position O.

completed by addition of any other detail not marked by a survey station pole, and by a description of the features planned; the detail can be put in by direct measurement from sight stations (by offsets (recommended) or triangulation), by estimation by the surveyor, or by subsequent radiation.

If the degree of accuracy, and the scale of the plan, are suitable, the use of a telescopic alidade can greatly reduce the time taken by the radiation method. The telescope of the alidade will probably be fitted with vertical arcs and stadia hairs, so that slopes and distances can be measured. The stadia hairs consist of two short horizontal cross hairs separated by a main one stretching across the diameter of the tube. To use these stadia hairs in measuring distances, an assistant holds a levelling staff (p. 98) at each sight station. The surveyor reads the staff where it is cut by the upper and lower stadia hairs, e.g. (a) 2.76 m and (b) 1.35 m, and the difference between these readings, 1.41 m, is multiplied by 100 to give the distance from the main station to the sight station, 141 m. The process is accurate only for horizontal lines of sight, but modern telescopic alidades have in-built provision for the rapid reading of the horizontal distance. A telescopic alidade may cost £120, but again second-hand tested instruments may well be available.

For sights that are *not* horizontal, using an ordinary telescopic alidade with stadia hairs and vertical arcs (graduated in degrees), the true horizontal distance is obtained by multiplying the difference in the readings, $a-b$, by 100, and also by the cosine, squared, of the angle α made by the line of sight of the telescope with the horizontal. Thus, horizontal distance $= 100 (a-b) \cos^2 \alpha$. This procedure is unnecessary where the angle of slope does not exceed 3° (about 1 in 20).

If the alidade is fitted with a Beaman stadia arc, the process of measuring the distances is eased. The Beaman arc consists of two scales which are read instead of the angle (α) in degrees. The H scale is so devised that it provides a reading that can be directly applied to 100 $(a-b)$ for obtaining true horizontal distance. Thus, horizontal distance $= 100 \;\; (a-b)-(H$ scale reading $(a-b))$.

Traversing   This method of plane table survey is not likely to be employed in much archaeological work. It is not as accurate as chaining a series of ranged lines, but details can be found in most surveying textbooks.

Intersection   This is a very important method, and is suitable for one person. Only one measurement on the ground is required, and the plan can be completed rapidly. The preliminary examination of the area, such as a field with barrows, or a camp or hill-fort, or a spread of standing stones, and an approximation of its size and shape through pacing will indicate the scale of the plan to be developed and its position on the plane table.

Sight stations are selected, and poles erected, where main features change alignment or character. Main or survey stations, at least two in number, are then chosen so that every sight station can be seen from at least two main stations (fig. 42).

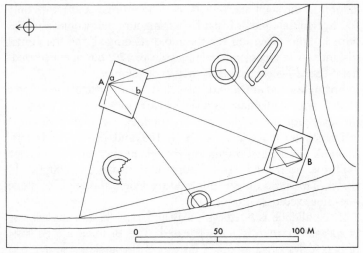

Fig. 42 Plane-table surveying by intersection of a site at Dalnaglar, Perthshire, to show the main stations A and B, and other sight stations.

The choice of main stations is vital, and sight stations may have to be adjusted to meet the requirements of the main stations. The principle of the method is the accurate intersection of two rays drawn from the main stations, and if the rays intersect at an angle less than 30°, or more than 150°, the error introduced at the scale used, generally 1/100 or smaller, will make the position on the plan extremely unreliable; 60°–120° has been suggested as the range for acceptable ray intersections. Therefore, in positioning the sight stations and the main stations, the surveyor should prevent bad intersections, and generally this will mean the establishment of a third main station. The advantage of a third station is also that it provides a check on the intersections from the other two.

The actual plane-table work begins with the measurement

of the distance between two main stations, A and B. This is scaled off on to the paper as *ab*. The table is set up with *a* over A, and levelled. It should be noted that at scales of 1/100 or smaller, the point *a* can be considered to be over A if the approximate centre of the table is over A. The alidade is placed along *ab*, the table rotated until the line of sight cuts B. The table is clamped, and with the alidade arm touching *a*, rays are drawn towards all the sight stations; the rays need not be complete, but should be short lengths at or near the presumed intersections. They should be labelled by descriptive notes, e.g. field corner, barrow, tree in hedge, to avoid confusion. The table is then moved to main station B, orientated so *b* is over B, levelled, and the alidade placed along *ba*. The table is rotated until the sight lines cut A, and is then clamped. With the alidade arm always touching *b*, rays are drawn to all the sight stations to intersect the rays drawn from *a*. This produces the framework of the plan (fig. 42), and the points thus located can serve to fill in detail as noted above. The use of the intersection method for detail on a plan is not recommended, as the rays tend to accumulate in quantities that can only confuse when the second main station rays are drawn.

If the intersections are bad, a third station will be needed, and over large areas and complicated large sites, a number of main stations, and many site stations, will be required. The main stations must of course be accurately located in relation to one another, and would therefore be sighted as an ordinary sight station during the work from the first main stations, i.e. a third main station C would be planned from stations A and B. The table would then be moved so that *c* was over C, levelled, and orientated on B, before sight stations were plotted. The sighting of some stations from C already planned from A and B would be a check on the accuracy of the work; if slight errors appeared, i.e. if the intersections were not exact and a small triangle was produced instead, the surveyor should consider if the error was great enough to warrant concern at the scale he was using. Assuming that the true point lies within the triangle (not necessarily so but probable), his error can be halved by accepting an average central position for the point within the triangle. Otherwise, he can check the intersections by reoccupation of all the main stations, or the one at which he suspects the error was perpetrated; a choice can be made on the basis of the size of the errors appearing at the other sight positions.

Resection   This is a subsidiary method in plane table survey, and is used only for the location of main or survey stations, and not for sight stations. It will arise when the surveyor wishes to occupy a position in the area under survey which he has not yet plotted on his plan by radiation or intersection. It may be that his original main stations are no longer available, e.g. in a gravel pit, or in a field where the posts marking his stations A and B have been removed (fig. 43). The positioning of a new main

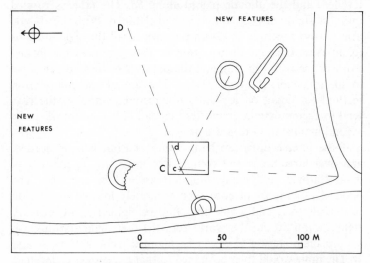

Fig. 43 Plane-table surveying by resection, of a site at Dalnaglar, Perthshire, to show the position of the new station C and ray drawn towards station D.

station depends upon the preservation of three sight stations previously planned. The table is set up at a new main station (C), carefully selected to allow any new sightings to take place. The table is levelled, orientated with the trough compass, and clamped. The alidade is positioned so its arm touches one of the former sight stations on the plan, and it is aligned so that the same station appears in the alidade sights. A ray is drawn towards the surveyor from the sight station towards the new main station *c.* The table remains clamped, and the alidade is moved to the second sight station, and then the third. Rays are drawn back from each of these as before, and should intersect with the first ray. If the intersection is not a point, where three lines cross, the centre of the triangle of error can be accepted as the position on the plan of *c*, or the table can be re-orientated by a slight movement to right or left, and the entire procedure repeated until the triangle is reduced to a point. Check-sightings on a fourth sight station already plotted should be made. From the new main station C, now located on the plan as *c*, another new main station D can be sighted and a line drawn towards it and scaled off. The new base line *cd* can then be used for sighting any new features as before.

The advantages of plane table survey to the archaeologist who is acting as an amateur surveyor are that it is reasonably accurate, quickly completed, undemanding on manpower, and productive of an immediate plan in the field. Radiation is the more accurate of the two main methods, but requires more people and more time than does the intersection method.

Vertical measurements

Levelling
Levelling is the procedure followed in determining the relative heights, or differences in elevation, of points on or around a site.

Equipment The instrument used by surveyors is basically a telescope which is attached to a bubble tube so that the horizontal axes of the tubes are parallel. The instrument has levelling screws so that it can be tilted to bring the bubble into the centre of its tube, and when this is achieved the line of sight through the telescope is a level line.

The most common type of level used in archaeological work is the Dumpy level, called this because of its appearance, a short squat instrument (fig. 44). The features of an ordinary Dumpy level are: internal focusing of the telescope (by a screw on the right-hand side of the telescope), twist focusing of the eyepiece, bubble reflector (so that the surveyor can observe the bubble position as he sights on the staff), levelling screws.

There are a very large number of levels available that are suitable for archaeological work and are not expensive. Second-hand levels are commonly available, and if checked for accuracy these are perfectly satisfactory; they will cost from £20 upwards, and will generally be rather heavy instruments. These, and a majority of Dumpy levels, have three or four levelling screws to enable them to be correctly positioned. Other Dumpy levels have mechanisms that allow a more rapid levelling operation for the setting-up of the instrument, either through a single screw or more or less automatically; these are noted below.

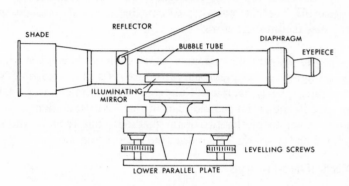

Fig. 44 Sketch section through a Dumpy level.

Before any work can be carried out, the instrument must be set up and levelled. A few instruments still in use have four levelling screws, but most have three. The legs of the tripod are firmly planted into the ground, or positioned so that they will neither slip sideways nor squeeze down further. The tripod should be placed, using the adjustable legs, so that its top is approximately level by eye. The telescope is attached to the tripod by the screw arrangement provided.

There are four main types of level likely to be encountered on archaeological sites:
(1) The oldest type relies upon the centring of the tube bubble by three, sometimes four, screws in the base of the level. To level the telescope, turn it so that it lies parallel to any pair of the three screws; these two screws are then turned

in opposite directions, i.e. one clockwise and one anti-clockwise, until the bubble is centred. The direction in which the left-hand screw moves is the direction of bubble travel, i.e. to bring the bubble from the left in to the centre, turn the left-hand screw inwards (anticlockwise) and the right-hand inwards (clockwise). Once the bubble is centred, turn the telescope through 90° and level up using only the third screw which lies beneath the telescope. The telescope is then moved around again, over each screw until all minor adjustments have been made and the bubble remains centred in any telescope position. Levels of this type are only available second-hand.

(2) The most common type has a circular bubble level, on the base, centred by three screws as above, and the final adjust-ment to make the telescope level is carried out by a screw, placed under the eyepiece of the telescope, which centres a second bubble in the tubular level beside the telescope. Good levels of this type cost from £100 upwards, including tripod and carrying case, and weigh as little as 2.1 kg (about 5 lb) with case.

(3) A slightly different level is the 'Quickset' type; this has a ball and socket type of mounting at the base, which enables the circular bubble to be roughly centred, after which the central bolt is clamped firmly. The instrument is then levelled accurately for each sighting by a tilting screw, as in (2) above, which centres the bubble in the tubular level beside the telescope. This type of level, and case, may weigh about 1.5 kg (3 lb), and costs around £55 with tripod.

(4) The most modern type of instrument is the automatic level, in which there is a compensator ensuring that the line of sight is always horizontal. The level is positioned on the tripod to be roughly horizontal, and three screws are used to make approximately central a pillbox bubble; the readings are then made at once without any fine adjustment. Some of these instruments are extremely compact, weigh about 3.5 kg (7 lb), and cost as little as £120.

Some of the varieties of levels available of the more modern types are:

Dumpy levels: Wild Heerbrugg NKO1 *c*. £75
                              N 10 *c*. £100

Quickset levels: Hilger-Watts Quickset *c*. £65
                              Stanley Sitemaster *c*. £55

Automatic levels: Stanley AL–31 *c*. £120
                              Wild Heerbrugg NA2 *c*. £200

The next stage in levelling after the accurate positioning of the level is to focus the telescope. This is a two-process operation at first. The cross hairs are focused by turning the eyepiece until the hairs are sharply defined. After this, the staff (see below) should be sighted and the telescope focused on it, by turning the screw generally mounted on the right-hand side of the telescope. The surveyor should then sight through and, by slightly moving his head, see if the relationship between the objective (staff reading), and the cross hairs changes; if it does, correction for 'parallax' is essential. To correct, turn the focusing screw until no object can be seen in the telescope, turn the eyepiece to bring the cross hairs in sharp definition, then focus the telescope upon the objective again and test as before. Once the correction is made, the position is fixed for the particular observer's eyesight.

Datum   The usual method of comparing heights is to refer them to a common datum, a point the height (altitude) of which is known or can be found out, and which is considered both convenient and permanent to the area under survey. This can be any fixed mark on the ground or on a building; archaeologists tend to use temporary marks on a site, and then to level these in to a permanent mark outside, and this is a reasonable procedure if the temporary mark (such as a wooden post driven well into the ground) is immovable for as long as is necessary.

The whole point of the levelling operation is to express each point on the site as a definite number of metres above or below the datum. On an archaeological site, the temporary datum can be assumed to represent any altitude the surveyor wants, but generally it is taken as zero, and readings of features on the site are therefore expressed in terms of metres above or below this ($+x$ m or $-x$ m). Eventually, however, the exact height of the datum, and thereafter all the points, must be established, and to do this the surveyor will seek a permanent mark which has a known altitude above mean sea level. The archaeologist need not use this on his contour plan of the site (see fig. 60), and may prefer to express the contours as above or below an assumed zero mark in order to make the contours more easily assimilated by the reader (see fig. 58), but somewhere in the text of his report he will record the absolute values.

The absolute datum points available in Britain refer to mean sea level, the Ordnance Survey Datum, established at Newlyn, Cornwall, from many years of tidal measurements. By geodetic levelling this datum has been transferred over all of Britain, and is available as a series of Bench Marks cut into permanent features such as walls, bridges and the like. A Bench Mark is a fixed point of reference, and its usual form is a triple arrow pointing upwards to a horizontal groove (fig. 45), the centre

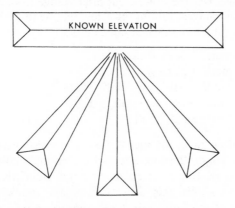

KNOWN ELEVATION

Fig. 45 Ordnance Survey bench mark.

of which is the known level above Ordnance Survey Datum (mean sea level). On maps at scales of 1/1250 as well as 1/2500, the positions of Bench Marks are shown by an arrow, and the height is also recorded in feet or metres to two decimal places. There is an advantage in starting levelling work at a Bench Mark, as the absolute values are known at the beginning of the survey, but the reverse procedure is also satisfactory and is more often used by archaeologists, particularly on small sites and on sites remote from the nearest Bench Mark. Bench Marks tend to disappear as buildings are replaced and bridges and gateposts rebuilt. The absolute heights of some are not shown on the maps, and can be obtained by application to the Ordnance Survey.

The levelling staves used in this country are now almost totally metric, but some archaeologists continue to level in feet; the latter practice will no doubt disappear in time, but in any long-term field project that commenced with measurements in feet, and with contours drawn in feet, it is clearly essential to continue this. Similarly, excavation areas laid out in feet, and drawn at a scale commensurate with feet (e.g. 1/12), will continue.

There is a great variety of staves available for levelling – folding or telescopic, of wood or metal, in lengths from 3 to 5 m. For archaeological work there is no particular staff that has an advantage over the others, but prices range from £15 to over £50. Wooden staves, folding or telescopic, tend to be cheaper than aluminium. Examples of 4-m staves:

'Vulcan' metal 2-piece staff, *c*. £18
'Vulcan' metal 4-piece staff, *c*. £24
'English' wooden telescopic staff, *c*. £24
'Carstaff' wooden 4-piece staff, *c*. £20
Wooden 2-piece staff, *c*. £15

The reading faces on metric staves are also varied. All of course have major divisions into metres, but the smaller divisions may consist of 10 mm intervals or 5 mm intervals; there are several types within this depending on the symbols adopted. Illustration of the four main types appears in fig. 46. In types B and C, the metre reading is repeated in red; in type RU, which is the British Standard Metric Reading, the division lines are in alternate black and red, by metres, and the full reading to 0.1 of a metre is printed at the relevant divisions. Type R is the same as RU but the numbers are inverted so that they appear right-way up through the telescope. Some levels now provide an upright sighting, and the combination of one of these and a type R staff is unfortunate. Type RU is probably the most convenient staff to use, but familiarity with all is necessary. The divisions of

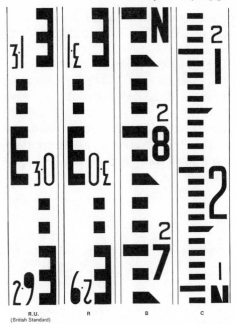

Fig. 46 Metric readings on staves: Types B and C have metre reading in red, types R and RU have alternate metres in red and black, with full reading to 0.1 m repeated. Divisions on types B, R and RU are in 0.01 m (10 mm), type C in 0.005 m (5 mm). Numbers on types B and C refer to top of mark opposite top of number; numbers on types R and RU refer to base of mark opposite base of number. Number 9 appears as N on types B and C.

types R, RU and B are in 10 mm (0.01 m), so that the observer can read off the height to the nearest dividing line, and then estimate to a further decimal place if desired. For archaeological work, the degree of accuracy should be considered before levelling begins, so that unnecessary fractions can be ignored. Normally, reading to the nearest 10 mm is sufficient. For Types B and C, the number on the staff refers to the top of the mark opposite the top of the number. The number 9 is changed to N(ine) on types B and C, to avoid the reverse confusion with 6. On types R and RU, the numbers refer to the base of the mark opposite the base of the numbers. Fig. 46 should make this clear. The use of metric measurements which automatically are in decimals of a metre disposes of the difficulty sometimes experienced by archaeologists using the old Sopwith or Scotch staves in feet, that the divisions thereon were also in decimals of a foot and not in inches.

The staff is held by the assistant upon the point required to be levelled, and must be vertical. The surveyor looking through the telescope can see if the staff is straight in the plane at right-angles to his line of sight, that is, if it leans to right or left, but he cannot see if the staff is tilted towards or away from him. The assistant must therefore ensure the upright position of the staff, and he can use a small spirit level for this held against the back and then the side of the staff.

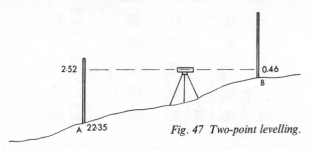

Fig. 47 Two-point levelling.

Differences of level between two points   The simplest operation in levelling is to obtain the difference of level between two points, and from this all other operations derive. The level is set up about midway between the two points A and B (fig. 47). The staffman holds the staff on A and then on B, and the two readings are made by the surveyor. The readings are essentially measurements made vertically downward (the staff) from a horizontal line (the line of sight from the levelled instrument). Therefore the difference of level between A (at, say, 2.52 m) and B (at, say, 0.46 m) is by subtraction $2.52 - 0.46 = 2.06$ m, and B is 2.06 m higher than A.

If the absolute height of A is known (if, for instance, it is a Bench Mark at 22.35 m above mean sea level), then the difference between the readings can be added to the absolute height to obtain the height of B. B is therefore $22.35 + 2.06 = 24.41$ m above mean sea level.

Alternatively, the same result is achieved by referring to the line of sight of the level. If A is 22.35 m above mean sea level, the height of the line of sight is $22.35 + 2.52 = 24.87$ m. B is 0.46 m below this line of sight, and is therefore $24.87 - 0.46 = 24.41$ m above mean sea level.

If A is arbitrarily assigned an absolute height for purposes of the work, the same procedure will be carried out, but subsequently all the important readings will be converted to absolute levels when the true height of A has been calculated through levelling it into a local Bench Mark.

Series levelling If the two points whose levels are to be measured are some distance apart, or separated by obstacles, there may be no position for the level from which both are visible (fig. 48).

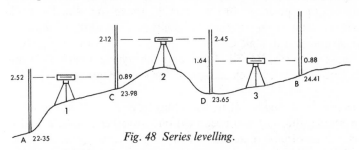

Fig. 48 *Series levelling.*

The level is set up near A, and the staff is held at A for a reading of, say, 2.52 m. If the absolute height of A is known, say 22.35 m, the collimation height (the height of the line of sight) is $22.35 + 2.52 = 24.87$ m. The staff is moved to C, the level remaining in position, and the reading is made, say, 0.89 m; the height of C is therefore $24.87 - 0.89 = 23.98$ m. The staff remains at C, but is turned carefully to face a new instrument position (2) beyond C and towards the destination B. This position need not be on a straight line between A and B, nor need the staff be put on the line. The new reading of C is made, say, 2.12 m; the new collimation height is therefore $23.98 + 2.12 = 26.10$ m. The staff now moves to D, the instrument remaining in place, and a reading is made of 2.45 m; D is therefore $26.10 - 2.45 = 23.65$ m above mean sea level. The instrument again moves, the staff is turned carefully, and the reading of D from the new position (3) is made, 1.64 m. The new collimation height is therefore $23.65 + 1.64 = 25.29$ m. Finally, the staff is placed on B, the instrument remaining in its previous position, and the reading of B is made, 0.88 m. The absolute height of B is therefore 25.29 − 0.88 = 24.41 m.

At no time can both instrument and staff be moved together, or the process is totally ruined, and a new start must be made. In the example above, points C and D for the staff are *change-points*, not necessarily on a straight line between A and B but on firm, unyielding ground.

Back-sights and fore-sights   A back-sight is the first observation made in levelling after the instrument has been set up. A fore-sight is the last observation made before moving the instrument to another position. In the example above (fig. 48), the back-sights were from instrument position 1 to staff position A, instrument 2 to staff C, and instrument 3 to staff D. The fore-sights were 1C, 2D, 3B. There must always be a back-sight and a fore-sight at each change-point for the instrument.

Intermediate sights   If in travelling from A to C in the above example, the staff had been held on two other points, E and F, the observations made are called intermediate sights. An intermediate sight is any observation made on a staff after the back-sight, except the last one which is the fore-sight. In booking levels (see below), extreme care must be taken to keep back-, intermediate and fore-sights separate, in different columns of the book, as these have different functions in the calculation of levels.

Running a section   If levels are to be established over a line through a site or area, in order to produce a section, the above procedures apply, except that the line itself will be accurately ranged and arrows put in at the intervals or points required (fig. 49). The level is positioned so that a number of these points can be seen, and an arbitrary or an absolute height is obtained for a starting-point on or near the line. In the example shown, the staff is placed on a Bench Mark of known height of 8.00 m above mean sea level. The reading is taken and is booked as a Back Sight. The instrument stays in place, and the staffman moves to positions on the line at A, then B, then C, and so on,

1 Native settlement, Jenny's Lantern, Titlington, Northumberland. The oblique sunlight casts a long shadow from the ruined house (*right centre*), and picks out the details of the earthworks known as Jenny's Lantern (*top*) and related enclosures (*left centre*). *Photograph by J. K. S. St Joseph, Cambridge University Collection. Copyright reserved.*

2 Round barrows, near Winterbourne Stoke, Wiltshire, now ploughed out but revealed by soil contrasts of chalk and earth. *Photograph by J. K. S. St Joseph, Cambridge University Collection. Copyright reserved.*

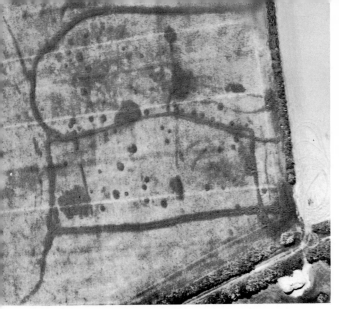

3 Native settlement, near Andover, Hampshire, revealed by differential growth of crops, the ditch systems supplying and retaining more moisture, allowing the crop to develop more strongly and to maintain its colour. *Photograph by J. K. S. St Joseph, Cambridge University Collection. Copyright reserved.*

4 Native settlement, West Overton, Wiltshire, partly revealed by a cereal crop in the field, but obscured by a root crop in the second field. The ditch and internal pits are particularly well-marked. *Photograph by J. K. S. St Joseph, Cambridge University Collection. Copyright reserved.*

5 Late Neolithic pit at Grantully, Perthshire, revealed by differential drying-out of the gravel and sand filling in relation to the undisturbed gravel. Surface exposed for 24 hours, photograph taken at noon after light rain the previous evening. Scale totals one foot.

Bronze Age urn with cremation at Grantully, Perthshire, revealed in its pit; stone slab covering its broken base removed. The next stage in excavation is enlargement of the pit to allow a metal or wooden plate to be inserted beneath the urn so that it can be lifted intact for transport to a museum laboratory. Scale totals one foot.

6 Henge monument at Mount Pleasant, Dorset, showing open excavation on massive scale using mechanical methods with a large team of archaeologists. *Photograph by P. Sandiford, courtesy of Dr G. Wainwright.*

7 Photogrammetric plan of Neolithic settlement and Bronze Age cemetery at Grantully, Perthshire. The cremation pits (*lower right*) were initially exposed by a pipe-line trench (see fig. 2), and the Neolithic scoops and pits (*centre and top left*) were dug into a gravel spread. *Photograph by F. M. B. Cooke.*

8 Prehistoric wooden roadway, the Sweet track, in peat at Shapwick, Somerset, with string grid in place for scale drawing; tapes stretched along both sides. The string divisions are at 0.4 m intervals.

until position E is reached. The readings taken on B, C and D are booked as Intermediates. In sighting E, the instrument is at its limit of accuracy, according to the surveyor's ease in sighting, and it must be moved. E is booked as a Fore Sight. The staff remains in place, and the instrument is moved to a new position (2), levelled and sighted on E again. The reading is booked as a Back Sight, on the same line as the booked Fore Sight reading of E, because they refer to the same position. The staff is moved to F, G, H, I, J and K, and the entries are booked as Intermediates except the last which is a Fore Sight.

Level books   The entries in the surveyor's book can be listed in two ways, the Reduced Level method or the Rise and Fall method.

The Rise and Fall method has entries booked as follows:

Back Sight	Inter-mediate	Fore Sight	Rise	Fall	Reduced Level	Distance	Remarks
2.34					8.00		Benchmark on wall (8.00 m)
	3.22			0.88	7.12		position A
	2.12		1.10		8.22	10 m	B
	4.03			1.91	6.31	20	C
	3.34		0.69		7.00	30	D
3.28		4.23		0.89	6.11	40	E
	3.56			0.28	5.83	50	F
	3.62			0.06	5.77	60	G
	4.08			0.46	5.31	70	H
	3.24		0.84		6.15	80	I
	3.22		0.02		6.17	90	J
		3.86		0.64	5.53	100	K

The Reduced Level in this method is obtained for each position by calculating its height in relation to the position immediately preceding it, whether Back Sight or Intermediate. Thus, at position A the staff reading of 3.22 is compared with the Back Sight reading of 2.34; the difference is 0.88, and this is a fall as the reading at A is greater (i.e. the foot of the staff is lower). A Fall is subtracted. The R.L. is thus 8.00−0.88 = 7.12. At B, the difference between B (2.12) and A (the immediately preceding reading, 3.22) is 1.10 and for B this is a rise as its reading is smaller (i.e. the foot of the staff is higher). A Rise is added. The R.L. is 7.12+1.10 = 8.22. At E, the R.L. is 7.00 (D)−0.89 (the difference between D and the Fore Sight reading of E) = 6.11. F, however, is 6.11−0.28 (the difference between the new Back Sight reading of E and F) = 5.83.

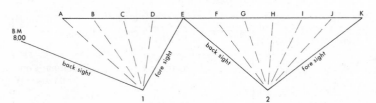

Fig. 49 Running a section. Back-sights and fore-sights as shown, all others are intermediate sights.

A check must be made of the accuracy of the arithmetic in the above methods. This is done by adding up the Back Sight readings, and then the Fore Sight readings; the difference between these gives the net Rise or Fall from the beginning to the end of the work, and this must equal the difference between the first and last Reduced Levels. In the example above, the sum of the Back Sights is 2.34+3.28 = 5.62, the Fore Sight sum is 4.23+3.86 = 8.09, and the difference is 2.47. The first and last Reduced Levels are 8.00 and 5.53, and the difference is also 2.47. In the Rise and Fall method, a final check can be made on the accuracy of the arithmetic, by totalling the Rise column and the Fall column, the sums being 2.65 and 5.12, the difference 2.47. The fact that all three agree is no assurance at all that the fieldwork has been accurate, but merely the arithmetic.

To check the fieldwork, the surveyor must always run 'flying levels' back to his starting-point, in the above case back to the Bench Mark. The positions of the staff need not be the same, except for starting at K, and ending at the B.M. The difference in the levels of these two positions, carrying out exactly the same procedure as described above, and checking the arithmetic, should be equal to the difference obtained in the first run, 2.47. If they do not agree, a mistake in reading the staff or in recording the reading has been made, and the whole operation must be repeated. It may well be, however, that the two results are almost the same, perhaps differing by 0.05 m. The archaeologist will then have to decide if the scale at which he is working justifies repeating the work, or if he can accept the result as sufficiently accurate for his needs; if the latter, he could split the difference and adjust the Reduced Levels of his positions on the plan. In the above example, position K was 5.53 on the first run. On the second, starting at K as 5.53, the Reduced Level of the Bench Mark would be, say, 7.95; but the Ordnance Datum recorded height of the Bench Mark is 8.00. K might therefore be 'adjusted' to read between 5.53 and 5.58, say 5.55 and therefore positions A to J require adjustment as well by adding 0.02. This procedure may appear messy and inaccurate, but the check on fieldwork *must* be made by the reverse run, and at the work scale, the archaeologist may feel that the result is sufficiently accurate for his purposes. It is likely that the averaged level of 5.55 is close to the truth, and there is no reason to prefer 5.53 (first run) over 5.58 (second run).

The procedure of levelling and recording described above can be carried out without a starting-point, the absolute height of

Back Sight	Inter- mediate	Fore Sight	Rise	Fall	Reduced Level	Distance	Remarks
2.45						0	position A
	3.15			0.70		20 m	B
	1.22		1.93			25 m	C
		2.87		1.65	15.75		B.M. 15.75 m

which is known. In this case, the Reduced Level column will remain blank until the Bench Mark is reached. This provides a Reduced Level for that position, as the Table on p. 105 shows. The Bench Mark reading is booked as a Fore Sight. The sum of the Fore Sights is 2.87, that of the Back Sights is 2.45, in this abbreviated example. The difference is 2.87−2.45 = 0.42, and this is a Fall *from* position A. The Reduced Level of A is therefore 15.75+0.42 = 16.17, and this can be entered, and the other Reduced Levels then worked out.

Sources of error in levelling There are many sources of error in levelling, but the precautions to be taken are simple. As a general rule, particularly careful observations are required when taking Back Sights or Fore Sights as errors here will affect the whole work more seriously than will an error at an Intermediate Sight. The necessity of checking the arithmetic, *and* the fieldwork through a reverse run, has been noted. Errors in levelling can be divided as follows:

Instrumental errors. The level should be periodically checked for accuracy of horizontal sighting, the work done by a professional instrument maker. Even so, Back Sights and Fore Sights should be deliberately kept as nearly equal as possible, that is, at approximately equal distances from the instrument (fig. 50). If the collimation adjustment (line of sight) is not correct,

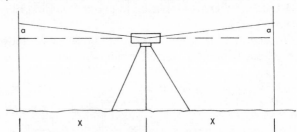

Fig. 50 Instrumental error reduced by equal distance Back Sight and Fore Sight.

and the telescope is slightly inclined, then the readings will be at a slight angle to the horizontal and will be greater than they should be. If, however, the Back and Fore Sights are equally spaced, the error will be eliminated.

Human errors. (1) A common error is to take a reading when the bubble is off centre, although automatic levels eliminate this and the simultaneous viewing of the staff and bubble in most modern instruments reduces the chances of error.

(2) The staff must be held vertically, particularly if the readings are taken near the top; it should be moved backwards and forwards so that the smallest reading can be taken.

(3) Soft ground will allow the level to settle of its own weight, and should be avoided. More serious, the legs of the tripod tend to be kicked by the surveyor in moving around the instrument; if this occurs, it is necessary to go back to the last known staff position, record its previous reading as a Fore Sight, re-site the level and take a Back Sight on the same position before proceeding.

(4) In moving the staff around to face the level, it may be displaced on soft or pebbly ground; to avoid this a triangular metal plate should be used as a support for the staff. These cost about £2.50, but any flat thin object could be used.

(5) In reading the staff, careful focusing and the eliminating of parallax are necessary. The observer should note first the whole number of metres, then the decimal places. He should then book them, in the correct column, and check the reading and its notation before moving on.

(6) Wind will cause problems in levelling, due to alterations in the position of the level and the staff. In hot sun, the apparent vibration of the staff is caused by refraction, and difficulties in accurate reading arise.

The elimination of all these sources of error requires vigilance on the part of the surveyor and his staffman. A single careless moment can entirely ruin a day's work, and there is nothing then for it but to start again.

Plotting a section (fig. 51) The plotting of a section such as has been described above is a simple matter. The scale of the plot must be determined according to the physical size of section required and the detail considered necessary to show the contour features. A lengthy section will reduce the impact of the vertical differences because the scale will be so small, and it is sometimes (but not always) appropriate to present a section with two scales, a small horizontal and an exaggerated vertical scale; the ratio can be 1/5 or 1/10. The result is a distortion, but sometimes serves the purpose of bringing out the features of a site or area. The horizontal scale is generally the same as that used for the plan of the area.

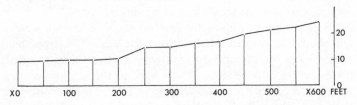

Fig. 51 Plotting a section. The Bell-Baker site at Westhay, Somerset (fig. 53), section along line X. Different scales used for horizontal and vertical measurements to exaggerate the elevations.

A base line or datum line is first drawn, and along it the horizontal distances of the positions are scaled off and marked. From these positions, perpendicular lines are erected (or squared paper can be used) and the Reduced Levels are scaled off on these. The points are then joined and the section is completed by the addition of a horizontal and vertical scale. If the section is on ground considerably above Ordnance Datum, it may be useful to record the local datum line as a fixed number of metres above O.D., rather than have to draw extremely long vertical lines. The representation of a section is to indicate the local contours, and extraneous features need not intrude.

Other levels Simpler forms of instruments for determining levels exist, and these are of course considerably cheaper than a Dumpy level. One of these hand levels consists merely of a square-sectioned tube with a horizontal cross wire at the front opening. A small tubular spirit level is on top of the tube, and is seen in the view through the tube by a reflecting mirror at 45°. The bubble indicates when the instrument is horizontal, and the cross wire then points to the spot which is at the same level as the instrument. The use of a wooden stand, a pole with a cross-piece on it, aids in holding the instrument steadily. The level can be used with a staff or ranging rod, and the height of the stand should be a convenient amount, probably 1.5 m. This is a handy instrument for occasional work, but does not replace the Dumpy level for more sustained levelling. The hand level could be employed for determining the height of a barrow or a rampart, using a ranging rod with divisions of 0.20 m.

A similar instrument but capable of a greater variety of measurements is the Abney level, costing about £16. This is basically a hand level but with the addition of an index arm, attached to the bubble tube, with a vernier pointer (fig. 52).

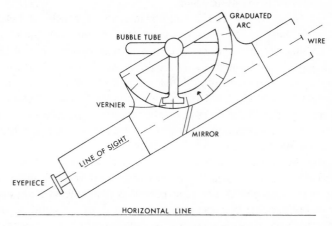

Fig. 52 Sketch of an Abney level.

The vernier travels over a graduated arc fitted to the side of the sighting tube. The observer, holding the instrument in his hand, sights the staff and position, the height of which is required, by tilting the level. A milled screw controls the bubble tube, and is turned until the bubble can be seen in the sighting tube to be horizontal. The observer can sight both the position, cut by the horizontal cross hair, and the bubble. It is then possible to read the angle of elevation, or depression, on the graduated arc scale. It is important to remember that the angle which is recorded on the vernier is equal to the angle which the line of sight makes with the horizontal. The instrument can be used as a level by setting the vernier to zero and mounting the level on a cross piece until the bubble is horizontal. The staff can then be read.

The vernier used on the Abney level is a short scale with a

central line of zero, and six divisions on either side, reading up to 60; each division represents 10 minutes of arc. The graduated arc scale on the level itself reads in degrees from 90° elevation to 90° depression. A magnifier is attached to some instruments for aid in reading the vernier. Reading the angle of sighting is simple. The number of whole degrees is read on the main scale and is the line leading up to the vernier zero index. The parts of a degree, in tens of minutes, are read on the vernier scale forward from the zero index to the line which exactly coincides with a division of the main arc scale.

The Indian clinometer is another instrument which can determine the heights of features, and is used mainly with the plane table. The clinometer consists of a base with two vertical sights. The base is positioned on the table, levelled, and the observer sights the feature through the rear sight, and moves a horizontal wire on the upright front bar until it cuts the feature. The angle of elevation can then be read on the front bar opposite the wire, and represents the angle between the height of the plane table and the feature.

The theodolite is an instrument used mainly by professional land surveyors for measuring horizontal and vertical angles in the field. Theodolites are high-precision instruments and some types are capable of measuring angles to $\frac{1}{10}$ of 1 second of arc. This high degree of accuracy is only required for precision triangulation or geodetic surveying. A very useful and popular type of theodolite is the 20 second instrument which as its name implies is capable of measuring angles to an accuracy of 20 seconds or $\frac{1}{3}$ of 1 minute of arc.

Such an instrument can cost upwards of £500 and not many are in use by archaeologists. However, on particularly large sites undergoing extensive archaeological examination, theodolites may be employed and assistants in this work are not likely to be involved in the actual manipulation of these instruments. They should be aware, however, of the necessity for extreme care and consideration in transporting, setting-up and packing away theodolites which are definitely not expendable equipment.

Gridding and contouring

Most archaeological sites are prepared for excavations or other studies by the imposition of a grid over the site itself and its adjacent area. The whole purpose of a grid is to provide an orderly pattern over the site so that trenches or areas for excavation can be planned accurately, finds can be plotted, and contours can be drawn. The grid consists of a series of parallel lines of arrows or pegs forming uniform squares over the site.

The procedure for setting a grid is straightforward. A line conveniently near the major features of the site is ranged (p. 65). Along the line are put in arrows or pegs at pre-determined uniform intervals, generally at 5, 10 or 20 m depending on the site. Parallel lines are set out at equal distances from the first or datum line and pegs are put in at the same positions. The cross-lines of pegs thus formed must be at right-angles to the datum line, and this can be achieved by the use of instruments (p. 76) or by measurement (p. 73).

The result of this is a network of pegs forming equal squares over the site (fig. 53). The pegs are in place only during the work, and are thereafter removed as they clutter up the fields. The grid, however, must be able to be revived on future occasions, and so parts of it, generally the ends of the datum line, are tied by measurement to local features such as gateposts, trees, fence posts. The tie-lines are drawn in the field notebook, and can also appear on the working plan of the area. The permanent features used in the tie-lines are generally painted or nailed so that the exact position of the tape for measuring to the datum can be found (fig. 54). It is often worthwhile tying the datum positions to three features rather than only two, in case one of them disappears through farming or other activities. A useful method for retrieving a grid is to sink a metal pipe well below any conceivable normal activity, with the permission of the normal landuser, and outside the 'archaeological area', on the grid line at each end; these can be discovered not only by measurement, but also by detecting instrument (p. 38).

The grid is then contoured by levelling (p. 102). A contour line, or contour, is an imaginary line laid out over the ground, every point on which is at the same level. The contours on a grid can be obtained by direct or indirect methods. The direct method is extremely laborious, and involves finding positions on the site where the staff readings, taken from a central position

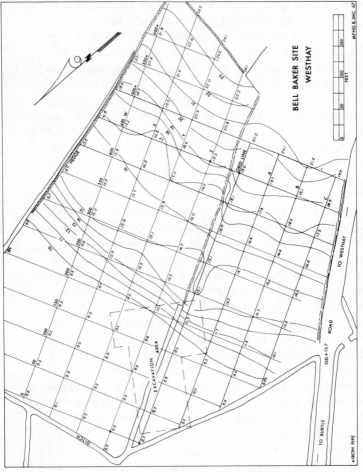

Fig. 53 Grid and contour plan of Bell-Baker site at Westhay, Somerset, for use during excavation. Grid lines at 50 ft intervals, and contours drawn at one-foot intervals; for section along line X, see fig. 51.

of the level, are uniform; much trial and error is involved and the method is not recommended.

The indirect method is simple. From a convenient position on the site, levels are obtained for all the grid points, and these are expressed as Reduced Levels, either absolute heights based on a Bench Mark, or relative heights based on an arbitrary local datum point (p. 96).

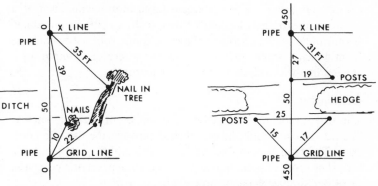

Fig. 54 Permanent tie-lines for Bell-Baker site at Westhay, Somerset (see fig. 53). Four points are fixed (X0, X450, Grid 0, Grid 450) by sinking metal pipes below normal agricultural activity, and tying them by measurement to trees and posts in ditch and hedge.

It is important that the surveyor be clear in his identification of all the grid points; the datum line and parallel lines may be given lettered identities, A, B, C, and the uniform distance along each will provide an unique reference for each point, A 0 (one end of the line), A 100 (A line, 100 m from zero). If the datum line is positioned through the centre of the site, it is generally preferable to call it by the intermediate letter, G (for Grid line), which allows the lines on either side to run forwards or backwards in the alphabet.

Before contours can be drawn, the grid must be produced as a plan to an appropriate scale, on squared paper. The Reduced Level of each grid point is then pencilled in. The vertical interval of contour is determined, dependent upon the site and what the contours are supposed to show. A barrow might be contoured at intervals of 0.25 m, a uniform slope at 1.0 m. The contour lines are then drawn in by interpolation (fig. 53, see also fig. 69). The basis for this is the assumption that the ground slopes uniformly between adjacent points on the grid, and therefore the position of each contour can be estimated by considering the distance and the difference of level between adjacent points.

The above procedure of gridding and contouring is suitable for most archaeological sites and areas, whether they are small sites such as barrows and hut-circles, or large sites such as camps and henges. For extremely large monuments such as a hill-fort, or extremely long structures, such as a cursus, a modified form can be used, consisting of a ranged line with perpendiculars from which a small grid can be set out wherever required, or a ranged line with offsets to particular features.

Orientation

The orientation of a ranged line, chain or plane table survey, or grid system, should be established through the use of a compass. The trough compass used in plane tabling is not suitable for other types of planning, and for these the prismatic compass, or rather simpler versions now available, is required.

The prismatic compass consists of a circular box, filled with spirit or glycerine, in which a compass card with needle rotates. A hinged lid with vertical hairline is raised to a position perpendicular to the compass, and the line cutting the feature is viewed through a prism which is also lifted to lie upon the compass glass. A small button or other release catch frees the needle which rotates with the compass card. The observer, stationed at one end of the line, the bearing of which is required, sights through the prism to the other end of the line, and the compass reading can be taken. There are many variations of prismatic compasses, costing from £15 upwards; second-hand compasses are often available.

A cheaper, and in some ways a more handy, instrument is a compass made by Suunto of Helsinki, costing about £10. This is on the prismatic principle, and consists of a flat metal box with rounded ends. A compass card and needle floats within, and can be seen from above. The straight sides of the box allow it to be used as a trough compass. A sighting aperture is in one end of the box. The observer holds the instrument so that one

eye sights into the compass, where the bearing can be read, and
the other eye sights the ranging rod or feature; the images
coincide upon a vertical hairline, and quite accurate readings
can be made.

In any work with compasses, the bearing should be checked
by a reading from the other end of the line, and the two bearings
should be separated by exactly 180°. Interference by local metals
should also be avoided by removing metallic objects from the
observer's pockets, and by taking readings well away from metal
structures such as iron-framed buildings or railway lines.

The bearings taken by compass are of course magnetic, and
relate to the magnetic meridian which in Britain was declined
westward of the true meridian by about 10° (fig. 55) in 1959 and is
decreasing by about one-half° every four years. The angle

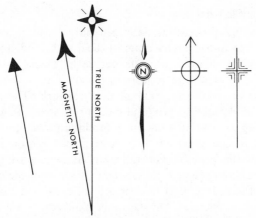

*Fig. 55 Symbols used to denote Magnetic North and True North. Variations
from these are abundant, but generally the letter N denotes True North.
The two joined symbols above appear on Ordnance Survey maps, and the
use of both symbols on archaeological maps would save potential confusion.*

is called the Magnetic Variation or Magnetic North on Ordnance
Survey maps. It is important to indicate on any plan that the
arrow denoting north is described as either True North or
Magnetic North; it cannot be both. The Ordnance Survey maps
also carry a Grid North arrow, which merely denotes the
direction of the map-maker's vertical lines of the National Grid;
this line would not be transferred to plans.

Another way of aligning a grid or ranged line is to relate it, through offsets, extensions, or triangulation, to fixed points upon a large-scale Ordnance Map, but in no case should this be considered as a substitute for the use of a compass. The use of Ordnance Survey maps for plotting finds is considered on p. 57, but here it may be useful to indicate the scale of precision in measurement required for the use of such maps.

Scale	*Accuracy of measurement required*
1/2500 (25-inch map)	1 m
1/10 000 or 10 560 (6-inch map)	5 m
1/25 000 (2½-inch map)	10 m

Any further divisions of measurement will be lost in the size of the pencilled line.

The assistant in surveying

The surveying procedures described above will probably be sufficient for most archaeological fieldwork and for many archaeological excavations. The degree of precision required in the finished plans and sections of the site area will determine the degree of detail necessary in the fieldwork. The assistant who may undertake to grid and contour an area, or who may lead or help in ranging a line or in levelling procedures, should be aware of the precision in measurements required by the director of the project. The time wasted in disposing of unnecessary detail presented by assistants, such as linear measurements to the nearest 0.01 m over a large area, is a tax on the director's own energies. On the other hand, there are fields of surveying where strict attention to detail is essential, such as the setting-out of perpendiculars, and areas of contouring, where figures should not be rounded off. The assistant should therefore ensure that the information he receives from the director is unequivocal.

The assistant on a field project should be aware of the surveying procedures likely to be employed, and should be acquainted with the types of instrument he may encounter as 'acting surveyor' or staffman or leader of a chain. The range of instruments employed by archaeologists is probably greater in its way than that of any other surveying team; this is not in the complexity of instruments but in their age, and many ancient surveying aids are still in use on ancient sites. The techniques that have been found useful by the archaeologist are also likely to be considered old-fashioned by professional surveyors and engineers; plane-tabling, for instance, is a procedure hardly used by anyone other than an archaeologist in Britain today. Nevertheless, if the technique is of use in a particular situation, then it will continue to be employed, and the nature of archaeological work, both in the degree of accuracy required, and in the manpower accessible, has its own character.

In any case, the assistant must be prepared to ask for explanations of the procedures to be followed. Only in this way will accuracy be achieved, and this is, after all, the purpose of survey.

3 Note-taking

This may seem an absurdly obvious point not requiring any comment at all, but at both professional and amateur archaeological levels there is scope for note-taking as an activity complementary to that of accurate survey. The booking of measurements taken during horizontal and vertical surveys has already been described (p. 70f.), but there are many occasions when an archaeologist will not be conducting such an organized survey, yet will notice features requiring some record. This will often occur during the search for sites through casual or consistent field-walking, through consultation with landowners and users, through examination of photographs from the air or the ground, through museum records and collections, and through his own thoughtful consideration of the potentialities of his area. All of these sources may yield data, some immediately important, some possibly so, some probably unimportant, but all worthy of record.

The most common method of noting all this data is by a diary-type of entry, covering the activities performed during a day or weekend of fieldwork, but this tends to be inconsistent in its inclusion of all the details essential for a proper record.

If the archaeologist considers that his activities are likely to be of importance as throwing light upon himself, then a diary is an essential, but if the details of a site or area are the aim, then some other procedure should be considered. A site card has already been presented (p. 20), and may be thought to provide some of the entries necessary for an adequate record of the site in terms of its position and its potential. The entries need not be discussed here.

However, it is true to say that archaeological sites tend to change their visual character over time, revealing sometimes more, sometimes less, of themselves through erosion or weathering or vegetation changes, in different lights and weathers, and through human interference whether gradual or sudden. The record of a site as it appears on a site card is therefore not complete, and can change through any number of circumstances. The obvious solution for a field archaeologist is a record card similar to that which described the permanent details of a site (p. 20), but which allows the archaeological features to be recorded systematically and chronologically. These should have the following details entered:

Site name (unequivocal, perhaps with N.G.R. as check).

Date of entry or entries (daily, seasonal, or yearly).

Observer's name (and assistants).

Conditions (land, weather, time).

Features noted (*any* data considered useful).

Small finds collected (position on site, reason for exposure)
Landowner informed (owner of finds)
Disposal of finds (held by whom, and why).

Other detail (e.g. photographs taken).

Future visits (explicit detail on points requiring observation and suggested time of next visit).

The consistent recording of sites or presumed sites over a period of time in this way will allow a more accessible and probably clearer report on the site than is provided by any other method. The record cards are transported to the site each time, and further details filled in on the site card as necessary, e.g.

landuser changes, changes in attitude to archaeology, threatened activities on the site. A new card for archaeological detail can be filled in each time, using the previous one as a guide to observations. The cards should be photocopied as insurance against loss in the field; no doubt the local museum would hold a set if asked, but few archaeologists would probably wish to release their own intimate raw data unworked. In any case, the data should go to the local museum or society eventually, and provision should be made for this.

The last point is not unimportant. Site records, particularly those based upon single-man fieldwork, are notoriously liable to total disappearance when the observer leaves the area, loses interest, dies, or all three. It is not only his private collection (p. 49) that is dispersed, but his own records, and it is probable that the latter is more important than the former. Reports and notebooks on small-scale excavations, unpublished and incomplete, may also be lost for any number of reasons. The point about local poaching of sites because knowledge of them has been allowed to percolate through to others is certainly a valid one, and examples of poaching are not hard to find (p. 136), but they must be fewer in number than the sites lost through total secrecy on the part of fieldworkers.

Many sites have been discovered by local archaeologists who continue to visit them and collect material; the position of such sites may become common knowledge through publication, lectures or local gossip, and it is an unwritten rule that these sites are reserved for the discoverer, so long as he is actively interested in them. Others should not attempt to collect material, or organize excavations, unless permission has been obtained from the discoverer as well as from the legal owners. The local museum or society is probably the only proper agency for controlling a situation, by no means unusual, where further investigation is required of a site still jealously guarded by its discoverer.

In addition to note-taking, the archaeologist should maintain an adequate and accurate set of maps. The scale of the maps will depend upon the size of area covered, and the type of information likely to be recorded (see p. 55f.).

The procedure for plotting an archaeological find or feature

upon a map is basically simple. Field corners or other significant positions on the map, that can be related precisely to
features on the ground, can serve as stations for chained lines
to the feature which has been provided with a marker for sighting.
Chained or taped lines from two points allow scaled compass
intersection on the map for the position of the feature (p. 75).

A second method is to take the bearing of the feature from
two similar positions, check by reversing the sightings through
the compass, and then with protractor correctly aligned on the
map, draw two lines to intersect at the position of the feature
(p. 114).

A third method is to use a straight field boundary as a ranged
line; a line perpendicular to this can be dropped from the feature
on to the ranged line (p. 74). The taped measurements of the
ranged line and the perpendicular can then be scaled off on to the
map.

The same procedures for recording small finds, of flint or
metal or pottery, can be carried out, both in mapping and in
noting on cards or in the notebook. The ownership of such finds
is not in question and this should also be recorded.

By measurement, all such finds, whether portable or monumental, can be mapped and then their National Grid References
can be deduced from the 1/10 000 or 1/10 560 map. This Reference should also be recorded.

In some cases, local information may be obtained about the
existence of small finds made in the past, or objects may be
produced whose provenance is only imprecisely known. It is
essential that the details are recorded verbatim, and efforts be
made to find out as many facts as possible as near to the moment
of discovery as possible. Even so, the precise find-spot may be
lost; a N.G.R. to four places should be recorded if possible,
otherwise the general area will have to do.

The use of sketches is another item in the noting of finds,
just as it is in the positioning of gridline stations (p. 111). Sketches
of objects in private possession are always valuable as the dispersal of finds from such collections is an unknown quantity
(p. 49).

Finally, the same strictures about notebooks and record cards
can be made about maps and notes on small finds. The point is

well known, that a site or find is not really discovered until it is published or otherwise made available to the public. Information should not be held back if there is no genuinely honest chance that it will be published or deposited in a public place such as museum or library or university department. There is not much thrill in making a wonderful discovery and keeping it to oneself.

IV Excavation

1 The organization of excavation

Excavations of prehistoric sites in Britain are the choice and responsibility of government agencies, national and local archaeological societies and museums, training colleges, university departments of archaeology and student societies, and purely private individuals (p. 243). Their depth of commitment depends on the interest of the particular site, the inclination of the archaeologists concerned, and the financial and other support available. Excavations are not generally simple operations, and the initiation of one is not merely an *ad hoc* decision on the part of an individual. No excavation, on whatever scale, should be attempted unless all of the known archaeological problems have been considered, and an approach to the answers suggested. The problems are not purely 'excavational', but include also legal matters as well as those of financial and staff support.

Permission
In Britain, a number of ancient sites are protected by governmental legislation. Some are under guardianship (p. 247), and others are merely 'listed' as worthy of preservation (p. 247). Responsibility for the conservation of both types lies with the Minister of the Environment, on the advice of the Ancient Monuments Board. No interference with such sites is allowed, unless permission has been granted by the Chief Inspector of Ancient Monuments. A list of sites selected as of national importance is made available by H.M.S.O.

Many sites, of equal potential importance but often of less imposing appearance, are not so protected, and control over their fate is in the hands of the landowner concerned. Permission to excavate must be obtained from the owner, and the archaeologist must be prepared to make out a clear case for excavation; few landowners automatically take kindly to the idea of disturbance of their property, unless the eventual gain, in knowledge, can be impressed upon them. The ownership of the finds has already been noted (p. 46). It is unquestionably to the advantage of both parties that any agreement to excavate should be written and signed. Such an agreement should indicate the following:

(1) area of excavation (precise position and size, with allowance for extension if necessary);
(2) dates of commencement and termination of work (with allowance);
(3) protection of site during work (arrangements for fencing, access route for workers and visitors);
(4) restoration of the land (back-filling, re-seeding etc.);
(5) compensation for damage to land and crop (explicit with regard to scale of compensation and nature of crop);
(6) ownership and, if possible, ultimate disposal of finds (with permission for excavator temporarily to retain all finds for study).

The interests of the tenant must also be considered, and these should be protected by any agreement between archaeologist and landowner; by their mutual consent, items 1–5 should also be settled with the tenant.

Finance

The financing of excavations in Britain tends to vary greatly, and it is the duty of the archaeologist to ensure that his financial support will not dry up and will sustain him through the entire course of work including the study and publication of the site.

At a private level, purely personal finance has been the sole source for many small-scale excavations in this country. An excavation at weekends, with local help, with equipment stored on the site and notes and finds at home, can cost very little money, if no problems arise; the problems, however, are generally unforeseeable and may involve the archaeologist in considerable expense. For example, the site may suddenly require a far greater excavation than is possible on a shoe-string budget. The labour force may dwindle through boredom, delays and weather, and fresh incentives may have to be offered by the director. Material may be found that needs expert collection and treatment (p. 209), or which can involve unexpected expense in such matters as dating. The other cost of small-scale excavations of this kind is in the potential loss of evidence through delays during the excavation (p. 210), and through lack of time and energy in the study and publication of what may turn out to be an uninspiring and un-exciting site to the excavator. Nevertheless, the basis of much knowledge about early Britain, particularly in distributions of sites and finds, has been established through this kind of work, often conducted under considerable difficulties. The archaeologist should be aware of the problems that occur in such operations, without being entirely frightened off. In Britain it is generally true to say that any such site that yielded, or promised to yield, exceptional information, would attract extra support from local or national museums or other interested bodies.

Financial support for excavations in Britain is sometimes available from local, county and national archaeological societies, from museums, from government agencies and from specially constituted bodies. The sums available from societies are liable to be small, generally in the £25–50 range, but occasionally an excavation project will appeal sufficiently to gain much greater support; these projects, however, are likely to be those devised and directed by professional archaeologists on known sites. Information about local society funds are generally available through local museums where the activities of such societies are often housed.

Museums, controlled by county or town councils, may also have funds available for excavations. These are generally aimed at the acquisition of material, and the archaeologist should be aware of the implications of such support in his applications to the museum and to the landowner. Occasionally the financial support from these sources is considerable, but many small museums have no such funds. National museums, on the other hand, are able, from time to time, to finance large research projects or other excavations designed to yield important material for study and display; again, these funds are liable to go to professional archaeologists. Information about potential museum support is obtainable at the museum itself, and the archaeologist should be aware of the limited resources of the majority of museums in Britain. Lack of financial support does not necessarily mean lack of interest.

Government finance for excavations in Britain is generally restricted to those sites that have been scheduled and which are threatened by agricultural, building or road-making activities. Full support is provided, and helpers at all levels are paid at standard rates. The directors of such excavations are generally professional archaeologists or others who have had considerable experience.

Occasionally, special projects of research or rescue excavation will find finance through specially constituted committees, set up to raise money for this one particular issue. The research excavations at South Cadbury and the rescue excavations at Winchester are examples of the value of such bodies; again, the director of such projects is likely to be a professional archaeologist, either working from a teaching post, or appointed as a full-time director.

In making an approach to any body for funds for an excavation, the archaeologist in charge is generally asked to provide the following information:
(1) name of the site and precise position;
(2) nature of the site, its age and extent;
(3) importance of the site in yielding new data;
(4) name of archaeologist responsible for the work;
(5) date and duration of the work, and size of excavation team;
(6) name of landowner, and assurance of permission to excavate;
(7) eventual disposal of the finds, and publication plans;
(8) detailed costing of the work;
(9) other sources of finance.

Not all of these items can always be assessed, but an honest attempt should be made. In particular, the costing of the work must be accurate, and other sources of finance (applications or promises) clearly stated. The panel that allocates funds will include excavators who probably know the site and can themselves estimate the probable cost.

Recruitment of staff

The excavation team *must* have a director, preferably only one, whose role (p. 156) includes the appointment of supervisors and workers of various kinds (p. 160). The ways by which such a team is formed can vary. Probably the most satisfactory procedure, from the director's point of view, is to invite individuals known to him or recommended to him by professionals. There is much to be said for a team composed of people who have worked together in the past for the director, and the worker who finds himself on such a team can have a particularly enjoyable time. Excavation is a scientific technique to be learned by experience and application, but there is no reason why it should not be fun at the same time. The only way by which the archaeologist can obtain admission to such a select group is through experience on other excavations where his own contribution can be observed, assessed and (hopefully) recorded. Most directors of excavations will ask for information about previous experience, and follow up the references given (see below).

The sources of information about excavations in Britain are more accessible than those of most countries. The agency for this is the *Newsletter and Calendar* issued by the Council for British Archaeology, and obtainable from the Council at 112 Kennington Road, London, SE11 6RE; the cost of a year's subscription to this is £3.00. The Calendar appears monthly from March to August, and a summary of the excavations conducted is published at the end of the year. The details of the excavations listed include the size of the team, duration of work, accommodation and financial help for workers.

Other sources of information about excavations in Britain are local societies, local museums and university departments, particularly Extra-Mural departments. These excavations are generally not publicized, other than details appearing on notice boards in the relevant institutions.

Many excavations are designed not only to yield new information about a site but also to provide training of potential archaeologists. Instruction is provided in surveying, photography and other aspects, as well as actual digging techniques. Details of these courses, often on Roman sites, generally appear in the Calendar of Excavations. Other instruction courses, similarly announced, deal with particular aspects such as surveying, area studies, sampling and conservation.

A final source of information about archaeological excavation is in the personal columns of national newspapers, and often these yield surprising results.

Applications for permission to attend as a worker on an excavation should be addressed to the director and should provide the following basic data, in addition to any other information requested:

(1) name, full postal address;
(2) sex and age;
(3) excavation experience, with full details of sites and directors, year and duration of work on each site;
(4) particular qualifications possibly of use, such as surveying, drawing, photography;
(5) availability for work, with dates of arrival and departure;
(6) financial help required (if any);
(7) preference for accommodation (hotel, farm house, caravan, tent).

This information will probably save correspondence time but the applicant may have to wait for an outright acceptance or refusal. The director will think first of his site, and must choose the best available help on the evidence he has before him; he is likely to wait some time before deciding his list of workers from the applications received, and he may wish to interview some applicants.

The popularity of archaeology in Britain tends to have the effect that many excavations are over-subscribed. Yet it is also true that many excavations end up being understaffed. This apparent contradiction can be explained by two facts. First, directors tend to overestimate the amount of work they can get through, and particularly the amount that they can delegate to their site supervisors; the result is an excavation team under in-creasing pressure, lacking time and therefore vigilance (p. 133). Second, of less moment, successful applicants to a team do not always appear on the site when asked, and often a team lacks one or two hands that might have made a considerable difference. The worker as well as the director has a responsibility to the site, and it is imperative that as much notice as possible is given to the director of any change in plans; such changes should not be made unless of paramount importance.

Public relations

The precise relationships that develop between director, site supervisor and workers are purely internal to the archaeological site (p. 155), but there is always a different face to the site, that presented to the public. Any excavation or field project will necessarily involve the landowner and tenant, and should involve the local archaeological society and museum. This is mere courtesy, and almost always can add nothing but good to the work, either through local information that may be forthcoming, or through expert museum assistance that may be needed unexpectedly. In addition, and ultimately of greater value to the subject as a whole, is the community-at-large. Archaeology will only flourish in a society aware of and responsive to its problems, and the director of an excavation has a duty to the public and to his subject. In a small excavation, good public relations may be particularly difficult to retain.

The director of a small excavation cannot spare the time of either himself or his supervisors to escort visitors around the site, and he is unlikely to receive such a consistent stream of interested parties that he can set aside a particular time for conducted tours. Generally, one of the workers will be assigned the task each day of escorting visitors around the site, and he should ascertain from the director exactly what he is to impart. A general description of the site, how old it is, why it is supposed to be important, who is doing the work, and what has been found, is generally sufficient for most visitors. However, the worker–guide must also be prepared to steer the public away from the edges of the excavated areas, to prevent them from engaging the workers in conversation, and to conclude the tour after a reasonable length of time. He may also have to inform the public of any other rules that the director lays down, such as 'no smoking' (contamination of samples), or 'no photography' (most sites go through a messy phase), 'no dogs' (as bad as elephants on a site), and justify such rules. There are different ways by which such rules can be transmitted, and there is neither need nor excuse for rudeness. The guide should also be aware of the existence of the landowner or tenant, and other helpful parties, who should receive more attention, but not more courtesy, than ordinary visitors. The director and site supervisor will generally recognize and take care of the V.I.P., but may not be able to at the moment of arrival.

Members of the press are rather different, and the director is the only person who can deal with the release of information to the press, or to radio or television reporters. Such people should announce themselves, before or on arrival, and the director must be informed at once. For directors of small excavations, premature release of information may not only be misleading but encourage illicit visitors and unauthorized digging on his site, and extreme care must be exercised. Rules for interviews with reporters cannot be fixed, but the director must ensure his right to 'clear' any report before publication. The workers on a site should not give any interview or provide any information unless the director is present and is agreeable; human interest is good copy but may not entirely represent the aims and achievements of the excavation.

Finally, archaeologists like to visit other sites, and should behave on them as they require visitors to behave on their own sites.

Insurance and tax
All directors of excavations should take out insurance against their legal liability for damage to property or injury to workers and to the public. Even the smallest excavation can cause damage to property, particularly animals, and the cost of insuring against these occurrences is negligible in Britain. On a site where large buildings are not adjacent to an excavation, the premium for third-party liability insurance might be £1. The precise legal relationship between a director or sponsoring society and the workers, who receive nothing or only a subsistence allowance, is not very clear, and insurance companies will vary in their approach to this problem; directors should investigate the position. The C.B.A. (p. 249) now has a general policy.

For paid labour, the director of an excavation must contribute his share of National Insurance, deduct the employees' share, buy stamps and fix them to the card provided. He must also deduct income tax from his employees' wages, and observe other regulations affecting the relationship between employer and employee. Officials in the Ministry of Social Security will advise.

2 The approach to excavation

The aim of excavations

The aim of archaeological excavation is the recovery of data that can throw light upon man's past behaviour. Excavation is one of the first steps in the actual recovery of material evidence, but cannot by itself advance our knowledge; some preliminary processes of fieldwork have been noted (p. 11), and there remains all the interpretative work following the excavation (p. 233), and publication (p. 241), before a final assessment can be made as to the value of the exercise.

The actual approach to the excavation of a site, the archaeologist's attitude to the site, is determined in a number of ways in which logistics play a part. But there is still the theoretical basis of the projected work to consider, and here the archaeologist must be clear in his own mind. The usual approach to a site in the past was haphazard, with excavation conducted in the hope that finds would be made. Finds *were* made in this way, and often of spectacular nature. But the results, in terms of information about prehistoric activities and behaviour, were grossly inadequate. The excavator was not aware of anything other than portable and attractive objects, and often did not recognize important evidence as it was being destroyed through exposure.

The more modern approach, and one clear in the minds of most archaeologists, is that of questioning a site. 'It is now no longer considered sufficient, or even justifiable, to excavate a site in a repetitive manner, merely waiting, like Mr Micawber, for something to turn up. On the contrary, every excavation and every part of one must be planned to answer a limited number of quite definite questions' (Atkinson 1956, 203). The questions may relate to the position of a site, its external and internal features, its contents, its evidence for past environment, its chronology, or any number of subjects. The formulation and phrasing of the questions will depend on previous work, on the attitude and interests of the excavator, on his technical knowledge and capabilities.

A view considered by some to be contrary to this is the approach to an excavation of 'total collection', the collection and recording of everything observed on a site. There should be no real dispute here, because the question and answer approach will obviously not neglect or ignore evidence that may be peripheral to the particular problems. The total collection approach can be criticized, however, as it infers that all observable evidence is of equal value, and there is no doubt that this is wrong. There have been enough excavations in Britain and elsewhere that relied on careful and elaborate recording of everything observable, and never set out to answer any questions; the woods and the trees fit perfectly here.

In Britain, excavations on prehistoric sites are often divided into 'rescue operations' and 'research projects'. Both, however, are based upon the questioning approach, where the sites pose certain problems that may be answered by particular approaches to the work. The time and energy expended upon the excavation, and in considering the problems, may vary greatly, from a hurried organization necessitated by threatened destruction, to a project initiated several years before excavation begins.

The first essential for any proper excavation is the thorough investigation of the area, through the acquisition of local information (p. 12), fieldwork (p. 11), aerial photography (p. 21), the use of detection devices (p. 30), the study of museum and private collections (p. 246), and local antiquarian literature (p. 244). On the basis of this, and on the economic scale of the work, the actual site and area for excavation will be chosen. The care taken in the decision to excavate may well be reflected in the success of the work, in the formulation of the right questions to ask of the site, and in the approach to the answers. However, not all sites are in such a position that all this preliminary work can be done, and here, in an emergency, the archaeologist may have to select a very few questions, or in some extreme cases (in front of a bulldozer) fall back on the 'smash and grab' method of collection of whatever is available.

Rescue digs

Many of the prehistoric monuments of Britain are threatened by destruction. The redevelopment of city centres, the new towns, motorway and airport construction, all contribute to the levelling of land and the exposure and disintegration of ancient remains. Additionally, the millions of tons of sands and gravels required

for new works come from areas of land particularly favoured by
early people for settlement. On a slightly lower scale, the afforesta-
tion of marginal lands in the north and west of Britain damages
ancient sites, although total destruction is unlikely. Other less
spectacular modern activities also contribute to the elimination
of sites, and among these the deep-ploughing of arable land is
probably the greatest.

The scale of this problem can be appreciated by the consideration of a few examples. Of about 900 barrows in south Dorset, only
5 per cent are now undamaged; of 360 barrows in Gloucester-
shire, half are now destroyed; in Wiltshire, nearly half of 640
'listed' sites are now completely destroyed. Archaeological work
in advance of the M5 motorway between Worcestershire and
Somerset, about 200 km long and only 100 m wide, showed that
the road cut through 125 ancient sites. On the basis of this sort of
information, it is estimated that an archaeological site exists for
every 65 hectares (160 acres) in Britain, and that by 2000 A.D. a
majority will be destroyed or severely damaged. The formation
of 'Rescue, a Trust for British Archaeology', is designed to inform the public of the dangers, to press for new laws to protect
sites, to acquire sites for permanent conservation, and to aid
rescue excavations. The success of this Trust, and the success of
other interested bodies, such as the Council for British Archaeology, depends ultimately on the recognition by the public of the
actual and potential loss of part of Britain's past (p. 251).

Many sites that are threatened by destruction are excavated as
a rescue operation, often by local archaeological societies under
considerable difficulties. In these cases, the archaeologist may
have little opportunity to decide upon the approach to the work,
and it is often necessary to extract what data he can from the site
as it is undergoing destruction. There are no set rules for such an
operation, just as there are no rigid rules for any excavation, but
the archaeologist should make every effort to obtain the following
skeletal information:

(1) precise position of the site;
(2) its extent (linear and shape);
(3) its character (what activities went on);
(4) its date (stratification, collection of samples for dating and
    cultural material).

Extreme care must be exercised in observing and recording; under conditions of stress caused by lack of time and help, by adverse weather, by observation of destruction, errors may tend to creep in, and the archaeologist must be aware of this. Even worse than a site completely unrecorded is one incorrectly recorded. This last, however, does not mean incompletely recorded, because there is no such thing as a completely recorded site.

Other rescue operations are fortunately not under such pressure, and the archaeologist may have time to complete his fieldwork and prepare his attack on the site. Again, no rules can be laid down, but it may be thought imperative to possess knowledge of other comparable sites in the area, excavated under more peaceful conditions; the potential of the threatened site can be more readily realized, the type of finds and their condition can be better appreciated, and the archaeologist is in a more advantageous position all round. Some of the rescue operations of this sort are planned as research projects, if ample foreknowledge of the threat is available. One of the advantages, perhaps the only one, of rescue operations is that the archaeologist is not faced with the question of posterity, of the advisability of leaving the site alone for future, more expert, excavation with as-yet undeveloped techniques. This, however, assumes that a site not threatened today will remain so in future years, an assumption of considerable uncertainty.

All excavation is destruction, and the archaeologist should not need to be reminded of this. Once the deposits of an archaeological site have been disturbed or exposed by excavation, the evidence they contain has also been disturbed (p. 210). In effect, this turns any operation into a rescue excavation, as once the processes of decay begin by exposure, the archaeologist is working against time. If observations and recordings have not been fully made during the excavation, the evidence is lost, and if incorrect records are made, through inexperience, ill-luck or stupidity, then the evidence will mislead the excavator and his successors. However, with the best will in the world, the finest available techniques of excavation, the most sophisticated recording methods, and the most exemplary publication, the archaeologist will inevitably destroy his site and future generations may regret this. Any excavation then must involve the archaeologist in decisions about destruction of evidence, and this is a matter of conscience for the individual.

Research excavations
In the study of prehistoric Britain, there are many specialized subjects concerned with the character and situation of particular monuments. These may be farmsteads and fields, settlements and cemeteries, megalithic structures, hunters' kill sites and transit sites, or any other surviving traces of human activity. The investigation of some of these sites takes the form of short-term or long-term research projects, generally carried out by professional archaeologists who can bring to bear considerable resources upon the problem, both financial and specialist. Fieldwork as opposed, in this case, to excavation plays an important part, and generally at least an entire season's work is devoted to the project, more often several years.

Such research is not necessarily restricted to the professional, and many small projects have been completed by amateur archaeologists. These have included area studies of hut-circles, with selective excavations of individual sites, studies of barrow cemeteries again with some excavation, and studies of hunter–gatherer sites through surface collections and limited excavation. Local knowledge of the region and of the archaeological work that has already been done, allied to an experience gained through general archaeological training, is a necessary preparation for any archaeologist who undertakes such a research project; in many cases the archaeologist who possesses detailed local knowledge is best suited for some of these area studies.

Questioning As noted above, there is some difference of opinion about the attitude of the archaeologist in research excavations. The view that 'everything' should be collected has been criticized as too unselective, and the more usual approach is made through a set of questions to which the archaeologist requires answers. The questions, concerned with particular structural details of a funerary or ceremonial monument, the distribution of varied activities on a settlement site, the recovery of particular environmental evidence, and so on, are formulated through previous experience and knowledge of related sites; the archaeologist sets out to find answers to perplexing problems that have been raised by former work. Of course, in attempting to find these answers he may well end up with an entirely new set of questions.

Any site can yield at almost any moment a find that will transform our knowledge of human behaviour (p. 3). In Britain, as elsewhere, conditions of preservation are not consistent, and a micro-environment on almost any site may yield unique evidence that will alter ideas about past behaviour that have been built from other evidence. No site, however, can ever be completely recorded, and the process of subjective selection begins as soon as the archaeologist states his problems and chooses his sites for answers. It is therefore essential that the most relevant questions are asked, and in the right order; the choice of these can only be decided by an archaeologist conversant with the whole field of this study, previous excavations and fieldwork, problems in the approach, and the questions already asked and answered.

An example of this questioning procedure as applied to a particular site is given later (p. 235), but the questions to be asked of any site cannot be standardized. The questions to be asked of a hunter–gatherer settlement will be different from those of a burial mound, or a hill-fort. Most questions, however, will be somehow concerned with time (the age and duration of an activity), with exploitation of the environment (the seasonal and permanent use of resources), with technological abilities (the degree of sophistication of crafts), with social behaviour (the structure and function of society), and with human populations as developing organisms (demographic studies). But these are general and archaeologists will tend to focus attention upon specific problems within these or other groups, and, while hoping to neglect nothing, will filter the rest of the evidence seeking not only answers but new questions.[1] Only in this way will knowledge be advanced so that archaeology can succeed in its aim to recover, interpret and understand the evidence for past human behaviour.

Experimental excavations Occasionally, but perhaps not often enough, a research excavation is concerned primarily with experimental techniques, using new and untested methods of

[1] A number of the field surveys and excavations noted in the list on p. 256 have been included because of this questioning approach, with particular problems to be solved or restated.

digging, recording and sampling; such work can be extremely interesting, is generally carried out by professionals, and must be applied with great care to sites that will provide a fair testing-ground and yet be partly expendable in the interests of progress.

Treasure hunts
This is a term that may be levelled at eighteenth- and nineteenth-century antiquarians who undertook the excavation of ancient monuments as an amusing way to spend an afternoon or a week-end. Another purpose of the exercise was to obtain portable antiquities for the sideboard, and so the quickest methods of excavation were adopted and burial mounds were the main target. A hole dug down from the top of a barrow was a popular and well-proved approach, or a trench dug into the mound from the side; the latter took rather more time but allowed the director and his party the opportunity to examine more closely the principal finds *in situ*, if the weather and timing of the discovery were right.

The term can also be levelled at some modern archaeological work in Britain. Archaeologists tend to dig because they enjoy it, and one of the pleasanter moments of any excavation is when an important find is actually made, but this is not treasure hunting. Nor, in this discussion of excavation, is the use of metal detectors (p. 43). Treasure hunting exists as a serious and regrettable activity on many archaeological sites in Britain. The publication of lists of sites from south-west Scotland and from Strathtay (fig. 4), following the completion of field surveys, led in 1970 and 1968 (respectively) to immediate illicit excavation on the sites, to obtain portable antiquities for private collection or sale. The existence of self-styled archaeologists who excavate on sites reported to them in good faith by local people, solely to recover such material for their own collections, is well known. Such individuals do not publish, or rarely publish, their findings, perhaps because no records were kept, perhaps because the material has been, in effect, stolen from the landowner.

There can be no justification in British archaeology for such events occurring, particularly when rescue archaeology is urgent, and archaeologists of whatever standing can and should take steps to prevent any recurrences of such illegal activities.

Problems in the approach to excavation

The variety of prehistoric sites in Britain is probably as great as anywhere in the world. Settlement in southern England has been more or less continuous for several hundred thousand years, with population and complexity of activities increasing with time. The position of Britain, as an island, and the world's edge, almost the final land before the ocean, contributed to the density and variety of human groups who have left traces of their presence all over the land.

The sites with which the archaeologist must cope range from the most ephemeral of occupations by hunter–gatherers on the Yorkshire Moors to the deeply stratified settlements of early London, from the simple spread of urned cremations in Derbyshire cemeteries to the reorganized, recut, defensive systems of Dorset hill-forts.

It is essential for anyone who wishes to excavate any ancient sites to be aware of this variety, to know how in the past such sites were investigated, how mistakes were made and how now to correct them, the questions posed by such sites, the new methods that can be tried upon them. For an inexperienced excavator, there are several texts that can profitably be studied to provide a guide to the types of monument most abundant in this country (see p. 14). The amateur archaeologist who wishes to gain experience in excavation should avail himself of the opportunities to work on a variety of these sites, of different periods, and on different soils, rather than limit his potential by digging only on a single or restricted range of sites.

The particular problems that may be posed by particular types of sites can only be appreciated by reading reports of actual excavations, and can only be solved by experience in the field. There can be no substitute for practical excavation experience on a variety of sites, but the book *The Directing of Archaeological Excavations* by J. Alexander discusses the following types of sites in terms of excavation problems:
(1) settlements of hunter–gatherers and pastoralists;
(2) isolated dwellings, farms, fields and roads;
(3) hamlets, villages and towns;
(4) religious sites;

(5) military sites;
(6) industrial sites.

A list of some important types of site recently excavated in Britain appears on p. 256, chosen more for the archaeological methods used than for the importance of the site in terms of prehistory.

There are four main methods by which the excavation of a site can take place, and the selection of the correct one or combination is one of the greatest tasks facing the archaeologist. The approach into the site can be made by test-pits, trenches, a box or quadrant plan, or by open excavation. The archaeological assistant, as well as the director, should be aware of the features of all these, as it is essential that he understands the reasons not only for the excavation but also for the approach selected as appropriate to the site.

Test-pits
Test-pits are generally used to ascertain the horizontal spread of a site. Pits of about 1 m square, occasionally larger and often smaller, are excavated through topsoil down on to the cultural deposit without disturbing the latter (fig. 56). This may allow the archaeologist to determine the extent of the site, and to position his actual excavation areas advantageously. Test-pits are often used, however, for another purpose, and this is to record the cultural deposits visible in the sides of the pit which has been cut through the archaeological material. The finds recovered from the pit are correlated with the sections so far as is possible considering the minute area visible to the excavator. On almost any type of site, the continued sinking of test-pits as the major approach to excavation would probably result in many section drawings, some finds of uncertain attribution, and little or no idea of the actual appearance of the ancient occupation or remains of other activities. The 'process could have been prolonged indefinitely without any prospect whatever of coming to understand the anatomy of the mound'.[1]

On the other hand, the careful excavation of a single or small series of test-pits at the beginning of an excavation may yield enough information about the stratigraphy to more than offset

[1] S. Lloyd, *Mounds of the Near East*, E.U.P., Edinburgh, 1963, 64.

the loss of evidence through unavoidable mixing of material in the pit itself. Yet it can also be said that on occasion the single test-pit has subsequently been found to penetrate into and destroy unique evidence that might have been recovered *in situ* and intact through other less impatient methods of finding out about the strata. The archaeologist must make up his own mind on his own site, but it is extremely difficult for a worker to be entrusted with such a potentially harrowing task as 'digging blind'; the director or site supervisor should take the responsibility of actually doing the work themselves.

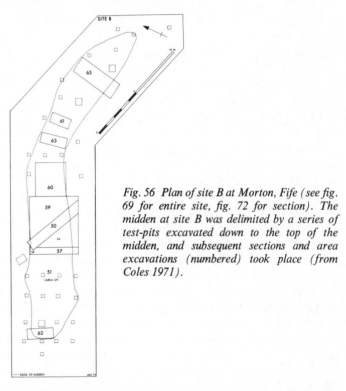

Fig. 56 Plan of site B at Morton, Fife (see fig. 69 for entire site, fig. 72 for section). The midden at site B was delimited by a series of test-pits excavated down to the top of the midden, and subsequent sections and area excavations (numbered) took place (from Coles 1971).

An example of the value, and at the same time the danger, of a test or exploratory excavation comes from one of the sites in the Olduvai Gorge, Tanzania. Here a small excavation revealed the existence of a few stones at a low level in the deposits at a site called DK1; the stones were recorded and then removed, but subsequent excavations were carried out and revealed the presence of a stone-built structure, probably the earliest-known artificial shelter in the world (*circa* 2 million years old). The exploratory excavation thus accomplished its aim in discovering an area for further work; at the same time, however, the removal of the material prevented a subsequent view of the entire structure, other than by a scale drawing.[1] This is not to detract from the extremely careful work done in the Gorge, by any standards the most important Lower Palaeolithic sites yet known from the world.

Trenches

Excavation by a trench, or series of trenches, is a method of entry into many prehistoric sites in Britain. It is a standard procedure for determining the sequence of building and other activities on defensive systems and funerary monuments, and it is a way of exploring a site outside the main areas of excavation. For rescue excavations, a trench system often can be the only way of working over the site on the time allotted. A series of related and ordered trenches can effectively cover a site and will show the sequence of events that led to its final appearance. But the emphasis is clearly upon sequence rather than event, because by its nature the trench cuts through archaeological deposits to sterile subsoils or bedrock, and therefore no single prehistoric occupation or other deposit remains intact for further or future examination. There are many types of site today that could be excavated to advantage without a single trench.

In the past, sites such as barrows, middens, embanked enclosures, have all been subjected to trenching in various ways, and there is no doubt that if the excavator requires a visible intact section, not merely built up by measurement (p. 150), cut through his site, such a procedure is reasonable. It is difficult, but not impossible, to envisage an alternative way by which the sequence of events of a rampart system such as that of Maiden Castle could have been elucidated by the excavator, but most such defensive sites are a good deal less complicated, such as that at Wandlebury,

[1] M. D. Leakey, *Olduvai Gorge, 3. Excavations in Beds I and II, 1960–1969.* C.U.P., Cambridge, 1971.

Cambs (fig. 57). There is far less reason for using trenches on any other type of site, except in three cases.

The first is where a site may show, by surface scatters, erosion, or test-pits, that it has a relatively uniform series of stratified deposits, not clearly separable by colour or texture. Such a site, a midden or rock-shelter, should be excavated by an open or perhaps a box system, but to ascertain the sequence of deposits initially, a trench might be cut into the site, and the deposits thereafter 'peeled away' from the clean edges of the trench. The advantages are clear, but the risk of disturbance of important evidence *in situ*, sleeping places or burials for instance, is also clear. If such a trench is to be exploratory, extreme care is required in its excavation.

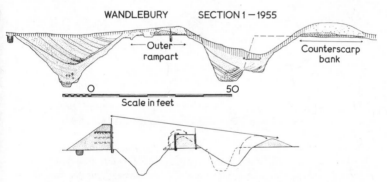

Fig. 57 Section drawing of a trench through the defensive systems at the hill-fort of Wandlebury, Cambs, with reconstruction of the defences (from Hartley 1956).

The second case is rescue, where a site is threatened and time does not exist for its complete excavation. Here the excavator will attempt to provide cross-sections through the site, to gain chronological evidence of the sequence of building or occupation; subsequent areas beside the trenches may be cleared if the finds and sections so indicate. For a small barrow, trenches would be cut through the site and expanded at the centre to allow a full examination of the area of presumed primary burial (fig. 58). The trenches here are also exploratory, but are deliberately chosen as the principal method of excavation when time presses.

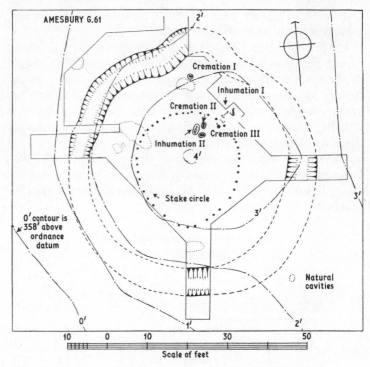

Fig. 58 *Plan of trenches and central area excavation of a round barrow at Amesbury, Wilts. The trenches are placed to allow sections to be drawn across the site, and the central area was opened to recover not only the burials but also the stake circle (from Ashbee 1960).*

The third case where a trench system may be thought to be of value is on a large site where suspected outlying structures or deposits must be located and examined. Here a combination of open or grid excavation at the centre of the site can be intercalated with a series of trenches that run out like fingers to explore the adjacent areas. On a multiperiod site, or one with a complex sequence of deposits, the trench system used in this way allows complete sections of the site to be observed, and the relationship of the outlying deposits to the central area to be demonstrated.

The excavation of a trench is almost always done in the recognition that it is the actual physical sections, on both sides of the trench, that are important. These sections can be observed, drawn, photographed, sampled, and taken away if need be (p. 216), but the excavator will also use the evidence revealed in the sections to decide his subsequent course of action, to peel back some or all of the deposits, to convert to a box or open plan, to close that part of the site and concentrate upon another, to cut further trenches parallel or at right-angles to the trench, or any other procedure. In the excavation of a trench, care should be taken to ensure the correct attribution of material to its deposit (p. 180), and so far as is possible the deposits should be removed over all of the trench in reverse order of their laying-down. The main advantage of this, as opposed to a complete removal of everything starting at one end of the trench, is that the excavator can call a halt, if the structural remains suggest that a change in plan is desirable. On the other hand, on a large site with deep deposits, a trench may be 'stepped', for ease in excavation, to allow transverse sections to be recorded, and to allow some open stripping of the deposits to take place.

Boxes and quadrants

On sites that are particularly large and which may possess relatively thick deposits of successive occupations, the archaeologist is concerned to expose areas of activities as well as to recover the stratigraphical sequence of deposits. The site may be too large or otherwise unsuitable for wholesale stripping on an open plan (see below), and in these cases a box plan is generally employed (fig. 59). The site is gridded and contoured (p. 110), and selected squares are then excavated. If adjacent squares are dug, a bank or baulk is left between them (see below).

The purpose of the method is to allow the excavator to recover some of the horizontal or near-horizontal activity surfaces through the removal of material in reverse order of their deposition, and at the same time to preserve in the sides of the squares the vertical sequence of deposits. At any stage, the vertical sections can be removed to allow a fuller view of a horizontal feature, but not all such features can be viewed if the sections are retained (fig. 59).

There are both advantages and disadvantages in this approach to a site. The practical problems of the grid or box plan involve the size of the squares and the width of the banks or baulks left

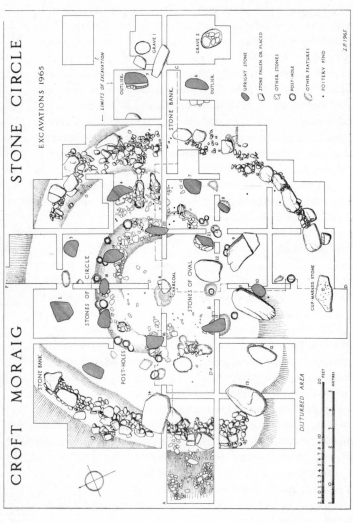

Fig. 59 Plan of box excavation at Croft Moraig, Perthshire. The areas excavated are not of uniform size, as the baulks left for sections have been positioned to obtain maximum information and to help support the largest

between them. The size is partly determined by the presumed depth of deposits; it is a question of the amount of light that will penetrate to the lower levels, as well as the difficulties in removing the spoil from lower levels by buckets (p. 169). Neither of these should be allowed to affect the size of squares over other archaeological considerations such as the excavator's opinion about the occupation area that he wants to see without interrupting baulks. Light can be provided by reflection, buckets can be hoisted, the cultural horizon cannot be so easily manipulated.

The width of the baulks between squares is also determined by the depth of the deposits to be excavated, and by the nature of these deposits (p. 183). Baulks provide access to the excavated squares, egress for the removal of spoil, and their sides provide the vital evidence for the stratigraphical sequence. The last should be the overriding concern of the excavator; the others are only technical problems that can be overcome by planking and mechanical methods of spoil removal.

The types of prehistoric sites that have been excavated using this method range from large barrows and fortified settlements to small caves and rock-shelters. Some shallow and single-period sites have been excavated in squares on a box plan but only because full open excavation was not possible; these are not really representative of the method of the box which is designed to allow some horizontal evidence to be exposed, and some vertical evidence to be retained.

The use of the box plan on a large site is often combined with trenches set on the same lines as the grid, so that complete or near-complete sections can be drawn through the site. This is particularly suitable for large barrows, where an internal grid system can be extended through trenches to include potential ditched areas and working or preparation areas outside the visible features of the site. A similar combination on fortified sites is not now often employed, as open excavation of interior areas has replaced the grid or box system.

The site illustrated (fig. 60) is a large barrow, initially excavated by a series of boxes in the central area, and trenches through the outer parts. The presence of trees prevented the full extension of the trenches to provide complete cross-sections (see fig. 65). Subsequently the central area was converted to an open plan

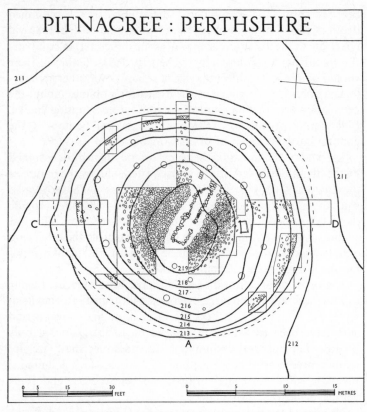

Fig. 60 Plan of a combined trench and box excavation of a large barrow at Pitnacree, Perthshire. The boxes in the central area were combined to an open excavation once the nature of the internal structures were recognized. Trees (shown as circles) prevented completion of an east–west section through the site, and prevented full examination of the entrance to the central area. Contours in feet above O.D. (from Coles and Simpson 1965).

excavation to allow as full an exposure of the central features as possible.

For small stratified sites such as cave entrances or rock-shelters, the box plan is often used. It allows the observation and recording of many vertical sections (p. 180), and provides some opportunity to observe the horizontal spread of occupation debris, but it is basically a vertical method of excavation. On such sites, there is equal justification for a different approach that allows a modified form of open excavation (see below).

Variations of the box plan   A method related to the grid or box system of approach is the block technique of excavating a stratified deposit. This is simply a reversal of the box, in that the square is left untouched while the sides (= baulks in the box system) are excavated. The block thus isolated can be seen not only from the top but from all four vertical sides, and the various stratified deposits can then be inspected and recorded before the block itself is removed. This allows an excellent opportunity for precise associations to be established between the cultural material and

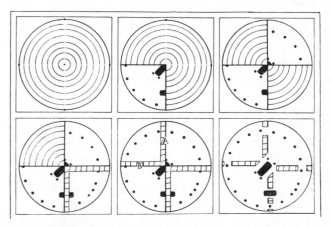

Fig. 61 Quadrant method of excavating a round barrow, to obtain transverse sections (A and B) for stratigraphy and sequence. The disadvantage is partial exposure of the central area, introducing weathering and decay before the area is fully examined.

its containing deposits, and is particularly suitable for sites where separate occupations are thin and where microstratigraphic units (see below) are employed. The size of block must be carefully assessed, as this not only allows an accurate sample (p. 226) of material to be obtained from the layers, but also determines the ease with which the layers can be followed, and the extent of 'horizontal' occupation to be exposed.

Small round barrows in Britain, and other small sites, are

generally excavated with a version of the box system, developed by A. E. van Giffen in the Netherlands. The site is divided into four sectors through the central point, and the sectors or quadrants are then excavated, in turn, to the old land surface or beyond (fig. 61). Baulks are left along the internal sides of quadrants 3 and 4, to allow the observation and recording of two cross-sections through the barrow. The baulks are then removed, and the whole of the old land surface exposed before it too is removed. The advantage of this method is again that it allows a vertical sequence to be actually observed, as well as, initially, part of the lower levels of the site. The disadvantage is that the excavation of quadrants 1 and 2 are likely to expose a position of the central and primary deposits, the burial or central coffin or cairn, and this can be damaged both by exposure and during the removal of the centre baulks. The central area is likely to be as important as any other, if not more important, and it may seem that this method does not provide enough protection. The alternative, completely open excavation, should be considered.

Open excavation
As the title infers, this approach to a site involves the stripping away of deposits to reveal the ancient occupation or activity area in its entirety. Each layer or feature of the site is completely exposed and then removed, to reveal the underlying stratum. There are no baulks or sections left that might obscure the overall view of a particular cultural horizon. This is the theory of open excavation, but there are a number of difficulties that generally prevent the completion of such a process. Most of these are technical, but one at least is a matter of the excavator's conscience, that he should consider the advisability of totally destroying a monument without leaving part for future investigation (p. 133). The solution to this depends upon the nature of the site, the questions that the excavation is supposed to answer, and the excavator himself. So many excavations in the past have concentrated upon sequence rather than event, and have used trenches and boxes, that the outstanding need in British prehistory is for sites to be opened entirely; only in this way can the full range of ancient occupations and activities be observed, and this is the major question that is asked of certain types of site.

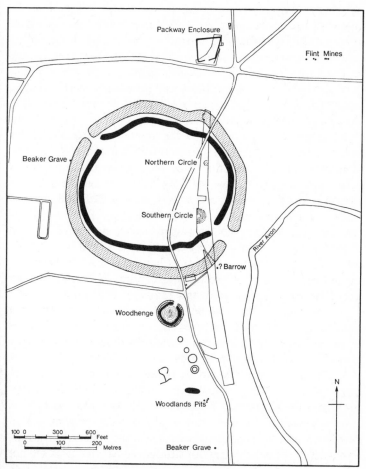

Fig. 62 Plan of Durrington Walls, Wilts, and its adjacent area, to show extent of open excavation within the henge monument, and the width of the machine-dug section through the ditch (see plate 6 for comparable ditch at Mount Pleasant). The work was a rescue operation in advance of road-building (from Wainwright 1971).

Open excavation means the clearance of large areas, not only of the site itself but its adjacent land (fig. 62 and plate 6). In some cases this clearance can be done by machinery (p. 191) but there are dangers in this of the removal of uppermost levels of *in situ* material, and of the compression of deposits through the weight of the machines; dragline operations avoid the latter. Other more serious practical difficulties involve the removal of excavated material from the interior of the cleared area, to avoid trampling; here the use of planks and boxes can generally prevent trouble, and there is no reason to shy away from an open excavation because of such technical problems.

Most important, however, is the absence of any observable vertical section of deposits. The establishment of a grid and contour plan (p. 110), and the fixing of permanent datum points around the site, will allow the drawing of sections through the site by careful levelling procedures at specified and marked positions. The sections can be built down as the various deposits are revealed and removed. This again is a technical problem well capable of solution by an experienced archaeologist or surveyor. But it does not remove the serious handicap that the excavator cannot refer back to the sections to confirm or reverse original decisions about stratigraphy and problems of various deposits. The individual deposits can be adequately sampled (p. 217), but their precise stratigraphical position in relation to other deposits must be based upon accurate surveying practices and single-period observations and records. The handicap is not insurmountable, but extreme care is required in the once-only examination, and the archaeologist should be aware that stratigraphical problems may arise. However, the open method is generally applied to sites of one period only, or sites with a restricted series of deposits which have clearly defined divisions, and the hope must be that major stratigraphical problems will not arise.

The use of open excavation on small sites such as a hut-circle, a cemetery or a camp site (fig. 63) infers that the excavation will start and finish without a break; this is a single-season operation. On a larger site such as a farmstead, the interior of a fortified site, a henge monument, open excavation can be spread over several seasons if necessary (fig. 64), or curtailed after a proportion of the

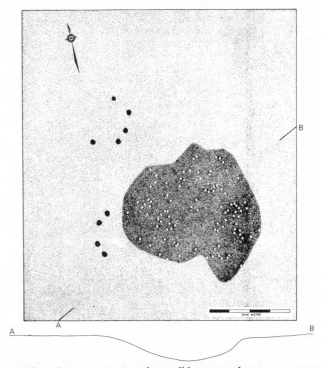

Fig. 63 Plan of open excavation of a small hunter–gatherer camp on sand at Morton, Fife. The black spots represent stake holes for two windbreaks, the grey patch is a scooped area where flints (white dots) and charcoal flecks were found. The sand surfaces were excavated in 5–10 mm levels (from Coles 1971).

site has been revealed; the entire plans are therefore not available, but future excavators may benefit.

The sites for which such an approach seems best-suited include interiors of embanked enclosures of all sorts (plate 6), flat cemeteries and open settlements of all kinds. More technical problems arise for sites where stratified deposits are liable to be present in some quantity; such sites include barrows of all types, and rock-shelters or caves. The advantage of seeing all the phases of building of a barrow (in reverse order), completely, may be thought to be as important as sections and quadrants. For shelter or cave occupations, it might well be considered necessary to have a test-pit, trench or block approach before switching to an

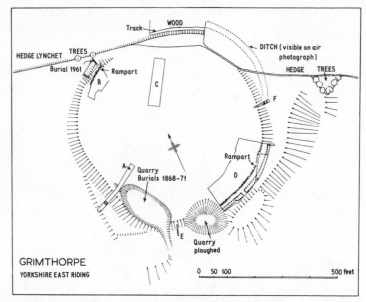

Fig. 64 Plan of hill-fort at Grimthorpe, Yorkshire, showing the area excavation of part of the interior and including the defences; the work was carried out over a period of years (from Stead 1968).

open plan, so that the stratigraphy can be assessed; such sites are not to be undertaken lightly, and are probably the most difficult with which to cope. In Britain, anciently occupied shelters and caves are so rare that only a fully qualified and experienced, probably professional, archaeologist should undertake their excavation.

Strata and stratigraphy

The different layers of rock and soil that make up the deposits of a site are from potentially very varied sources. They may all be of natural origin, representing decomposition products of the underlying rock, still water, running water, hillwash or wind-blown material, developed earths and soils of ancient or modern formation, or of other sources (p. 211). Some may be of human origin, ancient occupation surfaces, deposits of rubbish, cleared areas subsequently trampled, fired soils, decayed contents of storage pits, and others. The natural and human deposits may interfinger, or be disturbed by further activities such as erosion and weathering, earthworms and burrowing animals, humanly dug pits and scoops. Each of these deposits, whether of natural or human origin, whether *in situ* or disturbed, may be distinguishable from its adjacent deposits by colour or texture or by other means. The recognition and separation of such strata, and the breaks and interruptions of them, provides the archaeologist with the stratigraphy of the site, giving him a clear, or not-so-clear, guide to the sequence of events on the site (fig. 65). Not all events need be represented, as erosion may have removed some deposits, and some episodes may not have resulted in the deposition of any recognizable material. The interpretation of these deposits is crucial to an understanding of the site.

The vertical sides of an excavation, be it test-pit, trench or box, will present a series of these deposits which can be recorded by the excavator, but this is not by itself of any value unless the excavator can explain to himself and to others the reason for the appearance of each of the layers where it occurs. The 'sequence of strata can no longer be regarded just as a heaven-sent means of separating cultural levels, nor can deposits be regarded as meaningless and "barren", simply because no recognizable artifacts or organic remains are discovered in them. They are all equally important parts of a continuing record.'[1]

The popular view of stratigraphy as a simple series of layers, that can be easily distinguishable and be peeled off by the excavator, infers a far greater expertise than the archaeologist generally possesses. Some sites will indeed have a relatively straightforward series of deposits, laid more or less evenly or in otherwise easily distinguishable positions, and of different colours or textures. Other sites may have deposits that undulate and vanish, reappearing elsewhere, and their contours may bear no resemblance to surface contours. Both of these types of sites pose normal stratigraphic problems to the excavator.

More difficult are sites where deposits show no visible divisions, either by colour or by texture. Here the excavator must adopt a unit-level method of digging, in which the uniform deposit is arbitrarily divided into vertical units of a set thickness, perhaps 10 cm. Each unit is removed in turn and finds retained as repre-

[1] E. Pyddoke, *Stratification for the Archaeologist*, Phoenix, London, 1961, 17.

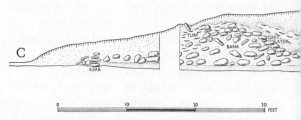

Fig. 65 Section drawing of the barrow at Pitnacree, Perthshire, to show disturbances (erection of standing stone over cremation, and construction of stone cist) cut into the body of the barrow, and the main features of the

sentative of the occupation at that time. The use of a box system of excavation is generally employed in such cases as these, and the unit-levels can be abandoned as soon as genuine stratigraphic units can be distinguished.

There is a difference here between deposits representing a single event and those of multiple origin, even although each may be thick and lack visible stratigraphic divisions. The body of a barrow, for instance, represents a single phase of activity, and can be excavated as a single unit. The occupation debris in a cave, however, may represent multiple events, yet be stratigraphically indivisible, and could therefore be excavated in thin unit-levels.

Decisions

The excavator has a number of established procedures that he can apply to his site. These varying approaches and techniques have been developed over time through the experience of himself and of others on different sites. It is up to the excavator to decide upon the approach most suitable for his own site, and to apply his own procedures and techniques to the evidence. But no two sites are ever the same, and it is not possible to predict the course of any excavation. The unexpected may turn up, the expected may require different treatment to extract different information from it, and the only rule about the approach to an excavation is that it must be adaptable and flexible enough to be changed to meet

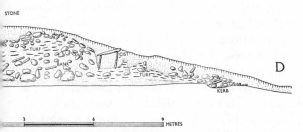

barrow. Note that the old land surface is preserved only within the kerb (from Coles and Simpson 1965 ; for plan see fig. 60).

changed circumstances. The decision to alter the approach can be made at any time, and it is the responsibility of the director to be constantly assessing the prospects and advantages to be gained from such a change. Stereotyped excavations are tedious to work on, to publish and to read, and add little to our knowledge. An imaginative approach to excavation, tempered with a sound judgment based upon experience, can make valuable contributions to knowledge, and at the same time provide the excavator and his workers with a sense of excitement and enjoyment over the acquisition of new information.

3 Labour relations

Most excavation teams consist of a director, his personal assistants (site supervisors), various technical assistants, and workers (paid or unpaid). Each of these persons has his own particular tasks to perform, which must somehow fit in with the rest of the excavation programme.

Many excavations in Britain are carried out by small teams, from six to fifteen people, with generally few technicians or specialists as permanent members. On such teams, the director or his supervisors operate as technical staff. A typical team might have a director acting also as photographer, one site supervisor doubling as environmental specialist, and six workers of whom one or two are selected as draughtsmen.

Some excavations in Britain are far larger, with a staff of fifty or one hundred, and on these there are places for specialists of all kinds. A team might consist of 'a director, a deputy director, a supervisor for each area under excavation, a trained foreman, a small-find recorder, a pottery assistant, a photographer, a surveyor, a chemist, a draughtsman, and, according to need, an epigraphist or numismatist' (Wheeler 1956, 153). On a prehistoric site, the last two would be omitted, but places might be reserved for a geologist, a pedologist, a palaeobotanist, a zoologist and perhaps a physical anthropologist.

Each member of a team, however large or small the team may be, has a particular role to play, and the successful completion of an excavation depends upon the professional relationships that exist or develop between all the members.

The director

'The qualities to be considered are first the honesty, shown mostly in the eyes and by a frank and open bearing, next the sense and ability, and lastly the sturdiness and freedom from nervous weakness and hysterical tendency to quarrel.'[1]

The director of an excavation should be an experienced field archaeologist, expert in organizing an excavation team and its work, and in delegating authority to his assistants. He should be able to exercise firm control over his workers, without alienation. He should understand the basic principles of the variety of scientific techniques that he can bring to bear on the problems of his site. All of these qualities can only be developed through experience in the field, through excavating as a worker, site supervisor and perhaps technical assistant on a variety of archaeological excavations. In addition, the director must be fit both physically and mentally, not only for the actual excavation but for the work of study, interpretation and writing that follows the completion of the fieldwork.

The director of a small team is probably under more pressure during the excavation than is the director of a large team who has been able to pass many small but important technical problems

[1] F. Petrie, *Methods and Aims in Archaeology*, London, 1904, 21, describing a workman, but equally applicable to a director (Alexander 1970).

on to assistants. On a small team, the director may have a multiple role to play, dealing with landowners, the work programme, the recording and sampling, and if he cannot cope with the seemingly endless series of problems, then the excavation will suffer.

The responsibilities for the site and for everything that happens to it are the director's, and if mistakes occur through a supervisor's wrong decision, or a worker's inexperience, the director must bear the blame for the loss of information.

The relationship that exists between a director and his helpers depends partly upon the site and the size of team, but clearly a closer personal relationship can be achieved on a small site where the director is in closer contact with the workers. On a large site, the director can remain a rather distant figure unless he makes a distinct effort to establish contact individually.

It is easy for both workers and director to get along well when an excavation is progressing smoothly, when the weather is fine, when the results of the dig are encouraging. The pressures come during more difficult times, when both director and workers must exercise restraint and consideration. There is little that is more heartening to a director or supervisor than unasked for assistance or particular care that is offered during a difficult period of the work, whether this involves working on to finish an area, or taking responsibility for a small item of work. The reverse is of course true.

The director has a series of responsibilities to his workers. Paramount among these is the safety of the individual, and there can be no question that this must override all responsibilities that the director may have to his site (p. 189). The director should be prepared, and will find it to his advantage, to tell his workers about the site, and to inform them of the progress of the excavations; this is necessary not only for information to be communicated to visitors but to enable the workers to appreciate what is going on. For the same reasons, the director must instruct his workers in the techniques of excavation that he feels are appropriate to his site; sites differ in their character, and tools and techniques suitable for one may well be highly inappropriate to another.

The director should above all be human, and admit to being human. He may feel completely dedicated to his site, and he will be anxious to complete his excavation successfully. He may come under pressures caused by understaffing, lack of time, inclement weather, inadequate techniques, or just 'bad luck' (generally explicable but not admitted). His ability to resist these pressures depends to a great extent upon his relationship with his workers, and this relationship will in the end make or break the excavation.

The site supervisor

Site supervisors are the main link between the director and his workers. The supervisor should have had considerable experience in excavation on a variety of sites, and training in other aspects such as surveying, drawing, sampling and photography. Most supervisors will be young professional archaeologists or experienced students, but other extremely successful supervisors will be older people who have come into archaeology through extra-mural work and consistent digging. All will have worked their way up from the ranks, and will be best able to appreciate the conditions under which the workers operate.

The role of a site supervisor is straightforward, to put into practice the decisions of the director. Generally, director and supervisor will decide the plan of action before the start of each day's work, and the supervisor's task is to carry this out. He it is who assigns the workers to specific tasks, as he is best-placed to appreciate the individual talents of each worker. The supervisor will also give instruction in the techniques of excavation to be used, will answer routine questions about the progress of the work from the diggers, and will keep a constant watch on the excavation of his area, trench or entire site.

Supervisors do not ordinarily excavate, but will be able to assist a worker in a difficult task, or may actually replace a worker in order to complete a piece of work more speedily or efficiently (see below).

The supervisor will report to the director on the progress not only of the work as a whole but also of individual workers, so that the director may be kept aware of particular aspects of his team that might be of potential value. Discussions on the excavations are regularly held between supervisor and director, and decisions to continue or to change the approach are generally made jointly, but the director's final word is binding. An argument need not be avoided, and often is healthy, but should be held away from the workers who no doubt would be interested but whose concern it is not.

The responsibility of the supervisor is both to the director and to the workers; the precise authority that the supervisor has on the site is a question to be decided by the director, with the supervisor's agreement. As an example, the supervisor should be able to call a halt if conditions become too wet either for the site or the workers, and should determine the time and duration of the breaks from work. He should also assign individual workers to the various tasks that the director decides should be done. The site supervisor requires most of the qualities that the director must possess, and again the most important of these is to be human.

Specialists

Technical assistants on an excavation have particular tasks to perform, and are equipped to deal with these as they occur. There are two main groups of such assistants, the natural scientists and the archaeologists.

Work on a site may include the sciences of geology, botany, zoology, pedology, physical anthropology, and on large excavations this will involve the presence of specialists in these fields, who can examine the site and its surrounds, take samples from advantageous positions, and generally assess the problems. These may be entirely concerned with the 'archaeology' of the site, or may also include separate research projects in other fields. In either case, on an archaeological site, the director's views must be expressed as to the nature of the problem for which the samples or deposits are being examined. The specialists will be expected to respect the methods of archaeological investigation, and to adapt their own procedures, so far as is possible, to the format of the excavation. This may involve assistance from site supervisors or workers who otherwise should be left alone to continue their work.

On small excavations, the director or supervisor may have to fill the role of such specialists, and collect samples for forwarding. This is in many ways unsatisfactory, but there are various sampling procedures that can be used to cope with such a situation (p. 217).

The other group of technical assistants is concerned with archaeological problems such as photography, surveying, drawing, conservation. In almost all cases these assistants will be either archaeologists who have had training in their respective fields, or technicians who have had archaeological experience. This is important, particularly for such aspects as photography and drawing, where only experience in the field will produce results likely to be completely satisfactory to the director (p. 207).

On small excavations, the director or supervisor will probably carry out all or most of these activities themselves, unless certain workers can be entrusted with the tasks. Drawing is the most popular of these to pass on to workers, and there is no doubt that an ability to draw accurately, either by scale or by sketch, is a useful attribute of any archaeologist. If this, or any other specialist activity, is assigned to a worker, it is essential that full information is sought and obtained about the procedures to follow and the results expected. There are few activities on a site that are more annoying than having to re-do a set of plans on which much time has already been expended. More serious, however, can be the loss of evidence through inadequate sampling or recording of material subsequently destroyed, and here again the director must accept all responsibility.

The workers
The sources of help on archaeological excavations in Britain are extremely varied. School children, university students and adults from all walks of life continue to apply for permission to dig, and the total labour force available in this country is truly immense. Many excavations that are advertised in the Calendar of Excavations (p. 249) are over-subscribed, and almost all of the full-time projects, that is, occupying the whole of at least a fortnight, and often two months, are fully staffed. Weekend excavations have a tendency to lose labour (p. 124), and rescue operations also may have insufficient time to prepare an adequate crew (p. 132), but most excavators have little difficulty in completing a team.

Most of the workers on excavations are amateurs, in that they do not earn a living from archaeology. Hired labour on excavations does not enter into this discussion. However, most workers do receive some financial assistance to help pay their travelling or living expenses, and they thereby incur some responsibilities for their conduct on the site. Excavations can and should be fun, and there is no obligation on anyone to dig. But the fact that it is an enjoyable experience does not mean it is a holiday. Directors obtain funds for excavations under rescue and/or research conditions, and they are expected by their backers to complete the work with competence and some dispatch. The volunteer labour on a site is expected to work, and not to treat the operation as a complete physical and mental rest-cure from the normal ordinary occupations of the year. Archaeological excavation does provide amateur workers with a change of occupation and this can certainly be of therapeutic value, but the first essential for the worker is his sense of responsibility to the site and to the director.

The relationship between worker and director is fairly simple. The director is, as his name implies, in charge, and the worker is expected to carry out instructions so far as he is able. There is one important exception, however, and this is the question of safety (p. 189); if there is, in the worker's opinion, any personal danger involved in digging or recording beside large vertical faces of buildings, he should state it and remove himself promptly from the position. He should not return unless and until a safety factor is introduced. The same should be said for working beside, behind or in front of machinery (p. 191). In all other cases, the worker should be prepared to do as he is told, subject to a reasonable attitude on the part of the director over conditions of work (see below).

Allocation of work will be done by the director or his supervisor, and explanations about why such work is necessary, and how it is to be done, will be provided. The worker should have a basic knowledge of the tools and the techniques that he is likely to encounter on a site (p. 165). If he is in any doubt, questions *must* be asked before work commences, or potentially important evidence may be lost through inexperience and lack of communication.

Most teams of workers will consist of experienced diggers and those with little or no archaeological training. The director or supervisor will be aware of this, and will often pair workers so that one can observe the other in the procedures used. The supervisor may prefer to instruct the beginner himself, and all workers on any site generally will receive some comment or suggestion about their capabilities from time to time; this is personal advice, given in the interests of both the site and the worker.

A problem that often arises during the course of an excavation is that of substitution. Where a particularly valuable find has been exposed, or a sample must be taken, the director or supervisor may feel obliged, on behalf of the site, to replace the worker with another of greater experience, often the director or supervisor himself. Although initially the situation may be galling to the original discoverer, reflection must show that it is the only course of action to take. Generally the worker will remain to observe and assist in the delicate procedures, but he should not feel despondent about his temporary relegation.

The work to be done on almost any site ranges from heavy manual labour to pencil drawing of plans and sections, with most intermediate stages also represented. Most workers on a properly conducted site will be engaged on a variety of jobs which involve both hard and soft labour, but the relative proportions of these will vary. Experienced workers will most often be employed in the more delicate tasks of trowelling, lifting and recording (soft labour), while beginners may well find themselves occupied with spading and shovelling, bucketing and barrowing (hard labour). No doubt it will seem unjust at the time, but the interests of the site and the approach to its excavation determine such assignments; most workers will, in fact, have ample opportunity to display their qualities for both types of labour. The most harrowing of tasks, backfilling of the excavated area, is mercifully today carried out by mechanical methods on most excavations.

The worker is expected to carry out his allotted tasks as efficiently as he can. These tasks may include any or all of the following: deturfing, spade and shovel work, barrowing, bucketing, grass-cutting, trowelling, cleaning and brushing, drawing and recording, lifting and labelling, conserving and packing, taking of samples, assisting specialists, water carrying and coffee making. Doubtless directors and supervisors could devise other jobs.

In addition to these, the worker is expected to obey implicitly all rules that are laid down for his conduct on the site. These rules may vary from site to site, but if they *are* rules and are expressed and explained as such, they must be observed. On prehistoric sites in Britain, the rules may include the following:

Do not smoke or eat near or on the excavated areas (contamination of samples).

Do not sit on or lean against sections or baulks (collapse).

Do not move around the site when you are supposed to be working (progress).

Do not talk *all* the time (boring).

Do think about what you are supposed to be doing.

In return for obedience and adherence to rules, the worker may expect to share in the accumulation of information about the site, to be tolerated for his inexperienced questions, to be treated with consideration in terms of working conditions, and to be allowed to enjoy himself both on and off the site. It seems a fair exchange.

Women In this book most references to archaeologists are in terms of the male. There are no implications in this; today more females than males study archaeology in universities and in extra-mural courses, and as many women as men apply for places on excavations. On the other hand, relatively few women direct excavations in this country, and hold university or other excavating positions in archaeology. The reason for this is obscure. Most directors will choose to have a reasonable proportion of both men and women on their excavations, and some directors consider that females are better able to excavate the more delicate objects sometimes found. Women may not be as suitable for the 'hard labour' activities on sites, but again this is not an infallible rule. In general, there is very little difference in the abilities and treatment of women and men on excavations and the comments of 1915 need not necessarily hold true today:

> ... I may perhaps venture a short word on the question much discussed in certain quarters, whether in the work of excavation it is a good thing to have cooperation between men and women ... Of a mixed dig ... I have seen something, and it is an experiment that I would be reluctant to try again. I would grant if need be that women are admirably fitted for the work, yet I would uphold that they should undertake it by themselves ... the work of an excavator on the dig and off it lays on

those who share in it a bond of closer daily intercourse than is conceivable . . . between men and women, except in chance cases, I do not
believe that such close and unavoidable companionship can ever be
other than a source of irritation; at any rate, I believe that however it
may affect women, the ordinary male at least cannot stand it . . . A
minor . . . objection lies in one particular form of constraint . . . moments
will occur on the best regulated dig when you want to say just what you
think without translation, which before the ladies, whatever their
feelings about it, cannot be done.[1]

Working conditions

The precise working conditions are the director's and supervisor's
choice. Generally, the hours of work on sites in Britain are from
8.30 in the morning to 5.30 or 6.00 in the afternoon, but most
directors will feel free to ask for longer periods if conditions on
the site require this. Workers may expect to have forty-five or
sixty minutes for lunch, and breaks of ten or fifteen minutes in
both morning and afternoon for coffee. The work generally
continues in cold conditions, but excessive rain may result in the
temporary abandonment of work on behalf of either the site or
the workers, or both. Portable shelters are often put over excavations to protect the workers from wind and rain.

Most sites are also provided with tents or other shelters
beneath which lunch and other breaks can be taken. Drawing of
small finds is generally done here, and equipment stored. A toilet
tent may also be provided on some sites, but others rely upon
adjacent wooded areas. Workers should be informed of these
arrangements, or the lack of them.

Transportation to and from the site is generally arranged by
the director, and workers are expected to present themselves at
the assembly area at the correct time. Directors, and even more
so supervisors, do not enjoy holding up an excavation for one
slowpoke.

Payment for workers is very varied in this country. Most
excavators will have sufficient finance to pay a small amount,
from 50p to £2 a day, to all workers, but some excavators operate
on a severely restricted budget. Applicants for an excavation
team should make it clear if they expect payment (p. 127). Whether

[1] J. P. Droop, *Archaeological Excavation*, Cambridge University Press, Cambridge, 1915.

or not they receive pay, they should regard themselves as employees.

Living accommodation is sometimes provided by the director for the entire team, and this is generally in tents near the site. Often the worker is asked to bring some of his own camping equipment, and these details also should be clearly established. Other sites will have adjacent caravan or hostel accommodation, and some directors will leave it to the worker to make his own arrangements, providing a list of possible accommodation ranging from three-star hotels to a field for a tent. On camping sites near an excavation, food and washing facilities may be provided by the director, with a camp cook and foreman, but on others the individual will be responsible for his own needs; if the latter, transport and time for shopping should be allowed. The conditions are varied, and the volunteer worker should be sure that he understands them before arrival on the site.

Once the arrangements are made, it is essential that both director and worker should abide by them, otherwise the organization of the work may suffer.

4 Tools and techniques

Just as no two archaeological sites are the same, so the techniques of excavation differ in extraordinary degree from site to site. The one basic rule about excavation procedure is adaptability, the good sense to observe the conditions of the site and to adapt techniques to suit them. Conditions of preservation of material vary not only from site to site, but also within a site, and the archaeologist must be prepared to recognize changes and to meet them by introducing new procedures whenever they are needed. The archaeologist, then, needs to observe and adapt; in addition, he needs to respect his site by taking care over his work, and he needs to be stubborn and persistent enough to see the work through.

The techniques of excavation to be used on a site cannot be standardized. Some sites require a bulldozer to strip away overburden or actually to expose the occupation surface, others have been excavated with tools no larger than a screwdriver bent to make a hook. Most excavators have their own personal ideas about what tools are useful, and they provide these for their own sites. The ephemeral nature of many prehistoric sites in this country make it essential that these tools are used efficiently, and instruction in specially devised procedures will be given. The archaeologist who has been trained in the prehistoric field is sometimes considered to be better able to cope with remains of any period because of the greater discipline he must exercise in the recovery of prehistoric data (Clark 1957). And 'there is no method proper to the excavation of a British site which is not applicable – nay, must be applied – to a site in Africa or Asia' (Wheeler 1956, 36). Both of these are opinions and might not be accepted by all, but it is certainly true to say that the character of British prehistoric sites, and the contrast in conditions in which they are found, provide an archaeologist with a wealth of experience which is well suited to many other fields of archaeology.

Equipment

The equipment necessary for the excavation of a prehistoric site in Britain will vary in its composition depending on the soil of the site. What may be considered suitable for a site on limestone may not be applicable to sand. The basic tools, however, as used on many sites, are as follows:

Spades   These generally have 19 cm wide blades, and a flange at the top of the blade for the foot. Handles may be T- or D-shaped, preferably the latter as this allows the spade to be chained up after work. The handles and stem should be sandpapered smooth to avoid splinters. Spades are used to cut and to lift turf, to trim sections into a vertical state (see below), and to shave an area horizontally. They are rarely used for cutting into the deposits, even where no finds are expected, as their blade edges are sharp (filed) and insensitive to archaeological material. On occasion, however, on a site where the sterile overburden is thick, and no other methods are suitable, the spade can be used to loosen and cut out material for removal. They are lethal instruments when used vigorously. On some sites, a small garden spade will be useful; this has a blade only 14 cm wide, and is a more sensitive tool, quite suitable for cleaning vertically or horizontally.

Forks Garden forks are also used in preliminary work on a site, for removal of turf if this is particularly thick, and for loosening earth for removal by shovel. The tines of the fork may be round, square or rectangular in section, and probably the first two are preferable to the last. The fork is pushed or eased into the ground, never jabbed or thrust, and is used as a lever for loosening earth. The depth of penetration should be restricted to a maximum of 10 cm, often less. Risk of damage to ancient material is great if the fork is used indiscriminately.

Picks Picks are particularly lethal tools on a site, and not only to the ancient remains. In use they must be swung gently, employing their own weight, to loosen and lever out stiff or concreted material. The operator should ensure that others are well clear of his backswing if he intends to act in a violent manner; a backswing should not be necessary in normal archaeological use. In picking an area, the work should progress away from the operator, so that he has a vertical face to remove each time. He can then observe the stratigraphy of the deposits that he is hacking through.

Small entrenching tools are used in the same way, and are often more easily controlled. These have a double blade, one rather wider than that on a pick, and can be effective in loosening and slightly pulling deposits towards the operator.

Shovels There are two types of shovel available. One has a rectangular blade which is flattened except for upturned sides and back. The other is heart-shaped, and evenly curved across. The advantage of the first is that it can be used right into the corners, or up to the edges, of an excavated area. It does not, however, scoop up coarse material such as gravel as easily as does the heart-shaped shovel. In either case, care must be exercised in use not to push the blade into the sides of the area, thereby damaging the section, and not to push the blade into unexcavated deposits on the floor of the area. Shovels are for removing loosened soil, and not for excavating unless a shaving operation with flat-based shovels is ordered. With experience, an excavator should be able to throw earth accurately about 5 m, i.e. well up and out of the excavated area on to a spoil heap (see below), if buckets are not to be used.

Planks   Planking is essential for all sites, to protect the edges of the excavated areas, to provide runways to spoil heaps and processing areas, and to shore up vertical faces (p. 190). People, diggers and visitors alike, tend to stand and observe the work at the extreme edge of the area, with toes hanging over the edge, and this will result in disintegration of the edges and the bringing down of extraneous material. Planks should be placed along all edges of areas if possible, and at least along edges in constant use. They should also lead barrowers and bucketers to and from spoil heaps (dumps), and workers to and from the tent or other shelter where equipment and finds are stored and treated.

If a site is undergoing excavation for a week or more, it may be thought an advantage to remove all planks from edges each evening, to prevent the grass beneath rotting and yellowing; the presence of post-work visitors, however, may indicate the advisability of leaving planks in place.

In any case, planks should be regularly moved away from the excavated area and scraped clean before being replaced; if allowed to get too dirty, wet weather or dew will make them slippery, with potential consequent damage to the site and the workers. The cleaning of planks should be done away from the excavated area, to avoid a mixture of dirt and wood splinters falling into the area.

The size of planks suitable for site work varies, but 2 and 4 m lengths are always useful. The plank width is generally 30 cm and thickness 2–3 cm. The ends should be bound with metal strips to save splitting and chipping.

Planks of 3–5 cm thickness are suitable for excavation work where the nature of the soil and the ancient remains is such that no weight can be allowed upon them; this could occur on soft sandy surfaces, in peat, or on wet chalk. Here the planks are spread across the area, supported on other planks at the area edges, or balanced on open-based boxes (see below) which can stand upon the excavated surface. The worker lies on the planks, and excavates beside and beneath it. Various devices can be improvised to allow the planks to be lowered as the excavation proceeds, and the use of boxes is recommended.

Boxes The standard open box used as a base for planking is made of four boards screwed together to form a rectangular box lacking bottom or top. A cross-member inside the box will prevent wobble. The timber is generally 2 cm thick, and the box measures about 40 cm long, 20 cm wide, and 20 cm high. This provides a working height of about 25 cm above the excavation. A series of interfitting boxes, like a Chinese puzzle, is easier to transport than a set all of the same size. The combination of open boxes and toeboards at relating sizes is often convenient (see below).

Toeboards These are simple boards, about 40 by 20 cm, 2 cm thick. The worker puts his knees on one, and his toes on another; this spreads his weight, and does less damage to the surface than a pair of knobbly knees and pointed toes. Toeboards can also be used to plank awkward areas not covered by planks, to lift fragile material (p. 185), and to serve as improvised drawing-boards. If made to selected sizes, they can be nailed to an open box to form a proper container for finds or equipment during or at the end of a dig. Toeboards can be made more rigid, and avoid warping, by screwing or nailing cross-pieces on their ends.

Wheelbarrows Used for collecting and transporting excavated material, these should be sturdy but not too heavy. Solid tyres should be avoided, as bumping up planks is bad enough with an air-cushioned barrow. A metal box is better than a wooden one in terms of barrow weight.

Buckets Buckets are essential items of equipment on almost any excavation. Used for the transport and disposal of excavated material, they should be light but strong. Metal buckets are suitable for almost all types of site, but tend to dig into the working surface as they have a sharp rimmed base. Rubber buckets are far less noisy, hold as much, are lighter, and if used with care are a better solution. The transport of gravel or rock in rubber buckets is not, however, recommended. Plastic buckets generally split. Plastic bowls are sometimes used for collecting material that is being removed slowly and carefully from an excavation surface.

Scythes, shears, secateurs and scissors   On the assumption that a clean and neat site bespeaks an orderly mind and therefore a well-controlled excavation, the use of these items is recommended. Scythes and shears should be employed to cut and trim the grass along and around the edges of excavated areas as soon as the turf has been cut. The clippings should then be brushed away from the area, or brushed into the excavation so that they are removed with the first deposits of soil to be taken out. The result will improve the look of photographs of the excavation, as well as allowing an uninterrupted view of sections and preventing long grass falling into the area. The final clean-up of the edges can be carried out with scissors which are also useful for cutting off stray bits of root and grasses that may have penetrated deeper, and which appear in the sides or surface of the excavation. Secateurs may be necessary for the removal of thicker roots, which should be cut off flush with the vertical or horizontal surface. Roots or anything else should never be pulled out, as this will disturb other deposits.

Trowels   The trowel is the main instrument used in excavating prehistoric remains in this country. The mason's pointing trowel is the only suitable type, and curved garden trowels are not suitable. Sizes of trowels used in archaeology vary, but 10 or 15 cm blade lengths are generally considered to be the most convenient sizes. These will cost about £1. The blade and tang should be in one piece, as riveted trowels will always break, generally within the first fifteen minutes' work. Mason's trowels have sharp points and most archaeologists file these into slightly curved points, to reduce damage to material. The straight edge of the trowel should not be filed into a curve, as this may prevent its successful use as an instrument for scraping on a flat plane, particularly on soft soils.

Trowels are the totems of archaeologists; most diggers have their own particular trowel that has been carefully filed and worn down to a special shape, and these are generally stored in back pockets of jeans. Such precious items should not be borrowed by anyone.

The trowel should be used with care. It is small and light, but is nonetheless sharp and can do untold (generally) damage to soft material such as bone and wood, and some damage to stone and pottery. The point can be used as a delicate lever for loosening earth, or for extracting earth from crevices or awkward places. The point should never be stuck violently into the earth as a method of wholesale excavation; it is neither strong enough nor the right shape for such a purpose, and if this is how the site is to be dug, better to use a pick.

Trowels are mainly used as scraping tools, to remove a very thin section of earth. The tool is held so that one of the blade edges is parallel to the ground, and the flat of the blade is almost vertical; the blade edge is scraped along the ground, cutting into it slightly. The movement of the tool during this should be towards the user, and the work proceeds away from the troweller as he moves forward to excavate the deposit. The disadvantage of this method is that the loosened earth is dragged upon a previously trowelled surface, and can obscure material only just cleaned. It is essential to clear away the trowelled earth at once, using brush and handshovel or hands. With experience, a troweller can remove a fine layer of earth, leaving an even surface without scoops and bumps caused by an uncontrolled action.

Brushes Hand-brushes generally sold for cleaning of carpets or hearths are essential items of equipment for use with the trowel. These are not whisks, and have rows of bristles mounted on the side of a handle, the whole measuring about 30 cm long. There are a variety of these brushes available, ranging from extremely soft and unsuitable brushes to extremely hard and also generally unsuitable brushes; the intermediate type is best. Brushes like these are used for sweeping loosened earth into handshovels, and for cleaning trowelled surfaces and finds. If the deposit is wet, brushes will only smear and should not be used. The brush will scatter earth in all directions if used too deliberately, and fairly short brisk strokes are best.

A stable brush, with very stiff bristles, will sometimes be useful for cleaning *around* an excavated area, brushing debris away, but only if the grass has been cut short and the earth is dry.

Handshovels   Small handshovels, with blades 10 or 20 cm wide, are used to collect loosened earth for disposal in buckets. They are never used to excavate anything, and the temptation to push them forward into a small heap of earth should be resisted; the brush or trowel will pull such material on to the shovel.

Hands   Hands are useful objects for actually lifting earth if handshovels or shovels are not suitable or available; in preparation for this and other functions, nails should be short and thin rubber gloves (e.g. surgeon's or hairdresser's gloves) can be worn. Thick woollen gloves are entirely unsuitable for delicate work where the 'feel' is as important as the 'look'.

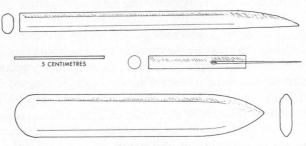

Fig. 66 Small excavating tools. Plastic spatula, handled needle, wooden point (at top).

Small equipment   Much time is necessarily spent in excavating fragile and delicate objects, often of uncertain shapes and sizes. These may range from intact extended skeletons, through heaps of flints or potsherds, to thin scatters of burnt bone and textile fragments in advanced states of decay (p. 210). The exposure of these is a matter of patience and experience, and in the exercise of both, special equipment is an aid.

A general range of such items of equipment would include bent spoons, dental probes and long-handled needles, paint brushes, spatulae of wood or plastic (fig. 66), small penknives and miniature bellows or bicycle pumps. The use of most of these is clear, but their whole purpose is to allow the removal of earth from small or fragile finds without disturbing the position or character of the finds. The use of the point of a small knife, and a needle or dental probe requires that the operator is fully supported at knees and elbows, if not wrists, so that no inadvertent movement to retain balance is necessary. The wooden or plastic spatulae can be of various shapes and sizes, and will act as miniature trowels on soft material around an object, or will allow a good measure of 'feel' if used to lightly scrape away surface earth from a find. The soft paint brushes available should be of several sizes; the 1 cm and 3 cm widths are useful for most small finds. Bellows or air pump will puff away loosened dry earth, but should not be allowed to puff away anything else.

Trays and markers   A 'find tray' is generally a plastic or wooden tray used to hold and transport objects and samples recovered from an area. On a site yielding quantities of potsherds, trays may well be considered necessary to retain this material from carefully controlled levels and areas. In almost all other cases, however, finds and samples should be bagged and labelled individually as they are lifted (p. 202), and the tray could then serve merely as a collecting box for a variety of specimens, each separately marked. In any case, trays in use should be labelled with their area or level, or other designation, just in case something goes wrong with other recording systems.

Markers on a site generally consist of small plastic or metal garden labels, used for marking bags (p. 202) but also for indicating the positions of finds subsequently to be recorded on a plan or section; markers also accompany trays of specimens from the excavation to the processing tent, and must not be removed until they are replaced by permanent labels.

Other equipment   Other items of equipment may also be required on certain sites. The use of screens or a series of sieves to sift through a deposit is often considered to be a lazy way to extract material, the view being that anything found in a sieve has lost its position on the site, and therefore much of its value. This is true to a point, but it is also true that the control over such sieved deposits can be tight enough to allow an attribution to a specific deposit from a specific area of the site, if not an exact spot. And it is doubtless better to make the find in a sieve than in the dump, if it is not to be made *in situ*. The last point is crucial, and the excavator should decide if he intends to recover everything visible actually in place, or organize sieving to allow a very close identification of the position of sieved finds. The best practice, of course, is to attempt to recover all *in situ*, and also check excavated debris by controlled sieving. Sieves can be obtained in a variety of interlocking trays with different meshes; a general-purpose set might commence with a 50 mm mesh to catch rocks, 20 mm mesh for pebbles and other pieces, 10 mm for small finds, the residue of earth falling through. However, the mesh size could easily be reduced to suit the site's conditions. For seeds, a different set is used (p. 224).

At depths near watertables, or liable to flooding, pumps will be necessary; these can range from small- or large-bore petrol pumps for 'instant' clearout, to hand-driven pumps for small puddles. A petrol pump will cost £35, and hand pumps about £5; a useful hand pump is the Whale dinghy pump (Munster Simms Engineering, Belfast). Sponges may be useful for general mopping of a damp site, if care is exercised over their application to the remains.

Other sites may be too dry for the excavator's satisfaction, and often structural and other features will only be revealed if the site is artificially dampened to allow differential drying (see plate 5). A small garden spray, under pressure, is an excellent piece of equipment to have available.

Care of equipment   Equipment is provided for the efficient excavation of a site, and all workers are expected to be able to manipulate the tools in a competent way. Some items of equipment are heavy and/or sharp, and can inflict damage to both the site and the workers. Equipment of any sort, large or small, should *never* be thrown about or dropped into an excavated area; buckets are the most prone to such action, but even picks have been chucked across a site. Tools should also *not* be stuck into the site during rest periods or left precariously balanced on planks or baulks; trowels should not be stored upright in an excavation level, or horizontally in a section.

The care of equipment is not a minor matter to the director or supervisor; on a large site it is good practice to 'book out' equipment to workers each day, but on a small site this may seem unfriendly and unnecessary. Tools should not be left lying about, and after use they should be returned to the storage tent or shed. All supervisors will insist that all equipment is cleaned, by scraping and washing, before the site is left at the end of the day, and most will ask that tools be superficially cleaned before any break in work during the day.

Personal equipment The excavator on a site in Britain must be prepared for a variety of weathers unequalled anywhere else in the world. Other regions may have hotter or colder or wetter or drier conditions, but not all, practically, at the same time. The experienced excavator should take precautions against some of these extremes by equipping himself or herself with clothing against rain and cold, including gumboots or waterproof shoes, anorak and warm sweater. Lighter shoes, such as plimsolls, may be essential for sites where finds or deposits are fragile or in abundance, requiring care in movement; it is impossible to be graceful in gumboots. A rubber kneeling pad is a personal luxury that many will find necessary. Directors of excavations generally provide information about other personal equipment required. Directors do not generally like radios, dogs or uncontrollable children on sites, but generally do not publicly advertise these facts.

All those engaged on excavation should have immunization against tetanus; this protection is obtainable from any doctor.

Recording See p. 193.

Conservation See p. 209.

Sampling See p. 217.

Some excavation procedures

The rules for excavation are not complicated, and all are based on common sense. The reason why the excavation is taking place in a particular area, and how it is to be done, should have been communicated from director to supervisor to workers.

Setting out an excavation

The procedures for setting out an area to be excavated have been described in general terms (pp. 110, 116), but one or two other points can be made here. Areas or trenches to be excavated should be strung out with strong but slightly elastic 'builder's string'. The general way in which this is done is by establishing a position on or convenient to one of the grid lines of the site (p. 110), and laying out a regular shape, be it a long thin trench, a square or a rectangle (fig. 53). Most archaeologists prefer to have the lines of their excavated areas running parallel and at right-angles to the grid, but there is no reason why this should be a rigid rule. Pre-historic sites are rarely squared-off, and a grid is merely a handy way by which to record and contour a site. The opinion of the excavator as to the exact position where he wants his excavations to begin is the controlling factor.

The areas generally have straight sides, for ease in recording and in drawing sections; there is no real reason why some other shape could not be chosen if it seemed to suit a particular site, but it is easier to string a site in straight lines than devise some other shape. It is generally necessary to ensure that the area is set out with adjacent sides at right-angles to one another, and on a large area this is best accomplished by measurement (p. 74); a small trench or square, up to 2 m wide, can be set out with a right-angle frame, consisting of three lengths of seasoned timber about 5×2 cm thick screwed and glued together to form a triangle with two sides each a metre long and at right-angles to one another (fig. 71). The frame should be protected by plastic paint, and must be checked before the excavation to ensure it has not warped.

The string should be held by surveyor's arrows at the corners of the area if a simple method of setting-out is required (fig. 67). The difficulty here, compounded by the use of wooden pegs or posts, is that during the excavation, the entire length of the vertical arrows will be exposed as the earth is removed, until the string pulls them into the excavation. The solution is to remove the arrows and string as soon as the edges of the area have been accurately cut, and retain these edges and corners with extreme care.

An alternative solution is to string-out as in fig. 67, using twice as many arrows or pegs; this allows the string to remain for as long as it is needed. The method is of use on sites where sides may

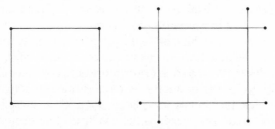

Fig. 67 Stringing out an area for excavation. Left, arrows or thin pegs in the corners may pull out as the work proceeds. Right, double arrows outside the area allow the string to remain for as long as necessary, and to be replaced for recording if necessary.

erode and crumble as they dry out, e.g. sand, and where the strings serve as recording aids. If they are to be so used, the pegs must be secured carefully. The difficulty is that strings tend to get pulled about by feet and equipment.

Dumps

Turf should be cut to a uniform shape, including thickness, and stacked neatly well away (5–10 m) from the excavation. The first turves should be placed face down on the grass in a row, and subsequent turves are placed face up on this row. The third row again is face down, and so on, so that grass to grass is the rule. Turves should not be stacked in a large block, and two rows side by side is the maximum; this is to allow the turf to be watered from both sides so that it does not perish during a dry spell of perhaps a month or so (see fig. 70).

The topsoil, next to be removed, should be deposited in a spoil heap or dump well away from the turf, and not burying it. This soil should be the last to go back when the excavation is filled in, and so should be kept separate from the deeper soils and subsoils. If soil is to be pushed back by a machine, it should be dumped directly on the grass; if, however, the backfilling is to be done by hand, then the dump should be placed on sheets of plastic (about 50p for 4×3 m sheet), so that cleaning up is more easily done. The separation of topsoil from other soils in dumps will allow a more successful returfing or reseeding operation (fig. 70).

The positioning of the turf stack, the topsoil dump and the

subsoil dump, is crucial to the efficient running of the excavation. The dumps must be accessible, yet far enough away to keep dump spreads from encroaching on to the periphery of the excavations. Dumps should be at least 3 m away, and planking on edge, held by stakes, will keep the soil from drifting forward. The wind direction may help decide the position of a dump if the soil is light. It is essential that the dumps are placed upon areas of site where excavation is not envisaged, as there is little more demoralizing than having to shift a dump to allow a trench or area excavation to be extended. This is one of the reasons for positioning dumps well away from the edges of an area, so that if an extension is needed it can be provided without disturbing the dumps. On a large site where a wide area is being cleared, some mechanical method of spoil transport can be devised, either a small dump truck or conveyor system, and these will move spoil well away. On a small site, however, where bucketing or barrowing is the method, and where backfilling by hand is necessary, the temptation to place the dump near the excavation is great; this should be resisted. Commonsense shows that once earth is in a bucket, or a barrow, it takes little effort to move it the extra 3 or 4 m that may make all the difference to an extension of excavation.

Backfilling by hand should be done in relays, some workers filling barrows or buckets, or shovelling directly into the trench, others tramping and ramming the earth into place. The topsoil goes in last, and then the turf is replaced, firmed in and watered. The area then can be brushed clean and the site left as immaculate as possible.

Levels, layers and spits
All archaeologists dig in levels, layers or spits at some time during their excavations. The upper deposits of a site, immediately beneath the turf, may be considered to be well above the ancient occupation and will be removed fairly rapidly. Other sites may lie just below the turf, and the removal of thin turves will be carried out with extreme care. In these two cases, and in their intermediates, direction may be given to take off a layer or spit of a set thickness, which may be as much as 150 mm (6 inches) or as little as 5 mm ($\frac{1}{4}$ inch). The use of the term layer does not necessarily imply that the deposit to be removed forms a separate

layer or stratum; similarly, the use of the term level, such as 'working to a level', does not mean that the surface must be kept horizontally level.

The various deposits on a site which make up the stratigraphy of the site (p. 152) need not, and rarely, lie evenly upon one another, and often are discontinuous, inclined or even invisible to the naked eye. The archaeologist will in all cases attempt to distinguish and separate these deposits and their associated ancient materials. He may cut through a series of deposits to establish a stratigraphical sequence, which is often described as a vertical sequence, although it need not be truly so. Or he may attempt to strip off completely each deposit in turn, to expose the 'horizontal' surface, which of course need not be truly horizontal. In both procedures, and often both are used on the same site, the individual deposits will rarely be entirely removed in one operation, and here the use of the word 'spit' is most common.

A spit is an arbitrary unit of depth for excavation, and a deposit that is believed to be as much as 20 cm thick, and lacking any visible divisions, may be excavated in spits of 1 cm to 5 cm thickness depending on local circumstances and decisions. The direction of work given in these situations must be explicit, and the worker must obey them. If the director or supervisor wishes the surface of the excavated area to descend upon a visible inclined lower deposit, the worker must understand that 'working to that level' does not mean clearing away to a horizontal level, nor does 'taking off a spit of *x* cm' mean that the surface need be evened up. The important thing is that separate deposits with their material should not be excavated together, and any spit or level that cuts through two deposits and lumps all finds together is a waste and destruction of evidence.

The worker has the only opportunity to see and feel differences in deposits, and must exercise care in excavating both to assumed underlying interfaces, and through a uniform deposit in spits. The supervisor or director is there to observe and guide, and must be told of any suspected changes. Workers, like directors, are a varied bunch, and again (p. 162) must be prepared to be moved out of a difficult excavation where soil or other differences are being sought. Some workers have 'good hands', able to feel differences where nothing is visible to the eye; experience helps in the acquisition of good hands, as in everything else about excavation, but some people seem to be born with particularly sensitive hands.

During the excavation of any ancient surface, whether it be an interface of deposits, or an artificial spit, the archaeologist should take care not to disturb the surface by shoes, knees, hands or buckets. Material can easily be brought into an excavation during removal of spoil, either in or on buckets or on boots. The use of toeboards (p. 169) should not be neglected by a worker if other ways of saving the surfaces are not available. On hard and stony surfaces, such a procedure may not be universally held to be necessary, but on any soft deposits such as sand or peat, the use of toeboards is essential. Any wet deposit, particularly chalk, should also be protected by boards.

The discovery of artefacts of whatever character during excavation also puts a responsibility upon the worker. He alone has seen the material at its moment of discovery, and has observed its precise relationship with the deposits. Finds should not be moved, should not be loosened completely, should *never* be pulled out or levered out from any deposit. Recording *in situ* is essential (p. 200), and the supervisor or director should have the opportunity to observe and advise. The association of the find with its deposit is vital, and if it occurs at an interface between two separate deposits or 'layers', it is usual to associate it with the younger, upper, deposit.

Finally, excavation should always proceed down to sterile subsoils (p. 211), and well into them. A general rule is to excavate at least 30 cm into subsoils or on to firm bedrock, so that the archaeologist can be sure that he has actually worked through the site (see fig. 76). Artificial deposits can resemble undisturbed subsoils such as gravels and sands, and it is essential that this step is taken to avoid a premature conclusion to the examination of the site, and the loss of evidence of the earliest activities.

Sections

The excavation of trenches through archaeological sites (p. 140) and the squares of a box system (p. 143) involves the archaeologist in problems of sections. The main purpose of these approaches to a site is the acquisition of sections that show the sequence of deposits making up the site. Care must therefore be exercised in the gradual exposure of these sequences. On many sites, sections can be rigidly vertical, on others it may be necessary to step or slope them to avoid collapse; sand and gravel are particularly prone to collapse through weathering over a short time. Safety and the preservation of a stepped section or a sloped section with its recording difficulties (p. 203) are far more important than a vertical face of uncertain stability.

The section will be gradually exposed as the excavation proceeds, and it is necessary to protect the face, and to maintain its shape. The removal of loosened earth by shovel or handshovel must not result in cutting into the side, thereby undermining the section. Similarly, the excavator must take care not to undercut the section with trowel or small spade as he works at a low level. It is practically impossible to estimate the 'verticality' of a section from a position at the base of and away from the face. The regular use of a plumb-bob by the worker, or supervisor, will ensure that the section is neither undercut nor left as an outward slope; the latter is less permanent than the former, but indicates sloppy work, and its removal can bring upper material down on to an older surface.

Sections at the sides of trenches or baulks are not sacred. Neither are the sides of large area excavations. They can be recorded at any time during the course of the work (p. 202), and can then be removed. The archaeologist should have no compunction about removing a baulk, or cutting into a section (see plate 8, lower right), if the site warrants it, but this is a directorial decision and not a worker's. The plan of an excavation may appear neater and therefore better organized if the squares and trenches are intact and uniform, but if evidence is obscured by rigidly adhering to this approach, then the basic rule for any archaeologist, adaptability, has been ignored. An excavator will try to position his sections advantageously, but they should be expendable.

The differentiation of strata in a section, and on an ancient surface, may not be immediately visible. Drying of deposits (plate 5) may reveal differences as much as wetting of deposits, and the use of patience or warm air for the former, and water sprays for the latter, may reveal information of importance. Sections peculiarly uninformative on exposure may yield useful data in time and in different lights, and the archaeologist should therefore carry out consistent examination, and take appropriate action, to gain the maximum evidence.

The cleaning of a section, for recording by photography or drawing (p. 203), or for the taking of samples (p. 222), should be done by the director or by the specialist concerned. In general, scraping with a trowel or other tool should be done along the lines of the visible strata. To clean downwards and upwards will lead to dragging of material from one deposit over another, and for sampling procedures such as pollen retrieval this can be disastrous; in any case, it is an unnecessary practice.

The excavation of stakeholes, postholes and pits presents the excavator with certain problems of approach. The usual procedure for a posthole or pit is to record its horizontal position as soon as it is recognized, and then excavate half of it by sectioning. The posthole excavation should aim to demonstrate if the post rotted in place or was withdrawn, if it was packed with stones or earth, if it was rammed in, and its size and shape. This procedure is useful on a single-period site, but on a more complex site the emptying of the hole may cause difficulties. The level at which the pit or hole is first noted is extremely important to record.

Stakeholes are generally too small for sectioning, and should be recorded as soon as recognized, and taken down along with the various spits or layers; their exact (to within 5 mm) position must be noted at each 10–20 mm depth, as only this will show the inclination of the stake and its shape and size along its length. The sectioning of stakes necessitates cutting through deposits vertically, and this may not be desired by the excavator who is working on an open plan.

Storage pits subsequently filled with rubbish are a problem in sampling and conserving (p. 224), and all of their contents should be treated for the recovery of organic material. The sectioning of such pits may be thought to be less important than that of post-holes.

Similarly, sections through middens, to observe tip lines, angles of rest of objects, and old land surfaces, are not a substitute for adequate sampling of a midden's content which can be carried out by an area approach (p. 148). Sections through rocky middens will disturb structural features that could be retrieved by open excavation, and recognition of tip lines and sampling can be made by either approach.

Soils

In Britain the main soil and subsoil types that are likely to be encountered are chalk and limestone, gravel and sand, clay, peat and mixtures of some of these. The archaeological interests in these different types can be expressed as questions which the excavator must ask himself.

(1) What techniques are best suited for the particular soils on the site?

(2) What types of evidence are likely to have survived in the soils on the site?

A few descriptive comments can be given here on soil types and the techniques used upon them, and the survival of evidence is treated under Conservation (p. 209).

Chalk and limestone are ideal subsoils, as they retain the shape of pits and scoops (plate 6); their surfaces are likely to be friable and decomposed, and can easily and wrongly be removed by an excavator. Both break up by frost action and other weathering agencies, and an undulating surface can be an entirely natural phenomenon. Being alkaline, they preserve metals, stone and bone if other more destructive processes are not also present.

Gravel and sand are completely different from chalk and limestone. They tend to be acidic, and most organic materials will not survive (p. 212). Gravel is particularly difficult to work, as it may be evenly bedded, or contorted by frost and water action. Its surface may contain hollows of entirely natural origin. Within gravel there may occur iron concentrations, or lime deposits (p. 213). Pits and holes in gravel tend to erode when first dry and when excavated; their fillings may well be visually indistinct at first but will emerge through differential drying, the gravel draining more quickly after dampening (plate 5).

Both gravel and sand are unstable soils, and cuttings should be sloped or shored, to avoid loss of sections or workers (p. 189).

Sand, and to a much less extent gravel, will retain colour and texture differences between undisturbed material and material partly composed of disintegrated organic matter, of bone or wood (fig. 63). The excavation of such soil discolorations is a horizontal process (p. 182) as sectioning may cause collapse. Plough marks will be particularly well identifiable in sand, but also may be preserved in chalk and other subsoils.

Clay, or clay with pebbles, is a difficult material in which to work; the procedures adopted depend upon the nature of the site and the condition of the clay. Wet clay is practically impossible to excavate successfully unless either extremely slow hand methods are used or water sprays are employed to loosen and drive off the clay particles. The latter procedure has been used successfully, but can result in absolute chaos if the water can not thereafter be removed. Dry clay, compressed by pressure, or dried by weathering, tends to chip and can only be excavated by tedious scraping; the lifting of finds in a block for removal in the laboratory is a useful expedient, if difficult to implement. A vibratory method of breaking up the material, as for any other concreted material, should be considered. Other clays, particularly clay with pebbles, are more easily worked but dampness can be a serious problem. A firm clay deposit, however, will preserve the exact outline of pits, and the precise shape of posts or stakes, as well as often preserving material embedded in it.

Peat tends to differ in its character from region to region. It is generally acidic, and bone and other organics will not survive. If it is anaerobic (oxygen excluded), however, wood will tend to be preserved (plate 8). Pollen and other vegetable remains forming the peat provide valuable environmental and cultural evidence (p. 227). The excavation procedures in peat are all based upon the fragile nature of the remains, and generally no metal tools of any sort are allowed; the hands perform most of the work unaided.

Small objects

The procedures to adopt for small finds are simple. Objects that are foreign to the soil decay rapidly after burial or loss, then gradually assume a more or less static position; upon exposure again, the processes of decay are greatly accelerated, and the excavator must take immediate steps to arrest these processes (fig. 74). The procedures of conservation are described on p. 213.

The discovery of a small object during excavation may be considered of tremendous importance because of its unique character or because small finds of any sort are rare; on the other hand, some sites yield enormous quantities of finds, and unless it is unusual and startling, a discovery may be uninspiring to the excavator. Nonetheless, each find *is* important, and never more so than at the moment of its recognition when its precise relationship with other finds and with its containing deposit can be seen.

No small find should be pulled or levered away from its deposit; the deposit should be lowered sufficiently around it to allow it to be lifted freely when required. If the containing deposit is not to be removed for the moment, then the find should remain in place. Its precise position should be recorded by measurement, and its association, character and condition noted before any attempt is made to move it.

During all this time, and during its removal, no tool edge should touch it. If of stone or pottery, scratches will occur, if of bone or even softer material the damage will be greater. The careful study of flints and other excavated materials increasingly involves examination for traces of wear and use, and a metal trowel, or edge of a steel tape, will produce scratches on any substance.

Occasionally a small find will be extremely fragile or in such a position that it cannot be excavated on the site. In such cases, the piece can be lifted in a block of its deposit by excavating and undercutting the deposit; final exposure of the find can then be made in a laboratory where conservation can begin at once. The general rule for conservation in the field is to reproduce the conditions under which the object was found, that is, if the object was wet, keep it wet, if it was dry, keep it dry. There is no excuse for the sad comments still heard today, 'It fell to pieces upon exposure', and 'It was seen but could not be recovered'.

Animal, including human, remains

The emphasis in British archaeology upon environmental and economic aspects of prehistory has had the happy result that bones, both animal and human, receive far more careful treatment than in the past. The quantity of such remains from prehistoric sites in Britain is unlikely to be such that sampling techniques need to be introduced except for molluscan material in middens (p. 225). The inadequate state of knowledge about prehistoric husbandry can only be improved by the fullest possible examination of surviving material, and the conclusion must be that all animal remains are treated in excavation as small finds. If so, there is no justification for inadequate excavation, recording or conservation.

Bone tends to decay or become fragile through weathering and elements within the earth. Particular care should be exercised not to scrape bone with any excavating tool, as traces of ancient damage, through breakages or wear, are always important to record. If the bone is extremely fragile, it should be consolidated before removal (p. 215), or it should be lifted in a block (p. 185).

Animal bone in middens is of particular importance, and great care and observation is required. The preservation conditions may be adequate for many mammalian remains, and for bird bone as well, but fish bones are notoriously difficult to retrieve. Some fish such as salmon and sea trout possess lightly calcified bones that do not survive well; the retrieval of even one such bone may therefore indicate the presence of others recognizable only with difficulty or not surviving at all; in dietary reconstructions, such bones are important. All bones in a midden should be conserved and recorded, and note should be made of their angle of rest as this may indicate the lines of deposition of the midden.

Human remains should in theory not bulk any larger than other animal remains in the care with which they are excavated, recorded and conserved. However, as they *are* human, they generally receive kinder treatment and more consideration. In Britain, the recovery of human remains should be reported to the coroner, through the police, if there is a suspicion of an 'unnatural' death through violence. The establishment of a prehistoric date for the remains generally will make this report a formality, and no further action is taken.

Their eventual disposition, in a museum or university department, may not be exactly in accordance with nineteenth-century admonitions: 'The real Antiquary will always respect the Skeleton, Ashes, and Bones of the dead, which he may discover in his subterranean excavations. With hallowed feelings sanctified by the knowledge that the dry bones shall live, he will do unto them as he would wish should be done unto his own remains when he has passed away and has been forgotten . . . .'.[1]

The excavation of human remains is time-consuming but must

[1] The Rev. Charles Wools, *The Barrow Diggers*, 1839.

be carried out according to the data likely to be available. This can include evidence of pre- and post-mortem activities, dress and decoration, as well as physical anthropological details. Inhumations, either extended, crouched or flexed (knees drawn up near chin), should be excavated from the centre line of the body outwards, so that cleaned bones do not become obscured by earth removal. The skull is generally the first part to be uncovered, and a knowledge of anatomy, and experience of likely postures, will lead the excavator to the appropriate position to begin. The trunk should be cleaned, then the legs and arms, the skull, finally the feet and hands; the feet and hands have many bones and are best left to the last in case of disturbance. The excavation should be carried out by a team of two, one actually to clean with paintbrush, spoon and spatula, the other to record as notes and sketches the positions of the bones relative to one another, and the recognition of other materials. The question of articulation of bones and a complete set of bones is important, to see if the body was exposed and moved before eventual burial. Any decoration of the body, often surviving in the form of beads, must be recorded in exact detail for reconstruction of the ornaments (fig. 68). Samples of earth where suspected organic materials existed should be taken (p. 222).

The excavator should be aware that the soils around and within an intact skeleton are likely to retain some traces of organic material, particularly in the area of the stomach. Zealous cleaning of the bones for photography may well destroy evidence of diet or clothing that could be recovered by excavation in a laboratory; the complete lifting of a skeleton for transport to a laboratory should be attempted, but if this is not possible, the soils should be carefully collected for subsequent examination. This procedure is not restricted to human skeletons, as dietary evidence from other animals may be of equal importance.

Cremated remains are generally better preserved than inhumations in acidic soils. True cremation reduces the bones to ashes, but prehistoric disposal of the body by burning generally produced a mixture of ashes and bone fragments. These should all be retrieved for examination by specialists who are able now to extract surprising amounts of information from such fragmentary remains. Cremations should be lifted in a block if at all possible, for excavation by the archaeologist under the direction of the specialist concerned. This will enable him to observe the relationship of the individual bone fragments to each other, a task extremely difficult to record in the field.

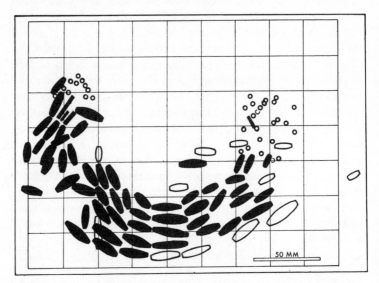

Fig. 68   Plan of positions of barrel and disc beads of jet from an inhumation in a cist at Masterton, Fife. The outlined barrel beads were found at a slightly higher level than the black ones (after Henshall and Wallace 1962–3).

The excavator must ascertain, so far as is possible, the position of the cremated remains as an entity, to determine if they were dumped from a container, or laid in a bag or box subsequently destroyed by decay. The condition of the earth beneath the cremation will determine if the remains were still hot when deposited. Dribbles of the cremation near the spot may show the method of transport and the direction from which it came, and therefore the likely location of the pyre, if wind did not blow fragments away from an uncontained deposit.

Cremated remains in a pot should always be lifted intact, whether or not the pot is upright or inverted (plate 5). Wrapping a pottery vessel with bandage may enable it to be lifted without cracking, but the pressure of the wrapping can cause breakages as well as preventing them. The contents should be excavated in the laboratory. Consolidation of pottery in the field is possible (p. 215).

5 Safety

Precautions against accidents on an excavation must always be taken, and any rules the director lays down must be observed. The safety factor in some relatively deep excavations has occasionally been neglected, through enthusiasm for the site, and through reliance upon inadequate experience. Similarly, injuries to workers have sometimes been caused by inexperience in handling equipment, and by lack of foresight in providing medical aid. More recently, the use of machinery in both rescue and research excavations has placed both amateur and professional archae-ologists at risk through lack of understanding of the potential dangers of such heavy and cumbersome pieces of equipment. Adequate supervision and enforcement of safety rules are better than the provision of medical assistance after an accident, but all aspects should be an important part of the organization of any excavation.

Collapse of sections
Deep trenches or squares are potential danger points on any excavation. The type of soil and subsoil will determine to a great extent the degree of danger of collapse, and sand and gravel tend to be as bad as any. But any trench can collapse, and archae-ologists, both directors and workers, must prevent this. The main cause of a collapse is excessive weight on the sides of the trench, weight from an adjacent dump, a barrow run on planks along the edge, near-by buildings, large stones, a horde of visitors standing too near the edge, or a piece of heavy equipment operating for a brief moment too close to the trench. All of these activities must be avoided, by instructions and by ropes around any potentially dangerous area. A worker who feels uneasy about precautions should go on strike.

Sides of excavations are particularly vulnerable to collapse if the soil is excessively wet. The effect of heavy rain can be spectacular and sudden, or it can be delayed; a trench that has been flooded and pumped out regularly will draw water towards it from the surrounding earth, and lead to a soil-flow into the trench that may cause a collapse.

Prevention of cave-ins can be effected either by cross-baulks in a trench, or by timbering of the sides held in place by cross-members. Timbering is the better procedure, and should be carried out by a professional from a relevant trade, an engineer with experience of trenching and revetting. Archaeologists tend to think their own experience is adequate, but sometimes position their timbers incorrectly (too high), and often use inadequate strengths and sizes of wood. Such wood may shrink, warp or expand with different weather conditions, and needs regular inspection with a view to remaking with extreme care.

Timbering is often said to be required if the trench is as deep as the height of the worker. This is an inadequate rule-of-thumb, as it takes no account of the fact that a worker may be prone or at least kneeling at the time of collapse. In sand and gravel, in peat, and in any loose soil under wet conditions, timbering should be automatic at depths where any concern is expressed by those who are experienced in such matters, and this can include the workers. In any case, no person should ever be allowed to work, or allow himself to work, alone in a deep trench.

Injuries to workers

Injuries to workers can be caused in a number of ways, and most of these can be foreseen and avoided. The major serious danger, apart from collapse of trenches, is accidental damage to the head. This can be caused by objects such as buckets (full or empty) falling from the edges of the excavation, by a barrow sliding off a plank placed too near the working area, or by the toppling of a large stone from a megalithic structure. Care by the bucketers and barrowers will avoid trouble, and engineering knowledge will adequately prop and tie the stone. The archaeologist is not generally a fit person to supervise the last. The common practice of erecting photographic towers is also a matter for concern, not only for the climber but for those below.

In any situation where objects may conceivably fall, that is where heavy objects have to be positioned above workers, safety helmets should be worn. These are light and will cost about £2 for various 'caving' types. They will also be protection against the inadvertent occasional thrower of equipment. Helmets are of no use if placed anywhere other than on the head.

Machinery

The types of machines that remove topsoil, dig trenches, haul spoil, and backfill, are all large and heavy; they also all have blind spots, directly in front, diagonally or to the back. The precautions to be taken with such machines are simple. No one should be allowed to work within the reach of the machine, and a supervisor should be present with the sole task of watching for danger to workers near at hand. The machine operator himself will need an observer (banksman) to guide him in the excavation or back-filling, and to keep the machine away from edges of cuttings. Machinery is expensive to hire, and the relatively small amount of time involved in their work should not disrupt the programme if hand workers are entirely removed from the area during this period. The pressure of time in backfilling is generally the reason for workers spreading and levelling earth as it is pushed or dumped in by machine; this should not occur.

Medical aid

The excavator should be equipped to provide medical aid, of at least a restricted nature, to all those present on the site. A small medical kit is listed at the end of this section. The archae-ologist, or someone else who will be on the site, should have adequate knowledge of medical procedures for minor injuries and for emergencies. Small grazes, bruises, blisters and scratches should be treated at once. The archaeologist should also inform the local hospital of his presence, and ascertain the shortest and quickest route there from the excavation. He should also be in a position to locate the nearest police in case he needs assist-ance with transport. Many excavations take place well away from regional hospitals, and in cases of collapse, or snake-bite, or serious reaction to local plants, advance notification to the hospital by police or private telephone may be important. Immunization against tetanus is important for all workers on an excavation.

Procedures for minor injuries   Wash hands if possible before applying first aid.

Minor cuts. Clean with cotton wool, apply antiseptic lotion, cover with dry dressing.

Bruises. Apply cold wet compress, and bandage.

Minor burns, blisters and scalds. Do not burst blister; apply ice or very cold water if available; cover with dry dressing.

Eyes. To remove objects from the eye, apply cold water with eye bath, or lift objects with sterile cotton wool moistened with water. Cover with sterile pad if irritation is bad. Do not rub.

Insect bites and stings. Apply cold water or ice if available, dry and apply antihistamine cream.

Procedures for major injuries   Call a doctor or ambulance, or take injured person to hospital at once. *Temporary* treatment is as follows:

Shock. This accompanies most serious injuries, the signs being cold clammy skin, sweating, weak rapid pulse, thirst, impaired breathing and fainting. Wrap patient in blanket, and treat injuries. Do not give drink or anything by mouth if there is an internal injury or fracture. Loosen tight clothing.

External bleeding. Apply firm pressure to wound with clean dry pad to stop bleeding. Do not remove clot. Cover with clean dressing and bandage firmly. Release pressure every ten minutes.

Internal bleeding. Signs as for shock; keep patient warm and still.

Major burns and scalds. Keep patient warm, cover only exposed wounds to face and hands with dry dressings. Do not remove clothing sticking to burn or scald.

Simple fractures. Splint broken bone to prevent movement.

Multiple fractures. Apply sterile dressing to prevent infection, and splint or support to prevent movement.

Artificial respiration   If breathing stops, start artificial respiration at once, and continue until patient breathes freely, or medical help arrives. Place patient on his back, loosen clothing, clear his mouth and throat to ease breathing. Tilt head right back, with hand under his jaw to prevent tongue blocking air passage. Blow through patient's mouth, holding his nostrils to prevent air leakage. Remove mouth, wait for patient to exhale. Blow every four to six seconds. If gurgling or vomiting occurs, turn head to one side, clear mouth and throat and continue. Do not give up.

For small children, blow until chest rises visibly and no more, placing mouth over patient's nostrils and mouth. Repeat every two seconds.

First-aid equipment
Plain lint bandages, various widths;
Cotton wool;
Crêpe bandage;
Elastoplast or equivalent, various sizes;
Gauze squares, 8-ply;
Scissors;
Tweezers;
Eye bath;
Safety pins;
Antiseptic cream, Savlon, Germolene, Boric Acid ointment;
Antiseptic liquid, TCP;
Aspirin, Dispirin, Codeine or equivalent;
Anti-histamine tablets;
Wasp-eze or equivalent spray;
Whisky or brandy (for post-dig recuperation only).

6 Recording

> ... from the moment when an archaeological excavator lifts the first shovelful of earth, he has begun a process of destruction for which the only compensation is complete and immediate record.[1]

The recording of an excavation is not an aspect to be taken lightly or without considerable forethought. It has been said that no site is discovered until it has been adequately published, and the basis for such publication is a record of the site as it was observed during excavation. The site report may be abbreviated for a number of reasons, including the excavator's own inability to prepare a full record (inexcusable), and the unavailability of a

[1] M. Wheeler, in *Antiquity* 42, 1968, 295.

journal to accept a lengthy report (common, and unfortunate). The prospect of this, however, should not influence the excavator in the compilation of his records during and after the excavation.

The purpose of recording a site is to allow it to be reconstructed, mentally, on any future occasion. All deposits and finds should be recorded so that they could be placed back in their correct positions. The record of an excavation should be clear enough to allow its use by another archaeologist should the excavator be unable or unwilling to pursue the research.

Yet the provision of clear records is no real substitute for the excavator's own publication. 'Those notes have not yet been made which will serve as the perfect guide to a dead man's unfinished labours, as if one was at his side while he was engaged upon them.'[1]

The basic elements in the recording of a site are scaled plans and sections of the site and its excavated areas, notes on the excavation details of each area (daily record books), notes made by the director about how the work is progressing, the problems arising, possible solutions, potential approaches and theories (ideas book), photographs and record cards of finds and samples.

The equipment necessary for the production of plans and sections on a site is as follows:

The planner:
    drawing-board (2 sizes, 1 by 0.5 m, 0.5 by 0.3 m approximately);
    squared paper (1 mm squares);
    draughting or masking tape (for attaching paper firmly to board);
    ruler (metric);
    scaled ruler (optional but useful, scaled edges 1/5, 1/10, 1/100);
    set square and compasses;
    pencils (selection, HB, B, H);
    eraser (soft, new, non-smudging);
    knife for sharpening pencils or good-quality sharpener;
    grid frame (optional);
    polythene sheeting for protecting paper from wet and mud;
The measurer:
    linen tape (10 m, or 20 m);

[1] G. Boon, in *Antiquity* 42, 1968, 294.

bulldog clips (for fixing tape);
spring tape (2–3 m, for offsets, etc.);
measuring triangle;
plumb-bob;
Both:
Dumpy level and staff.

In addition, the site equipment should include notebooks and record cards. Notebooks should be bound, about 20 by 12 cm, with lined or squared pages; their waterproof covers could be marked by identifying colour tape. Record cards, 20 by 12 cm or smaller, should be filed in a plastic box.

Site plans and records
The preparation of a grid and contour plan of the site in its surrounding area (p. 110) should be the basis for a general site plan. The scale of the latter will of course vary with the size of site, but should be large enough to allow the plotting, from the grid or from a ranged datum line, of the various trenches or squares or areas that are to be excavated. The degree of precision required for this plotting will depend upon the scale used (p. 61), but the surveyor's notebook should carry the detailed measurements of the corners of the excavated areas from the grid or datum line, although these measurements may be rounded off in the plotting of the site plan. The corners of excavated areas should be dropped as perpendiculars to the datum line, or triangulated into the line, and check measurements are needed. The orientation of the grid or ranged line will automatically serve for all excavated areas.

The excavation areas should be identified by simple numbers or letters, thus, area A or trench 3 (fig. 69); on a square or box approach to excavation, using a grid system, the individual squares can be identified by lettered lines running in one direction, and numbered lines in the other, so long as continuity is observed in identifying squares by a particular corner. Whatever system is used, it must be simple and clear to all, and must not be altered during the excavation. There is much to be said for sign-posting areas on the site so that workers and supervisors and directors can avoid startling mistakes in mis-identification of the area or trench.

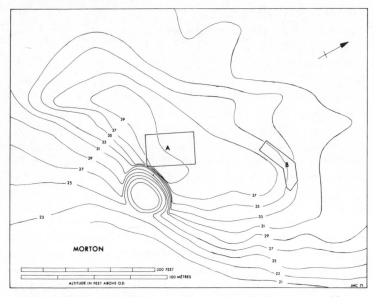

Fig. 69 Plan of a Mesolithic site at Morton, Fife, showing contours of former island, and main areas of excavation. For reconstruction of conditions in area at time of ancient occupation, see fig. 77 (from Coles 1971).

The notebook dealing with the preparation of site plans will include all surveying details, the measurements associated with the grid or ranged line datum, including their tie-lines for permanent identification and retrieval (p. 111), the levelling operations for contours, and the offsets for fixing excavated areas. The book could also hold details about the previous history of the site, but it should be a factual record throughout.

Excavation plans and records

The planning of finds and structural details within the deposits of an excavated area or trench is theoretically simple. The basis behind the operation is the provision of an adequate and reliable set of fixed positions near or within the excavated area, from which all other measurements can be made. Such fixed positions should conveniently be a part of the grid or ranged line, but if not they should be fixed to the site lines by double measurement, such as a perpendicular checked by triangulation, or triangulation checked by a further swinging line. These fixed positions should be pegged vertically into the ground, and identified by painting the relevant code number or letter on them. A nail in the top will allow the tape to be hooked for measuring in detail.

In planning a particular layer with its associated structures and finds, there are several ways by which these fixed positions can be used (fig. 70). One is by triangulation, another is by dropping a perpendicular. In triangulation, the tape is stretched in turn from three fixed positions (0, 5, 10 m) to a point directly above the find or detail to be planned. A plumb-bob will show the exact overhead position. The measurements are recorded, and

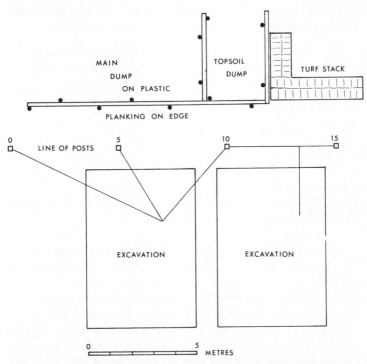

Fig. 70 Plan of a small excavation, with turf stack and dumps placed well away from the edges, and held back by planks. A line of posts are used for recording finds and features by triangulation (left) or by perpendiculars (right). The edges of the excavated areas, and walkways to dumps and processing area, should be protected by planks.

can be plotted by compasses on the plan. The third measurement is a check on the intersection of the first two.

The other method often used is to drop a perpendicular from the find point on to a line joining the fixed positions; a tape is stretched between two positions (10, 15) and the measurements from the find point to this tape, and its position on the tape, provide the necessary detail for planning. A large measuring triangle (fig. 71), with two sides one metre long forming a right-angle, can sometimes be used to align on the fixed positions and project a perpendicular to, or towards, the find point; bubble levels on the triangle allow it to be held horizontally so that the plumb-bob can be dropped upon the find point. The sides of deep trenches are rarely vertical, and detailed measurements should not be taken from these without a check to the fixed datum positions.

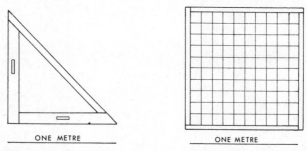

Fig. 71 Left, *measuring triangle with two bubble levels set into the frame.* Right, *grid frame with strings at 0.1 m intervals.*

These measurements provide a flat two-dimensional plan of the details of an excavated area, but a third measurement is required to complete the point of discovery. This is achieved by relating the level of a point to a fixed datum that should be established conveniently near or on the site (p. 96). There are two main ways by which this can be achieved. The first is to level in the find point by instrument, a Dumpy level being most convenient (p. 93). The second is to employ a temporary datum at the side of the excavated area, generally a position at the turfline on the edge of the area, from which measurements down to the find point can be made; the measuring triangle, held horizontally by observation of the bubbles, extends the temporary datum out over the find point, and measurement by spring tape down to the find point provides the third dimension.

The measurements noted above can be obtained quickly once the fixed positions are available, and once the archaeologists are conversant with the procedure. Two people are required for this work. Alternatives can be devised so long as the principle remains the same, an accurate recording of find points and other details on a horizontal plan and by level.

The recording of a find-spot in this way does not, of course, represent the complete record of the position and therefore the significance of the find; this can only be obtained through observation and recording of the associated material, other small objects, structural details and the particular deposit in which the object lay. These associations are not likely to be preserved in sections, and must be recorded before the find is lifted.

If an occupation surface yields a large quantity of finds, or if structural features are abundant and complex, the planning can be carried out with a grid frame (fig. 71). This is a wooden or aluminium frame in the shape of a square, generally one metre across, with string divisions at 10 or 20 cm intervals. This is placed over measured areas of the excavation, and finds and features can then be drawn directly upon the plan, often by eye, using the strings as guide lines. The features must still be levelled.

The material represented in fig. 63 was recorded by offsets from a datum line, but a string grid frame would probably have been easier to use. Such a grid, without a frame, can be used to draw larger areas; an example is shown in plate 8.

The scale of plans of excavated areas or trenches will depend upon the size of the area and the requirement of the archaeologist for detailed plotting. Generally a scale of 1/10 or 1/5 is adopted, but some large areas, with few or only major features, can be planned at 1/20 or smaller. The measurements in all scale drawings should be taken to the nearest unit of measure applicable to the scale, and the understanding of this on the part of the measurer will save much time for the planner.

Plans of finds and features should be drawn on site, and not produced elsewhere on the basis of a set of measurements. The plans should be drawn by an experienced archaeologist, who has 'served time' as measurer and who knows the depth of detail required. All plans should be checked and approved by the director, and should bear orientation and identifying letters.

The amount of detail to be planned precisely varies, from exact measurement of every flint on a floor (fig. 63), to measured positions of stone banks that are then drawn in by convention (fig. 60). This is a directorial decision, and sometimes the saving in time by adopting the latter approach is lost through subsequent uncertainty about precise details of quantities, sizes and positions. If multiple plans are drawn, of successive layers or sets of features, the precise orientation of each plan must be the same, and the plans should be numbered in order of drawing, so that overlaps can be clearly produced.

Notebooks   The notebooks used by the site supervisor for each individual excavated area should take the form of a daily record of the archaeological activity in the area. This should indicate what was done each day, how it was done, and who did it. The various deposits should be described as they are exposed, their dimensions and levels should be indicated, and sketches should be made of particular features that seem relevant. The sequence of deposits visible in the sections should be described, and measurements of slope and thickness recorded; this is not a substitute for a scale drawing of sections but will aid the latter through measurements and observations made as the deposits were exposed. The book should also have a list of the finds that have been made, with notes on their containing deposits and positions as measured for the plan; this is not a substitute for the card catalogue of finds (see below) but is a part of the record for the particular area. The notebook should record the site supervisor's and worker's opinion as to the reliability of association of finds with the deposits and with other finds, as well as comments on the relevance and importance of such associations.

These site notebooks should remain with the excavation at all times, so that details can be entered whenever they are necessary. The director should keep a regular check on these, as they are a basis for his own notebook.

The director's notebook is his personal reminder of features that seemed important at one time or another, of finds of particular significance, of workers and work that deserve attention. It is also his ideas book, in which he records his own and others' suggestions about interpretations of the factual observations of the site.

All notebooks should be bound, with waterproof cover. Squared paper is useful for sketching or drawing features or finds. Writing should be done with hard (2H) pencil which will not erase. Ideas or comments once written should not be crossed out or erased even if shown to be wrong; dated rejoinders can always be entered in the book, and referring to previous dated notes.

Record cards Individual finds of objects or of anything that is actually extracted from a site should be recorded on cards, generally 5 by 3 inches (127 by 76 mm) or 6 by 4 inches (152 by 102 mm), but there is much to be said for a larger size 8 by 6 inches (203 by 152 mm) that allows the recording of the following details:

Trench or area designation:
Layer number: (if necessary, see below)
Find number:
Measurement: horizontal
                  vertical
Association: (with deposit, structures, finds)
Description of object: material
                    type
                    dimensions
                    condition and treatment (p. 214).
Plan or Section: (on which find number appears)
Photograph: (from which angle, to show which feature)
Finder:
Sketch: (on back of card if necessary).

The cards from each excavation area must be kept separate from those of other areas, but consistency in numbering will always prevent mixing. The numbering system adopted will be to each director's own preference, but the simpler the better. For an area with a restricted series of deposits, the best system is a simple numbering from 1 upwards. Preparation of a set of cards already with area designation and with consecutive numbers will prevent duplication of numbers. For an area with multiple deposits, some with quantities of finds, the system might well employ a deposit or layer designation followed by find numbers for each layer.

Examples of finds would then read Area A, layer 1, find 1 *or* Area A, find 1, and either would be a unique reference so long as the site itself was remembered.

Labelling   The lifting of finds has been considered on p. 184, and the treatment of finds is considered on p. 213. The labelling of finds is important, and on no account should any find be transported from trench to tent for processing, from tray to director for inspection, or from anywhere to anywhere, without an accompanying label. Labels must always remain with objects. The practice of pencilling numbers on finds on the field, and inking during processing, should be avoided, if at all possible, for everything except possibly pottery. The reason is that much attention is paid today to signs of wear (scratches or polish) on stone, wood, bone and clay, and the inscribing of numbers on an edge or face of an object may ensure that the traces of wear are obscured if not enhanced. The finds should therefore not be altered, and should be bagged in polythene and sealed with an appropriately numbered label. Self-adhesive paper labels will seal and record the bags, but dampness will obscure the writing. A better solution is to seal and label the bags with aluminium or other metal twist tags on which numbers can be recorded by indelible pencil or metal stylo. It should not be outside a director's competence to devise some alternative method to individual bagging for sites yielding many hundreds of finds, but if this involves compartmented trays, extreme care is needed to avoid disastrous upsets. Plastic bags cost as little as £5 for 5000, paper labels (to be kept dry) £1 for 1000.

Sections and records

The sequence of deposits on a site provide the basis for the chronology within the site, and adequate record of the sequence is of primary importance. The sections on trench sides and on the sides of grid squares, boxes or blocks (p. 180) provide deposits that can be observed, photographed and drawn. These, however, should not be the only record of the sequence, because they may inadequately represent the deposits that were present on the site. The more informative series of deposits may well have been in the middle of the excavation, and have been physically destroyed. The archaeologist should take steps to avoid this by positioning his excavation areas and trenches carefully (p. 153), but if the situation arises where he has not accurately estimated this, the site notebook will be the only record of the deposits that are gone. The site supervisor's daily record book should contain description and thicknesses of the deposits as they were removed, and notes of the associated features and finds; this record should be as detailed as possible, as it is the only source of evidence of the stratigraphy here.

The sections preserved on the sides of the excavation should be drawn to a scale not less than 1/10, and generally 1/5 is more satisfactory, but this will again depend on the size of site and degree of detail to be recorded. Sometimes it is useful to draw at different scales, a small (1/10) horizontal, a large (1/5) vertical scale, to emphasize or clarify features. Such differences must be clearly stated in the drawing. The actual section drawing requires two people, one to measure, one to plot. A horizontal string is placed along the section either near the top or half-way down, and the string is levelled into the permanent datum level of the site (fig. 72). A tape is placed along the string, the zero at one end of the section, or pins can be inserted at regular or other convenient intervals along the string. Measurements with spring tape are then made from the string upwards or downwards to the interfaces of the various deposits or other features in the section, and these are scaled off on squared paper at the appropriate horizontal position.

The drawer should refer to the daily notebook for description and depths of deposits as they were seen when fresh, and the measurer can, if required, trowel along the line of a presumed interface to locate the precise point for measurement. It is important to photograph the section before this is done, if the cleaning of the section results in its partial destruction. The use of a grid frame (p. 199) may accelerate the drawing of sections if the strata are reasonably clear, but direct measurement is generally the better procedure.

Sections that have been gently sloped to avoid collapse will slightly misrepresent the deposits if drawn as vertical sections. The angle of slope, if less than 5°, can generally be ignored, and the section measured and drawn as vertical. The distortion of a greater angle than this can be eliminated if some of the major lines in the section are levelled in, and the detail measured from these levelled lines.

The positions of all samples, of earth, pollen or anything else, taken from the section should be measured in and accurately drawn (see fig. 76). The character of the various deposits should be carefully assessed and described in the notebook, including the shape, size, texture and colour of the material. A colour chart costing about £2 is available from the Japanese Colour Research Institute, 1 Alaska Sukuyoshi, Cho Minato-Ku, Tokyo, and this is an adequate substitute for the American Munsell charts which are enormously expensive.

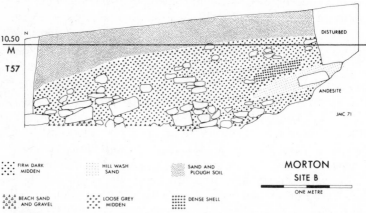

Fig. 72 Schematic drawing of a section through a midden at Morton, Fife. Ordnance Datum line (10.50 m above O.D.) used for measurements and drawn in, and conventions for deposits shown below (after Coles 1971).

The conventions used to represent various deposits are not standardized in British archaeological publications. Some conventions are given in fig. 73. The sections can be drawn stylistically, that is, with interfaces marked by lines (fig. 76), or naturalistically, with merging sets of conventional representations (fig. 65). Most archaeologists draw sections in the field stylistically, and compromise on the publication section.

Finds of small objects may actually occur in the section to be drawn, but most finds will not be in direct association with the section. The practice is to project significant finds into the sections, so that their association with certain deposits can be demonstrated. This may be useful but must be noted on the

Fig. 73 Conventions suitable for representation of different deposits on archaeological sites; these are not standardized in Britain, and it is necessary to provide a guide as here, or as in fig. 72, or to label the section (fig. 65).

drawing and in the notebook. The section drawing should carry a scale, and identifying and orienting letters or symbols; the area or trench letter or number is not enough, as the particular section within the excavation also needs to be identified, e.g. north-west side of Area A.

Photography

Any record of an archaeological excavation will not be complete without photographs. The presentation of immaculate plans and sections, with features and strata clearly defined, may disguise the fact that the procedures used in excavation were inadequate and the planning was inaccurate. Photographs accompanying a report help to suggest that an excavation was laid out and conducted in a reasonable fashion, but the straightest lines and cleanest sides to an area do not necessarily mean that the excavator knew what he was about. In this case the photographs may flatter to deceive.

On the other hand, a careful record of the course of an excavation through photographs will provide an excavator with reminders of his progress, will illuminate his plans and drawings with the shadows and highlights of a third dimension (e.g. plate 8), and will emphasize and help to demonstrate the significant aspects of the site (e.g. plate 6). For these reasons, a photographic record is essential.

Equipment   The basic equipment necessary for the adequate recording of an excavation by photography is as follows:

Single-lens reflex camera, 35 mm	£30 upwards
Film appropriate to site	
Exposure meter	£5 upwards
Tripod	£5 upwards
Cable release	£0.50
Notebook	
Scale (see below)	
Close-up lenses (optional)	£5
Wide-angle lens (optional)	£20 upwards

The reflex type of camera allows a more accurate view of the actual area to be covered by the camera than does an ordinary viewfinder camera. The through-the-lens viewing of the reflex is particularly important when using a wide-angle lens, or close-up lenses; a telephoto lens is not often required on an excavation, but can be useful in awkward positions. The combination of a wide-angle lens and a portable tower (of scaffold metal) may allow a view of a wide area of the site otherwise not obtainable except by aircraft (plate 6).

Not many small excavations can afford the luxury of a resident photographer, who can not only take the pictures but develop them on the site. This procedure is important, as the success or otherwise of the photograph can be gauged before the particular deposit is removed. The use of a Polaroid-type of camera may help to offset this difficulty (see below). The general practice, however, on small sites is for two cameras to be used, normally one with black-and-white film, the other with colour (for slides rather than prints). This should ensure that at least one set of pictures survives. The cost of film as a proportion of a total excavation cost is generally very low, and most archaeologists should automatically repeat photographs with both cameras, allowing $\frac{1}{2}$ stop both upwards and downwards, to ensure adequate exposure. This equals six photographs each time, the cost being therefore about 30p per set.

The main element in the success of archaeological photography is experience on the part of the photographer. This is gained by practice and experiment under different conditions, and cannot be taught through a textbook. The archaeologist who wishes to understand the practice of photography should consult the excellent guides to the subject that are available (e.g. Cookson 1954) but these too will emphasize that field experience is the best teacher.

Site conditions in Britain can vary both in temperature and dampness. Camera equipment should be protected from extremes, but normal care should ensure trouble-free operation. Wind-blown sand and dust will often cause problems to do with the shutter; a plastic bag over the camera and its case will help to prevent this. The ordinary leather or plastic case for camera equipment may not give adequate protection against accidental drops and bumps in transport; a cushioned case, with foam rubber cut out to fit the individual camera equipment, is a good investment. Films should be protected from heat and dampness.

The approach to archaeological photography should be varied. The types of photographs required under normal circumstances might be as follows:

(1) General views of the site and its area, and views from the site to adjacent features (colour and black and white). This might include aerial photographs of the excavation in progress.
(2) Views of the site under working conditions (colour only).
(3) Progress views of the excavation, as reminders for the archaeologist (both, and Polaroid useful).
(4) Views of final cleared excavation at end of each day's work (black and white, as insurance against vandalism).
(5) Set piece views, of fully excavated plans and sections (for publication, both types).
(6) Detailed views of individual features, finds *in situ*, stratigraphical detail, etc. (both).
(7) Photogrammetric views with or without an imposed grid, for recording and/or publication (both).

The photographs taken under 1, 5, 6 and 7 may be for publication, and particular care should be taken over these to ensure that the site is cleared of unnecessary equipment, that the site is clean, and that an adequate scale appears in the photograph. The other photographs and colour slides will serve as records and for lectures about the site.

Scales   Scales should be available to the photographer in a variety of lengths, with separate black and white divisions as indicated: 2 m (0.2 m divisions), 1 m (0.2 divisions), 0.5 m (0.1 m divisions), 0.1 m (10 mm divisions). These should be made horizontal with a spirit level, and placed at the far end, or in the middle, of the area to be photographed; they should be parallel with the horizontal lines of the reflex viewfinder, and if two scales are to be used, they should be parallel with each other. Scales for section photographs should be held in position by surveyor's arrows near the top of the section. It may be useful to have small bubble levels set into scales for ease in levelling, and if circular-sectioned scales are used, these can be turned to hide the level.

A photographic record should be kept of all views taken on or around a site. A notebook retained with the camera equipment is the only practical way of ensuring that all photographs are recorded. The record should include the following:

Area and level
Features in the photograph
Reason for the photograph
Direction of view, and angle
Film type and meter reading
Exposure, stop and time
Length of scale used.

A separate list of entries should be kept for each camera used.

Most cameras in use on archaeological excavations in this country are of 35 mm type, and are therefore extremely light. This can be a handicap for area photographs, in terms of the stability of the camera. Many excavation photographs are of areas of considerable size, where it is necessary to close down the lens to obtain an adequate depth of focus. This will mean the exposure time is lengthened, and it should be automatic that a tripod is used for all publication photographs, and probably all others as well. The combination of a lightweight tripod and a lightweight camera is not a good one, however, and is little better than a hand-held camera. A 35 mm camera really requires an extremely heavy tripod for stability. A cable release should always be used.

The use of photogrammetric techniques for recording sites is now becoming common, and there are a variety of systems available. The principle is that a series of vertical overlapping photographs will make up a complete horizontal plan of the site to a uniform scale, from which plans can be drawn. Certain sites, where features tend to be indistinct or slight, may not be suitable for planning this way, and in any case there should not be reliance upon photogrammetry as the sole method of planning. The equipment necessary is a lightweight collapsible frame, with two, three or four legs, that draws the camera up to a height of from 6 to 13 m, levels it and takes the picture through a long release cable. The frame is moved around the site, which has been marked with identifying grid points, until all the surface has been photographed vertically and from the same height. All the frames require at least four people to move and position them. On an open site, with rather large features, photogrammetry is a very useful and speedy method of recording.

The photograph (plate 7) shows an open site at Grantully, Perthshire, photogrammetrically planned, with a group of Bronze Age cremation pits partially cut through by a gas pipe line trench (see fig. 2), and a series of Neolithic scoops, storage and rubbish pits dug into a small gravel spread; the surrounding sandy deposits would not have been as easily drained as the gravel. About twenty photographs were taken to produce this plan (see *Antiquity* 41, 1967, 220 and 44, 1970, 214 for details of photogrammetric frames).

7 Conservation

The conservation of material from an archaeological site includes not only objects but also structures, deposits and records of them made during the excavation. This section is concerned mainly with manufactured objects, and these and other types of evidence are also considered on p. 184 and p. 215. The preservation of ancient artefacts depends upon their composition and upon the type of deposit in which they came to be buried; the interaction of these elements determines the degree of preservation, and often the interaction has been such that the object has decayed and been completely lost. There is another way, however, by which valuable evidence can be lost, and this is through loss of provenance. An object, be it a tool, a treasure or a sample, loses its value and its significance if its precise provenance is lost through accident or design. The procedures outlined in the preceding section are designed to eliminate this potential danger, and it cannot be emphasized too strongly that labelling and care of finds from an excavation or from any other site is not a matter for casual attention.

The problem of physical conservation of finds is intimately bound up with the nature of the local environment. Any material produced above ground has a form of stability in relation to its environment above ground. Once buried or otherwise discarded into or on to the earth, a material comes into contact with a new environment, generally entirely or greatly different from the previous, and it will undergo modification until it reaches a position relatively stable within its new setting (fig. 74). The modification required may be so great that destruction occurs, or there may be relatively little change. Once a level stage is reached, there will be little alteration in the material until the

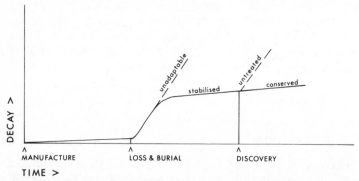

Fig. 74 Schematic representation of rate of decay of an object from its manufacture, through loss and burial, to discovery and treatment by an archaeologist. The material from which the object was made will determine the basic rate, and much variation exists (e.g. pottery versus wood). The two danger points occur when the environment is abruptly altered.

equilibrium is again disturbed. This final disturbance may well be of archaeological origin, and it may truly be said that destruction of material begins again with the spade.

Soils
Soils are made up of mineral and organic material; the mineral element is formed mainly by the disintegration of the underlying bedrock, the organic element mainly by decay of vegetable matter that rooted upon the mineral material. A soil type is defined by its complete profile, that is, from surface to bedrock, and most soils have distinct horizons depending upon their particular character and origin. The weathered bedrock is known as the C horizon, the humus as the A horizon. Between, there may be a B horizon, consisting of minerals washed down from A (an eluvial horizon) into B (an illuvial horizon). There are many divisions and combinations of these horizons, and a simplified version of a developed profile shows some of these (fig. 75). The soils on an archaeological site should be examined by a pedologist who can identify their character and thereby indicate to the archaeologist

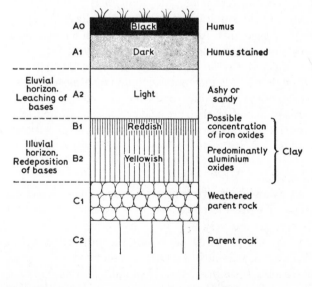

Fig. 75 *A schematic soil section, showing various simplified horizons (from Dowman 1970).*

the possibilities of material surviving. There are many difficulties in even this general assessment, as the precise relationship of an environment to material includes aspects other than that of soils, and is not yet fully understood.

From a chemical point of view, soils can be described as acid or basic. Acid soils have much silica and silicates, are poor in bases, and have a pH below 7. Basic soils are rich in bases (oxides of iron, aluminium and calcium), have a pH above 7, and are alkaline in character. pH numbers denote acidity, with pH 7 neutral (pure water), pH 1 very acid, pH 12 very alkaline. The character of the soil will naturally affect the preservation of material.

The effect of *acidity* on buried objects is complex, but a field archaeologist should be aware of its effects on materials likely to be present. The determination of the soil acidity with a book of pH indicator papers is well worth making. Bone will not be well preserved in a pH below 7, but may survive in a weakened state to pH 5, and sometimes even beyond. Pottery will survive but some tempering agents may have dissolved, leaving the clay in a porous state. Iron will dissolve completely in a very acid soil, but will survive in a very poor state, sometimes completely mineralized, in less acid conditions. Copper and its alloys will survive well in slightly acid soils. Aerated conditions, rather than acid soils, will totally destroy wood (see below for anaerobic conditions).

The effect of *alkalinity* on glass is more serious than is acidity, but total destruction may not occur, and on almost all other non-organic materials, alkaline conditions are much more favourable towards preservation than are acid conditions. More rapid decay of wood and other organic materials occurs in basic than in acid soils.

Environments
The most damaging environments for the preservation of material are those that are alternately, wet and dry, hot and cold. The best environments are very wet, very dry or very cold. In Britain, conditions are generally poor, but the physical conditions of archaeological sites in Britain are extremely varied, and entirely local circumstances may preserve organic or other material. The archaeologist should be aware of the potential of such conditions, and take appropriate action to conserve the evidence.

The only environment in Britain entirely suitable for excellent preservation is that of waterlogged lake deposits and peat bogs, where lack of oxygen (anaerobic conditions) inhibits bacterial and fungal action. Wood and other organic materials will survive, and these may provide unique evidence. They should not be excavated without the active assistance of a museum laboratory equipped to conserve the material. 'The evidence recovered from the mucky slime of one such well-preserved site may give more information than that from hundreds of poorly preserved sites' (Hole and Heizer 1969, 85). Alkaline bogs will preserve bone more successfully than acidic bogs, but the reverse is true for skin, hair and remains of plants and seeds. Pottery will survive in both, metals may also survive well.

Caves and rock-shelters provide a distinct local environment, but this is generally alkaline and allows good preservation of inorganic material and bone, but destruction of other organics.

An environment of total aridity, never encountered in Britain, and one of extreme cold, will preserve almost all materials, and sites within these conditions are again particularly important.

Saline conditions, such as occur in areas subject to sea-water submergence or flooding, may preserve wood extremely well but other materials may be concreted by sand and shell components, and some metals will become totally mineralized.

Practical conservation
The variety of materials, their condition, and the environments in which they may be found is extremely great in Britain. Sand and gravel, chalk and limestone, clay, and peat, provide different soils, and differing depths of burial of materials affect the processes of weathering and alteration through dampness and temperature. The possible circumstances of discovery are also varied, ranging from archaeological excavation with instant recognition of the situation, to ploughing and ditching operations that leave material exposed for months before recovery. Together, these add up to a variety of situations for which the excavator cannot hope to provide exact materials and processes of conservation in the field.

There are, however, several general rules for conservation of objects in the field. The first and most important of these is to preserve the balance that exists between the object and its environment in the earth. Any drastic alteration in this balance will result in accelerated decay. This means that any object that is wet should remain wet, and a dry object should be kept dry. The excavator may feel that he should take *some* action over an object that is in a bad state, but it is far worse to take the wrong course than to do nothing except maintain the balance. The ultimate action in re-establishing the equilibrium is reburial of the object to await the arrival of specialists in conservation, and this is a course that has much to commend it in cases of particularly valuable evidence. A second rule for field conservation is that what has been done on the site must be undone in the laboratory, where final preservative action will take place. The treatment of material in the field must be reversible, and to be so there must be a full record kept of the treatment given. Some of these are noted below.

Consolidation   If an object or its surface is badly preserved and weak, it will need to be strengthened by impregnation with a resin or a wax. During this process, the object will be weakened even further, and care is needed to avoid damage before it has set. Analysis of the object for dating or other purposes is not satisfactory after impregnation. Consolidants can be applied by brush, by spray, by immersion or by vacuum (Dowman 1970).

Lifting   If an object cannot be picked up alone or on a block (p. 185), and a consolidant will not strengthen it sufficiently, it must have some additional protection to allow it to be moved. Pottery may be consolidated and bandaged to facilitate removal, (p. 188), but in some cases it may be better to break the pot, lift it piece by piece and restore it later. Controlled breakage is preferable to accidental collapse with attendant minute fragmentation.

Larger objects requiring some support must have a firm backing material such as plaster of Paris; this, however, is irreversible chemically and so the object must be protected by damp tissue paper before plaster is applied as soaked pieces of scrim (open-work jute bandage). Polyurethane foam is an alternative to plaster with aluminium foil between foam and object.

Large objects such as a skeleton can also be lifted by isolating them on a platform of earth and then undercutting to allow a metal plate to be eased beneath. Consolidants should be used as necessary, and the whole may be encased in plaster for support. Extremely large objects may have to be broken up before lifting, and careful plans and photographs should be taken before and during this operation. Some large objects may have to be broken for conservation treatment in the laboratory, and field breakage need not be irreparable, even if it is disturbing.

Special materials Prehistoric pottery containing soluble salts may crack if the pottery is suddenly exposed to heat from the sun after removal from the earth. If this danger exists, the pottery should be soaked in many changes of water, and allowed to dry in the shade. The surface of the pot if in bad condition (flaking) can be consolidated by soluble nylon coatings. If the entire pot is friable a penetrating consolidant should be put on by immersion or spraying or brushing.

Stone objects should be allowed to dry slowly and can be soaked to remove soluble salts. Consolidation of stone that is flaking is a difficult and potentially damaging business and the stone should probably not be treated in the field.

Bone can be cleaned in water or by brushing and delicate prodding with a wooden point. Damage to the bone can be caused by any of these methods, and a test should be carried out on a small area first. Consolidation can be carried out with a polyvinyl resin. Ivory should not be cleaned with water.

Wet wood must be kept wet, even during its excavation and recording. It should be preserved in thin polythene bags from which air is excluded; a water spray with about 1 per cent fungicide may prevent organic growth, but fungicide should not be added if samples are to be taken for dating (p. 220). Lifting of wet wood is done by undercutting a platform of earth or peat, and easing a board or metal sheet beneath. A consolidant may be applied in the field but this is a temporary measure only. Dry wood must be kept dry.

Leather that is wet should be treated as wet wood, and dry leather must be kept dry.

Shale should be sealed in a wet polythene bag.

Metals are complex materials for treatment in the field, and the only rule is to do nothing to them except to dry them and bag them in polythene with a desiccating agent. No other treatment should be carried out in the field. If consolidation of the metal is required for lifting, soluble nylon will serve for small light objects, polyethylene glycol wax for larger ones.

Soil sections may also be consolidated and lifted for study in the laboratory; the same procedure is suitable for deposits on an occupation floor. Consolidants are applied and the surface is removed, producing a mirror image of the original. The most suitable is Quentglaze, sprayed on in three coats, possibly with scrim added for support, and coming off as a rigid section.

Supplies

The range of consolidants and adhesives for field use is extremely great, and archaeologists would be well advised to seek guidance from local or regional museums with conservation laboratories as to the facilities available. Additionally, the archaeologist might retain as a part of his excavation equipment some or all of the following supplies (Dowman 1970):

Consolidants   (reversible, non-shrinking, penetrating, strong)
  Polyvinyl resins: PVA (polyvinyl acetate) for dry non-metallic materials. (some shrinkage with time)
  Acrylic resin: Bedacryl 277 for wet non-metallic materials except wood and leather. (some shrinkage. ? irreversible)
  Modified soluble nylon: Calaton CB for surface flaking of any material except wet wood and leather. (surface use only)
  Polythylene glycol waxes: PEG 4000 for wood or metal; PEG 6000 for pottery and lifting. (penetration if very dilute over long period)

Adhesives   (reversible, strong, quick-drying):
  Cellulose nitrate: HMG
  PVA adhesive: UHU[R]
  Rubber/resin: Evo-stik for heavy joins.

Lifting materials   (strong, easy removal, shrinkless, lightness if possible):
  Plaster of Paris with scrim (cheap)
  Plaster bandage

Polyurethane foam (expensive, light; toxic and needs ventilation; needs warm weather to foam properly)
PEG 4000 and 6000
Quentglaze (insoluble, for soil sections)
Metal sheets (flat iron or alloy), or boards (e.g. 20 mm thick).

Desiccating agents   Silica Gel or Sodium Hydroxide.
Wetting agents   Water (pure, distilled).

Conservation of evidence
The evidence extracted from a site consists of drawn plans and sections, notebooks and cards, photographs, samples and cultural material ('finds'). All of these must be protected from loss or damage by care in the operations that produce them. The lifting and labelling of finds is generally emphasized, but the safety of the other records is more important, and there may be justification for regular duplication of plans and notes by photocopying or other methods. Plans and notes have gone astray in the past, and the result generally is non-publication of the surviving and recollected evidence. The publication of a site is the final stage in the conservation of the evidence, and without it, most of the effort put into the operation is pure exercise.

8 Sampling

Archaeology has been defined as a technique for the recovery of evidence about past human behaviour. Man does not function as other than a part of his environment, and many archaeological projects are concerned to see in what ways he was affected by and in what ways he altered his environment. These and other projects are also concerned with the economic basis on which man depended, on the steps taken, at whatever level, to ensure adequate and continuing supplies of food and materials. The rate of development of man's behaviour in these and other activities is a problem of chronology, and archaeologists are constantly seeking ways by which to measure time, to date particular events or to estimate rates of progress. All of these elements in archaeological research are specialized activities, and the material for such studies is provided by various sampling techniques carried out in the field.

Specialists

The sampling of material is not a difficult task for an archaeologist to carry out if he understands the general techniques of extraction or recovery of material, and if he avoids contamination of specimens. But this is not enough, because the archaeologist must also know *why* he is taking samples. Geologists and pedologists, botanists and zoologists, chemists and physicists, are not archaeologists, and may not be particularly interested in archaeology. They may agree to help the archaeologist in some way by examining material, but they cannot be expected to provide any information if they do not know what is required. Archaeologists in the recent past have been too ready to submit samples with the comment, 'What can you tell me about this material?' The specialist's answer to this should be, 'It is rock (soil, peat, bone, wood, etc.).' What else he is supposed to say depends on the questions that the archaeologist asks of the material, what it is made of, how it got into the deposit, what it means in terms of environment or economy, how it was made, and so on.

The answers to these and to other questions can often be provided by the specialist only if he has seen the sample *in situ*, in the archaeological deposit from which he himself can extract it. Not very many excavations in this country, other than well-financed and large projects, can afford to have resident specialists in the various fields, and most samples are taken by the archaeologist in the hope of some information. This is not entirely satisfactory, and there should be no reason why specialists cannot be provided for on a site, for a short time, so that sampling can be done by the person most competent to record its characteristics and associations. No financial problems, or archaeological problems, should prevent this, as in the latter case the work should be held up until samples are adequately taken.

The main problem is that of interest, because archaeologists should not expect experts in other fields to drop everything and devote their time and energy to a project removed from their own research. Collaboration in archaeology is not a one-way exercise, and if the archaeologist cannot provide enough material from his site to encourage a specialist to undertake its study, he cannot expect the full-time assistance of an unpaid trained scientist on a project that is mostly irrelevant to the scientist's own field. Many research projects have been successfully completed by an equal collaboration of archaeologists and scientists, but others, also completed satisfactorily, have involved only a full-time archaeologist aided by scientists who were interested enough in, and who got enough out of, the study.

The variety of samples that can be extracted from an archaeological site is considerable, and some are more specialized in the method of their recovery than others. It is possible for archaeologists to take many samples themselves, so long as they are aware of the requirements of the scientists, but other samples should not normally be collected by anyone except the specialist concerned. The latter probably include soils, beetles and snails, and material for archaeomagnetic and thermoluminescent dating, although on occasion almost all of these have been supplied by archaeologists.

Sources of contamination
One of the questions asked by most specialists in examining samples of material collected by others is that of possible contamination. Each type of sample, for environmental, economic or chronological purposes, has potential sources of contamination that, if present, reduce or eliminate the value of examination.

General sources of contamination on an archaeological site include wind or rain which can transport alien material into a deposit subsequently, or actually, in the process of being sampled. The rule for this is that a sample is not exposed until it is collected. A deposit to be sampled should remain incompletely cleaned until the last moment. A deposit already cleaned should be collected at once, or if this is impossible, protected by clean polythene well tucked in around it.

Humanly introduced contamination includes dirt on boots or toeboards, dirt on gloves and sampling tools, dirt in sample bags, and dirt brought in by smoking, eating, pencil sharpening or erasing, and general mess on a site. Other samples may be made useless by lack of information, inadequate labelling, omission of sample position on plans and sections, uncertain reasons for taking the sample.

The record of a sample should include a careful assessment of the dangers of contamination. Certain samples may not be as 'clean' as others, but have been taken because they are the only source of a particular material on a site; this is true of many samples for radiocarbon dating. The collector must be honest in his record of these, and provide details of possible and probable sources of contamination. The proximity of roots, animal burrows and tunnels, and other disturbances, must be recorded. A record card of a sample might be as follows:

> Site.
> Area or Trench.
> Layer or Deposit.
> Position of Sample – plan (sketches).
>   – section (scale drawing best).
> Nature of deposit.
> Nature of sample.
> Quantity/Size of sample.
> Reason for sample.
> Possible contamination.
> Collector.
> Date of collection.

Radiocarbon dating
Material suitable for radiocarbon (C^{14}) dating may be present on any archaeological site. The dates produced by the technique are measures of the radioactivity of the material, and have statistical uncertainties attached; the half-life of radiocarbon is about 5730 ± 40 years, but all published dates are based on the original estimate of 5568 ± 30 years and are expressed in years B.P. (Before Present = 1950). To convert a published date to the new half-life, multiply the B.P. date by 1.03. Although comparisons with tree-rings suggest that radiocarbon years and calendar years do not necessarily coincide at certain ages, it is still standard practice to publish dates at the old half-life in years B.P.

Material and quantity Wood, charcoal, peat, leather and hair, marine shells, and bone or antler, are suitable for dating, in decreasing order of reliability. The quantities to be collected are as follows:

Material	*Lab. weight*	*Collector's weight*	*Description*
Wood	3 g	25 g (piece 3 cm diameter, 30 cm long)	clean or rotten:[1] if water-logged, 90% weight could be water, i.e. collect 250 g
Charcoal	2 g 5g	20 g (about 300 cubic cm.) 50 g	black flakes brownish pieces
Peat	3 g 10 g	30 g 100 g	dark brown/black; if wet, 90% water i.e. take 300 g light brown
Leather, skin, hair, cloth	5 g	45 g	
Shells–carbonate	10 g 15 g	100 g 150 g	hard shiny surface powdery surface
Bone, antler	100 g	1000 g	
Soil		2–5 kg	last resort, generally difficult

Collection   The sample must not be touched with anything except a clean (scraped, not oiled) metal blade. Modern contaminants, particularly rootlets and animal runs, must be avoided. The sample should be put into a sterile polythene bag (double thickness) or sterile glass bottle (with plastic or metal cap, not cork) and completely sealed. The container should not be opened to add samples; use a new container. Metal tag labels with identification numbers should be put outside the container; paper labels should be avoided. Separation of dating material from soil or rootlets can be done in the laboratory with clean metal blades

[1] If large timbers are to be used, the outer rings of wood should be taken, as these will represent more accurately the date of use, inner rings may be many years older.

and tweezers, on a clean metal or plastic sheet; the sample, if wet, should then be dried in an oven (not a cooking oven) at about 105 °C, and resealed for the dating laboratory. Most samples will be damp and should be dried before decay and fungus growth begins; some laboratories will do this for potential customers.

Radiocarbon dating laboratories exist in national museums and universities, and as commercial enterprises. Some laboratories restrict their samples to particular research projects, and may provide free dates. Commercial laboratories will charge from £50 upwards for a date.

Soils
All the deposits on a site must have an explanation for their presence, some will be natural and undisturbed, others artificial, but all were formed or deposited by some agency, and the archaeologist must be able to account for their presence. As they are products of their environment, examination can often provide indications of the natural conditions of the time.

Collection About 250 g (about 9 oz) of soil is required for analysis. Samples are generally taken from vertical sections of trenches or areas, but can be extracted from a horizontal or sloping surface if the upper part is cleaned by trowelling away contaminated material. A vertical section should be scraped horizontally, to avoid dragging down deposits, and samples should be taken of each distinct deposit in the section. A thick deposit should have an internal vertical series of samples, at every 10–20 cm. If collected from a vertical column, it is not necessary to take at specific intervals because this may mean that an interface of two deposits is collected and therefore mixed. Sometimes, however, a complete monolith or column can be extracted. A clean trowel or knife should be used, and if the individual samples are taken from bottom upwards, the material will fall more easily into a clean strong polythene bag held beneath the area to be sampled. Labels must be attached at once, and bags firmly sealed. The exact position of each sample should be measured on to the section drawing (fig. 76).

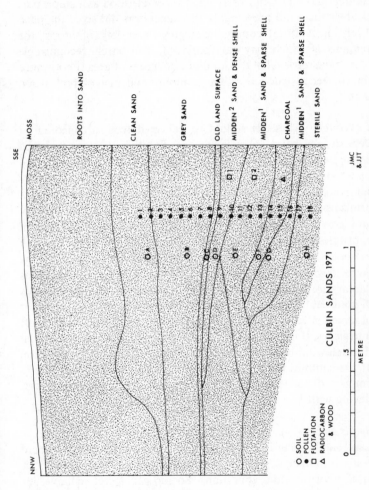

NNW   SSE

MOSS

ROOTS INTO SAND

CLEAN SAND

GREY SAND

OLD LAND SURFACE

MIDDEN² SAND & DENSE SHELL

MIDDEN¹ SAND & SPARSE SHELL

CHARCOAL

MIDDEN¹ SAND & SPARSE SHELL

STERILE SAND

○ SOIL
● POLLEN
□ FLOTATION
△ RADIOCARBON & WOOD

CULBIN SANDS 1971

0   .5   1
METRE

JMC & JJT

Fig. 76 Excavation drawing of a section through a midden in the Culbin Sands, Morayshire, to show the positions of samples collected for subsequent processing.

Seeds

The potential value of new methods of extracting minute organic material from archaeological deposits is extremely high. Modern hunter–gatherer groups rely upon vegetable food as a staple part of their diet, and presumably their ancestors did so in the past. Early agricultural communities grew a variety of crops, the remains of which may have survived, if in barely recognizable form. The retrieval of this kind of evidence is of great importance for the reconstruction of the economy and diet of prehistoric man.

Collection   All seeds should be collected from archaeological deposits, by hand, by sieving or by flotation. Flotation can be carried out in the field, but also elsewhere; sacks of potential material should be collected and sealed. Vegetable matter may survive in wells or peat bogs, or as carbonized material, as imprints on clay vessels, or as silica skeletons. Storage pits in chalk and gravel may yield traces of their former content. Human coprolites may also contain parts of vegetable foods. Retrieval of material by hand during excavation generally yields only the larger specimens, and sieving (p. 173) may collect more but causes damage to the spikelets of the plants. Flotation of large deposits of material from an excavation is now possible, where the lighter organic matter is floated to the top of the water and is poured off into sieves. It is important to avoid contamination of the material through wind-blown modern plant remains both in the collection of the samples and in the flotation process. This involves preliminary dry sieving with a 10 mm mesh to catch stones, then wet sieving with 1 to 2 mm meshes to collect plant remains.

Snails and beetles

Land snails occur in a wide range of soils, including those where pollen is unlikely to be preserved, and can yield information about local environmental conditions. So too can insect remains, including beetle cases and eggs. Large fragments of snails will be visible to the eye; smaller pieces, and insect remains, will only be recovered by flotation or by hand sorting with a lens. All should be collected.

Collection
These animals are likely to be found in surface layers of ancient soils, in ditch bottoms, in pits and in middens. Large samples of potentially useful deposits should be bagged and carefully labelled, for flotation and examination by a specialist. Individual fragments should be bagged separately and their precise associations with the deposits of the site must be recorded.

Animal bone
The total collection of animal remains has long been an essential in archaeological excavations. The evidence available from the study of animal remains includes economic activities (preferences, seasonal use, butchery practices, diet), and environmental data (range of animals both large and small), as well as chronological and cultural information.

Collection All material should be collected and recorded in as much detail as that for finds of stone or pottery or metal, and structural features.

Articulated bones should be collected intact, on blocks if necessary (p. 185). If complete skeletons are found, soil samples around the stomach should be taken for traces of diet. Small animal remains may only be recovered by sieving the deposit. Many bones tend to be fragile, and sieving must be done gently; rodent, bird and fish remains will only be retrieved by careful examination. Bones should be bagged and labelled, for cleaning in the laboratory or processing tent. Before they are sent to a specialist, they should be marked in ink so that they may be bulked in the identification procedures. Fragile bones, including skulls and lower jaws, should be padded with thin polythene bags or sheets; paper and cotton wool tend to cling to projections and may cause breakages.

Middens
Material from middens can yield valuable evidence of the diet, food-gathering practices and population size in prehistoric times. Middens may be excavated in total or in part (p. 182), but various types of samples should be collected from all sites of this nature.

Collection   A series of column samples should be taken through the deposits at intervals of about $\frac{1}{4}$ of the longitudinal and transverse dimensions, i.e. nine column samples, but local variations may indicate the desirability of additional samples from other parts. The position of all samples must be marked on plans and sections. Samples are columns of deposit about 20 cm square, collected in pieces of 10 or 20 cm depth, and running from top to bottom of the midden. The material found will mainly consist of rock, earth, shell and bone, and all these should be carefully bagged and labelled by column and by depth. The separation of this material should be done by sieving earth from shell fragments, and the three main constituents, rock, earth, and shell/bone, should be dried naturally, and weighed separately. By using the component weights from all the columns, estimates of the quantity of shell and the range of types can be obtained, leading on to estimates of the meat content of the midden. Careful labelling is required. All samples of rock, earth and shell should also be water sieved to recover seeds and other organic material. All bone should be preserved in the actual excavation of the midden, but the column samples will probably provide sufficient estimate of the shell varieties and proportions present.

Peat
Peat bogs tend to preserve some organic material, particularly wood (p. 228). The evidence of the peat itself, which is of plant origin, will provide data on the development of local vegetation in wet areas, and this sequence is valuable for dating and local environmental purposes.

Collection   A peat monolith can be most easily obtained from the side of an excavation. The peat should be trowelled sideways to clean the face, and a scraped knife or trowel used to cut two vertical lines, 15 cm apart and as deep as possible, e.g. 15–20 cm. The monolith is then cut into sections, about 30 cm long, and each is gently cut or levered out by a clean small spade pushed in behind the monolith. Each section is bagged in polythene, upper part in the bottom of the bag, sealed so the peat cannot slip about, and labelled as, e.g. Monolith A, section 1 (2, 3, etc.) 0–30 cm (30–60, 60–90, etc.). It is important to clean lightly the top of each section to remove fallen peat, and to record the position and depth of each sample on plans and section drawings; the precise relation of the monolith to the archaeological evidence should be noted, and if possible part of the ancient feature, or a label, should actually appear in the monolith for certain identification of the feature within the peat sequence.

Plants and pollen
Fragments of plants may survive in wet or very dry local positions on archaeological sites. Pollen is well preserved in acidic bogs (pH below 5), but may also have survived in clays and sands, and in cave deposits. The evidence of previous vegetation is important for establishing former environmental conditions and for relative dating.

Collection   Plant fragments may be recognized during excavation, and should be conserved and recorded as for any finds; if quantities occur, they should be carefully packed in polythene bags, and recorded by position and stratum. Flotation and sieving in water should be carried out for deposits suspected of containing plant remains; if this is not possible, a large sack of each deposit should be collected for laboratory examination.

Pollen should be collected by palaeobotanists if possible, but the archaeologist can take a useful series of samples if care is exercised. Individual deposits should be carefully scraped clean by a clean trowel, and then spooned into a polythene bag opened only when necessary; from 10 to 50 cm^3 is all that is needed. A section should be sampled as a sequence, starting at the base (in subsoil) and each subsequent 5 cm. The deposits to be sampled should be cleaned by trowelling sideways just before sampling. Small sterile glass bottles with wide mouths (bottles 5 cm long, mouths 2 cm wide) can be pushed into the deposits, until all are in place. Then they can be cut out, starting from the top (with a blade cleaned for each sample), capped and labelled at once. Ancient land surfaces or other special deposits should have additional quantities taken. The exact position of the column, and each sample, must be marked on a section drawing (see fig. 76).

Wood and dendrochronology

Wooden remains are rarely preserved except as carbonized pieces or under waterlogged conditions. They should be recorded as ordinary finds, and kept in the same environmental condition as they were found in, either dry or wet. Samples of wood can be used for environmental data and tree-ring dating.

Collection   Wet wood will begin to crack within ten minutes of exposure to air and sun. It must be covered by polythene or sprayed until it is lifted and bagged with a small amount of water. If an interval of more than a few weeks is to elapse before treatment begins, a little fungicide could be added, but not if the wood is to be used for radiocarbon dating. Large pieces of wood may have to be cut or sawn for lifting, or lifted on a plank. Wet wood is generally soft, and no tool should touch its surface. Dry wood, generally carbonized, should be kept dry or allowed to dry naturally, and then bagged.

Samples of wood for tree-ring dating must be well-preserved, and conifers growing in a semi-arid climate are the most suitable trees. The varying thicknesses of annual growth-rings of a tree may be matched with a similar pattern on another older tree, and the sequence thus developed may be dated precisely if one particular ring can be dated historically or, for older sequences, if a ring is dated by radiocarbon. Sequences dated to calendar years have been developed in various parts of America, and in Switzerland an open-ended sequence is used for lake-mud sites. Local sequences can be produced if the type of tree and the environmental conditions for growth are consistent for all samples. Complete tree stems, particularly the lower parts, should be sampled in lengths of 30 cm.

Thermoluminescence

The principle of this dating method is that many minerals, when heated, emit light that is proportional to the amount of radiation absorbed by the mineral. Pottery contains mineral constituents, for example quartz, that accumulate new thermoluminescence from the time of the firing of the pottery at temperatures above 500 °C. The accumulation continues with time, and estimates of the age of pottery can therefore be made.

Collection A group of potsherds from precise positions in a stratigraphical sequence, and sealed by about 50 cm of soil, is required, as well as a sample of the soil in which the sherds are found. Sherds and soil should be bagged separately. The sherds should be thick (minimum 3 mm) but can be otherwise small (25 mm across). They should not be exposed to sunlight for more than a few minutes, should be bagged in opaque material (brown paper will do), and should not be cleaned. The method involves the destruction of the sherds. Research in thermoluminescence continues, and laboratories do not normally accept anything other than reliable material of a specified period or type, and important samples should be collected by specialists if possible.

Archaeomagnetism
The principle behind this dating method is that the angle of declination between magnetic north and true north, and the angle of dip of a magnetic needle, have varied in the past. The firing of clay results in the magnetic fields of hematite and magnetite in the clay aligning with the contemporary angles of declination and dip. On cooling, these angles are fixed, and if the clay is not moved, the angles can be compared with known dated records and therefore dated. The records are very restricted, but radiocarbon dated sites with archaeomagnetic material preserved are gradually building a sequence.

Collection Areas of burned soil or rock, fireplaces and kilns, are suitable sources of material. The samples must be taken by the specialist concerned, who will determine the geographic north and magnetic north in the field, and record these while the sample is still in place.

Sources of assistance
In the past, the relationship of scientists to archaeologists has been rather casual, some specific problems occasioning detailed and equal collaboration, but most problems approached in terms of a simple and limited role for the scientist. His contribution was generally concerned with local environment, chronology or food sources. There is much to be said for more active collaboration today, in an equal relationship between archaeology and the

scientific disciplines concerned with all aspects of man's environment, his behaviour within it, and impact upon it. 'Sources of assistance' to the archaeologist must not be taken to imply a one-way system (p. 218).

The natural sciences most likely to be relevant to archaeological problems are geology, pedology, botany and all aspects of zoology. University departments are a major source of collaboration, and many departments or sub-departments are concerned with regional studies that will be of great value to the archaeologist. National museums, and some regional museums, also possess specialists in some or all of these fields, and an excellent working relationship is that between an archaeologist and a museum able to absorb not only cultural but environmental and economic material.

The dating of archaeological material is a more restricted field, and in Britain most of the work on Thermoluminescence and Archaeomagnetism has been done by the Oxford Research Laboratory for Archaeology and the History of Art. Other facilities do exist, however, mainly through national museums. Sources for radiocarbon dating are more widespread (p. 222).

9 Conscience and confession

Archaeological work in the field may or may not involve excavation, and only in the latter case can it be said that the destruction of evidence is initiated by archaeology. Field surveys, seeking to record particular monuments, or all monuments, in a limited area, are harmless in terms of destroyed information except where data obtained through surface collection or local informants is inadvertently or deliberately neglected. Excavation, on the other hand, sets in motion the processes of decay, through natural destructive agencies and through archaeological disturbance of deposits. The comments here refer particularly to excavation, but some may be applicable also to field surveys.

All archaeologists who have conducted excavations and who have worked over the records and materials obtained, must spend some time considering the procedures they might have adopted, but did not, that might have yielded more information than they actually obtained. Archaeologists may have a conscience about this and vow to do better next time, but this will not salvage sites already excavated. What is required here is honesty on the part of the archaeologists in admitting, confessing, that certain procedures were not carried out. These procedures need not be newly invented methods of retrieving invisible material, but can be simple standard practices of excavating, recording or conserving, that for some reason went wrong or were not employed. An archaeologist, in publishing a site, should bear in mind that his report will be of greater value to others if he admits that certain techniques were not employed, and if he admits that other procedures were inadequately performed. Such a report would allow others to profit in future work, and to understand the limitations of the evidence presented.

For these reasons it is also imperative that workers on an excavation should admit, to site supervisor or director, if a mistake has been made; this could be a bucket of earth tipped away before sieving, a layer trowelled away too vigorously, an object broken, a section damaged. All *might* be serious losses, but all *are* serious losses if those responsible for the excavation do not know of them. In some cases, immediate remedial action might be taken, in others not, but the worker must be prepared to admit his mistake.

It is not unknown for workers to 'plant' material designed to startle a fellow worker, a site supervisor or a director. The character of the plant is generally sufficiently distinct (yesterday's *Times*, for instance) to cause no concern. On occasion, however, some misleading but conceivably genuine evidence may creep in, and this sort of plant can sometimes be difficult to uproot. The rule must be, don't plant evidence of whatever kind, and if others do, they or you must admit it.

Far more difficult a problem arises when a difference of opinion exists about the nature or significance of a particular find or deposit. The conflict of views may be between director and supervisor, or supervisor and worker. Many workers on excavations are extremely experienced, and may find themselves disagreeing with the instructions to dig through or discard material, or to handle finds or record in certain ways. This can be a touchy situation, and can only be resolved satisfactorily if the worker puts his views forward delicately, perhaps indirectly, and if the supervisor or director is prepared to listen and consider, and to make an honest decision based on the importance of the site and not anyone's personal feelings.

The obligations on an archaeologist in excavating any site are to record the evidence as completely as is possible, to conserve the material and records, and to publish a report on the work done. If there is no intention to perform any of these tasks, the excavation at once falls into the category of 'treasure hunting'. An archaeologist must be aware that the time taken in study, and in writing an excavation report, is likely to be two or three times as long as the excavation took, and if there is no honest intention to devote this amount of time to the preparation of a full report, then in all conscience he should not begin work.

V Understanding the evidence

In attempting to understand the evidence recovered from excavation or fieldwork, the archaeologist is concerned with two separate aspects, the ability to reconstruct, and the flair to understand. The first of these is a technical problem of interpreting information. This is theoretically a simple process, involving the archaeologist in rebuilding his site according to the impeccable records he has kept, of translating his data into an imaginable and legitimate form. The relationship of one deposit or structural feature to another, the position of a find within a sequence, the association of significant materials, are, or should be, entirely clear to the archaeologist who has observed and recorded the evidence. Through this he should be able to rebuild his site, both vertically and horizontally. On single-period sites this is a relatively simple exercise, but even the most complex stratigraphical sequence should have been disentangled by the excavator through his observation and recording on the site. If uncertainties exist about the relationship of deposits and associations of features, he must admit it, accept the lack of information, and either do better next time or give up. He might in any case accept that more evidence could be obtained by allowing posterity the opportunity to develop and experiment with new techniques.

This procedure, the interpretation and ordering of the physical remains from a site, is only a first step towards understanding what the site means in terms of human behaviour. The flair to understand the archaeological evidence does not automatically follow from a high degree of ability in extracting it. This is where not only factual assistance is required, but also the exercise of ingenuity, and even the imagination. That the last sometimes obscures the evidence must be admitted:

> The researches of many antiquarians have already thrown much darkness upon the subject, and it is certain if they continue that we shall soon know nothing at all.   (Mark Twain)

Aims   The evidence that is obtained by archaeologists in fieldwork and excavation is all that has survived the passage of time and the processes of recovery. Both of these destructive elements are a part of a rather depressing equation that may illustrate the magnitude of the problem facing archaeologists. First, however, the aim of archaeology should be stated again, and this is to re-create so far as is possible the events of the past, to outline the development of man as a cultured animal, learning, adapting and transmitting his ideas and accomplishments, and to achieve an explanation of human behaviour. Archaeologists are like anthropologists in that they are interested in behaviour, but they cannot observe people in action, and must content themselves with the surviving remains left by ancient societies, in the hope that in so doing they can somehow approach the elements of human behaviour in which they are interested. 'Man's tools are the instruments of his response to the world in which he lives, but they are much more – they are the weapons of his conquest of that world and the clue to its interpretation.'[1]

Diminishing returns   The problem facing archaeologists can be simply described as a law of diminishing return. The evidence of past human behaviour does not survive intact, and is reduced by four major elements:

(1) Prehistory by definition implies pre-literate societies, so language and oral traditions, music, religious beliefs and other ideas, cannot have survived by transcription.

(2) The natural processes of decay will have removed large bodies of material that would illumine the character of prehistoric communities; much or all organic matter may have

[1] D. Garrod, *Environment, tools and man*, Cambridge, 1946, 27.

vanished, and with it, evidence of clothing and shelter, food and equipment. In addition, natural geological processes may disturb ancient sites through wind or water erosion, or earth movements, so that even surviving inorganic material may lose its significant associations. The importance of sites with unusual or unique preservation of material is obvious here.

(3) The archaeological processes of recognition and recovery of evidence may be inadequate for the material that has survived. The archaeologist may miss finds of importance through lack of observation in the field, or through incomplete excavation. The techniques for the recovery of evidence that *has* been recognized may also result in loss, through the destruction initiated by the spade; sampling or conservation procedures may be inadequate. Additionally, the recording of the evidence through drawings, photographs and notes, may not be clear enough when the time comes to assess the information.

(4) Finally, the archaeologist may not understand the evidence that is available to him. He may not have asked the right questions of his site or his area, he may not have obtained the answers, he may be handicapped by all of the above three limitations, he may miss the significance of his material. In other words, he adds a fourth reducing element to his evidence. The equation could read:

total evidence $>$ surviving evidence $>$ recorded evidence $>$ understood evidence
$=$ archaeological evidence for past human behaviour.

Questioning a site With such a limited potential range of evidence available for recovery, the archaeologist must be sure to exploit it to the full. For both an excavation and an area survey, the series of questions that the archaeologist asks of his material will determine to a great extent the potential knowledge that he will be able to acquire from his work. The questions to be asked of sites or areas cannot be standardized, but some general ones are noted on p. 134. As an example, some of the questions that were asked of a Mesolithic settlement in Fife are indicated below. The first question to be posed concerned the area of occupation, in an attempt to delimit the settlement as well as gauge the scale of the excavation required.

Questions	*Possible answers, and methods used*
Size of settlement	Delimited by area excavations around potential site (fig. 69)
Nature of occupation, permanent or sporadic	Sporadic, as shown by stratigraphical details
Size of human groups	Probably small (4–10) by total open excavation of camp sites (fig. 63)
Reason for choice of site (island in prehistoric times)	Shelter/safety uncertain; shellfish source, and fishing point, by midden content (fig. 72)
Fishing methods	Shoreline and deep sea, therefore boat
Area exploited	Tay to Forth, by geology and zoology of tools and animals (fig. 77)
Duration of interest in island	200–1000 years possible, by radio-carbon; 200–400 years probably, by stratigraphy

Reconstruction   Yet with all of the difficulties of the survival of evidence, the archaeologist must still attempt to reconstruct human behaviour through the re-creation of the events of the past. To do this he must try to relate his material to the other lines of evidence that may help him to understand. These additional lines include environmental data, ethnographic material, and experimental techniques.

The use of *environmental evidence* in understanding the presence and character of a prehistoric occupation or activity is too obvious to require much comment. No human ever existed in isolation from his environment, and the shape of an ancient community was determined in great measure by its physical setting. The words 'environmental determinism' have occasionally been considered as too rigid, in denying man a choice in life, but there can be no doubt that an understanding of human behaviour can only be gained through recognition of the potential that an environment possessed. Knowledge about the realization and exploitation of that potential, or part of it, is of primary importance to archaeologists. Similarly, the influence of man upon his environment is a measure of his approach to his existence, of his technical and ideological skills. The student of man's past must then recover, so far as is possible, the extent and character of man's relationship with his environment, through the evidence of the natural sciences.

The investigation of the site noted above may be taken as an example. Through geology, botany and geography, the environmental conditions of 6000 B.P. could be determined, and a reconstruction attempted (fig. 77); from this it was seen that the site must have been an island at the time of its occupation, and the likely climatic conditions, allied to stratigraphical evidence, suggested that the island could not have been occupied on a permanent basis. Geological examination of the stone equipment recovered by excavation suggested that areas to the north-west and to the south of the site had been visited to obtain raw materials. This would have brought the human groups into areas where particular food sources were also likely to be present; the types of food remains recovered by excavation could therefore be explained.

The use of *ethnographic evidence* in archaeology has often consisted of seeking analogous material in widely spaced communities in an attempt to understand the technology and function of ancient objects, the purpose of structures, the significance of artistic expressions. Assemblages of material from communities living in comparable environmental circumstances were considered to be more relevant than isolated artefacts. More and more, however, this approach of looking for one explanation is being abandoned in favour of a search through all possible relevant societies to obtain as complete a variation and range of explanations as possible. The single answer is considered to be potentially misleading, and scientifically unsound in the absence of proof. Yet even so, the ethnographic approach can open the mind of the archaeologist to the range of possibilities that exist for him in his interpretive work on his own material. Equally, it should remind the archaeologist of the meagre amount of evidence that he has recovered from ancient communities possibly rich in ideas and materials that have not survived.

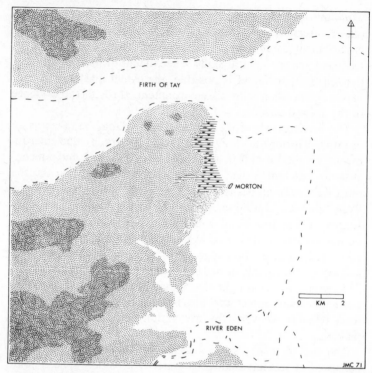

Fig. 77 Reconstruction of environmental conditions obtained through geological, pedological and palaeobotanical work around a site at Morton, Fife, occupied about 6000 B.P. by hunter–gatherers. The low hill (see fig. 69) is shown here as an island in the North Sea, linked to the mainland at low tide by a tombolo or sand spit. To the north-west of the island was a marsh, protected from the sea by dunes. The dashed line indicates the present coast-line, the double stipple is land over 100 m O.D. (after Coles 1971).

The excavations in Fife, noted above, also revealed archae-ological evidence of the sporadic nature of the prehistoric occupation, and of the short time-range of each individual occupation that could be recognized. This evidence, so far as it went, was consistent with the knowledge about the general nature of activities undertaken by modern and recent hunter–gatherer groups in various parts of the world, but it could not be taken much farther than this, except in terms of the food supplies (quantity and quality) and human subsistence at this latitude; the comparative data suggested small groups over several centuries of settlement on the island.

The use of *experimental techniques* in archaeology involves two aspects. The first is that of simple experiment, of reconstructing sites and equipment in order to see what technical skills may have been necessary in the past. The digging of ditches, building of barrows, erection of stones, all tell us something about the time and effort required by prehistoric man; they may also make suggestions about the degree of organization of people required for such undertakings. The advantages of a sound knowledge of practical methods in general technology (Hodges 1964), and with particular attention to 'Country Crafts' (e.g. Arnold 1968), are obvious in this aspect of experimental archaeology. Yet in almost all cases, there can be no absolute proof that a procedure successfully used today was precisely that used in the past; it is a question of probabilities and possibilities, not certainties.

In the example noted above, the quarrying of stone for implements, the hollowing-out of a dugout canoe, the cutting of timber for windbreaks, all have been tested by experiment, and some measure of the time and energy expended have been calculated. No estimate of the size of the group, or of any division of labour, could be obtained from this.

The second and far more important experimental technique is that designed to re-create the events responsible for the physical remains observed and recovered through archaeology. A descriptive 'model' is constructed by developing the evidence of subsistence and economy, the evidence of social organization and intercommunal relations, and the evidence of environmental influences and exploitation, into a picture of a society, still lacking features of language, custom and belief, but possessing the essential feature of time which can give information about rates of change. At this stage, the archaeologist is still dealing with evidence of a descriptive nature, obtained through the various lines of study pursued by archaeology.

For the site in question, it has been suggested that the people in the area occasionally, probably seasonally, occupied the low island to gather shellfish, to launch their boat for deep-sea fishing, and to shelter in small groups. They could capture sturgeon of up to 250 kg weight (3 m in length), they ransacked the near-by cliffs for birds, they hunted successfully in the hills for large mammals, they gathered wild plants for food, and they travelled widely to obtain raw materials for their tools. The archaeological site suffered from an absence of surviving organic remains, except for bone and a few pieces of carbonized wood. However, it can be suggested from other sites and sources that a wide range of organic material was probably used, that the community was not large, that it was mobile, that it was not under pressure to survive, that it was successfully exploiting its territory and that it therefore had developed accurate knowledge about its environmental potential. Beyond this, towards details of its social structure, the evidence did not extend. Nevertheless, the reconstruction was consistent with the evidence available, and could serve as a source for other comparable archaeological sites that might yield more of the same evidence, or evidence of a different type that could be applied to this one. All of the reconstruction of this site was made possible by the recognition, by an amateur archaeologist, of a few humanly struck flints lying on a molehill.

The introduction of factors that may explain the reasons behind ancient activities is a final step in attempts to understand human behaviour. This approach is first suggested by the recognition that certain groups in the past reacted in certain ways with their physical and their social background. Within a series of such groups, it may be seen that similarities in environment and in technological development do create similar responses taking the form of comparable economic and social processes. From this it may be possible to explain the reasons for such processes, using data from the series, and including data from ethnographic sources. The advantage of such a procedure is that it allows the archaeologist to draw upon a range of evidence from a wide variety of sources that may be particularly valuable through unusual preservation or recording, or, in the case of ethnographic material, through its addition to the evidence for custom and belief. The disadvantage may be that the archaeologist either seizes upon a particular feature out of context, or allows himself to be persuaded that his explanation can be the only one.

The limits to the reconstruction of prehistoric patterns of

behaviour must be bound by the limits of the data that are brought into the study. Archaeological imagination can be boundless on occasion (p. 2), and the temptation to look for an explanation, any explanation, because there must have been one, is hard to resist. There is scope for the exercise of ingenuity, but it must be kept apart from the exercise of presenting unimpeachable evidence in a straightforward account of an excavation or any other archaeological study. There is nothing new in this division: 'Thus far as to facts: I will next venture to give my opinion.'[1]

Publication

The archaeological report should therefore be in two distinct sections. The first is entirely factual, with plans, sections and photographs of the sites and the finds, with statements about the environmental setting, deposits of the site, structural features and other aspects that were observed and recorded. The preparation of this section can be tedious, yet at the same time it will force the archaeologist to filter all his data and to select those elements that he considers are relevant and important.

The additional data not to be published should be preserved in some public place such as a regional museum; and its whereabouts should be noted in the publication. The procedures to be followed in the preparation of this factual section of a report have been fully described by Grinsell, Rahtz and Warhurst (1966).

The report of an excavation could be organized as follows:

(1) Introduction: location of site (maps), its discovery, date and source of excavation, location of finds and unpublished records of the work.

(2) Environment: position of site within environmental setting (maps, including reconstructions of ancient conditions), and environmental potential.

(3) Purpose of excavation: reason for work, scale of work attempted, methods used, criticism of work (errors of technique and approach).

(4) Excavation results: description of site (plans), details of stratigraphy (sections) and structures (plans), description of finds (drawings), dating evidence, technical reports.

[1] Gov. T. Pownall, Description of the Carn Braich y Dinas, on the summit of Pen-maen-mawr, in Caernarvonshire, *Archaeologia* 3, 1771, 307.

(5) Interpretation: reconstruction (plans), experimental techniques.

(6) Discussion: comparisons with other sites and areas.

(7) Sources of information (bibliography).

There are other elements in the publication of excavated sites, but the above should cover most of the major sections. The use of appendices, where specialist reports tend to be buried and unread, should be avoided and relevant data included within the account of the site; extravagant detail could be deposited along with the excavation records in local museum or society or university departments:

> . . . it is the duty of archaeologists to be as economical as possible in their presentation of data. Otherwise the subject will be swamped by a vast accumulation of insignificant, disparate facts, like a terrible tide of mud, quite beyond the capacity of any man to contain and mould into historical form.[1]

The interpretative section of a report should also be factual insofar as it relies for support upon a sound body of evidence. This evidence need not come from the site or area under discussion, and may be of environmental or ethnographic character. Its reliability must be unimpeachable, its relevance must be demonstrated. The resultant reconstruction, the model of past events, allows the archaeologist an opportunity to exercise his ingenuity and to present his theories about the development of human behaviour in any of its aspects. The evidence available, and the manner of its presentation, will show the inadequacies or otherwise of the reconstruction.

Finally, not all reports of excavations or field surveys can be published; there are not enough archaeological journals, or finance for other publication. This, however, is no excuse for not writing a full report, with illustrations, within a reasonable time of completing the fieldwork. Field notes are not sufficient, and the full report should be an obligation on all field archaeologists. Such a report should be deposited with the local museum or society for future study, for possible reinterpretation by anyone, and for potential publication.

[1] J. Hawkes, 'The proper study of mankind', *Antiquity* 42, 1968, 258.

VI The organization of prehistoric archaeology in Britain

The variety of organizations that deal with aspects of prehistoric archaeology in Britain is extremely large, and there is probably no country in the world with such variety and such lack of control over archaeological work. Perhaps the two are related, but it is more likely that the lack of control is due in great measure to an uninformed and therefore uncaring public. Yet the conundrum here is that Britain possesses amateur archaeologists that at least equal those of other nations in relative quantity, and excel them in quality. One of the reasons why excavations and field surveys in Britain are often considered to be of a relatively high standard in the eyes of outside interests is this large body of interested and skilled workers.

Amateurs

The backbone of British archaeology has generally been acknowledged to be the amateurs who fill the local and national societies, who attend University and Extra-Mural courses, who complete excavation and survey teams, and who buy archaeological monographs and periodicals. This is in many respects true, and without doubt the withdrawal of their support would cause the collapse of much archaeological work in this country. Yet it is perhaps also true that the propelling element – one hesitates to call it the brains – is something outside the purely amateur framework. The days when most of the major and fundamental research surveys and excavations were conducted by amateurs are past, and most of the impetus now derives from governmental and university institutions. The decline, in this respect, of the amateur archaeologist is most assuredly not due to a decline in standards, or in numbers of particularly gifted unpaid archaeologists. It is perhaps due to the multiplicity of other interests now available, to the financial difficulties of attendance on excavations, possibly to some discouragement by professionals; in some cases, the lack of access to research laboratories for technical assistance has quite rightly dissuaded amateur archaeologists from undertaking excavations.

Local societies

The basis of the field of amateur archaeology is the local society, and it is likely that here the first effects of any long-range decline in the numbers of amateurs will be felt. Most counties in England, many in Wales and Scotland, have local archaeological societies; sometimes these are combined with natural history interests. The work of the local society is concerned with county projects, field surveys and excavations, and most societies are run by a very small band of dedicated amateurs, who devote time and money to the furtherance of county studies. Regular lectures are given by members or others, and many societies publish annual *Transactions*, *Journals* or *Proceedings*, in which reports of field projects appear. These volumes provide the basis for much archaeological research in Britain. The contribution of local societies is primarily that of attracting people into the subject at amateur level, of controlling local excavations through the ability to organize and guide the work, and of publishing to an adequate standard the results of excavations, field surveys and other studies. Some of the county journals are extremely well-produced, but all are faced with problems of rising costs. Membership of local societies is obtained for an annual subscription of from £1.50 to £3, and information can be obtained from most county museums.

National societies

There are a number of national societies that are concerned at least in part with prehistoric archaeology. All publish research reports as monographs or, more usually, as papers in their annual journals. Lectures are held regularly, and conferences are also organized by these societies. Membership is generally by election, but conditions for admission are varied; most professional archaeologists belong to one or more of these societies, but the bulk of the membership is amateur.

The major national societies are:	Their publications are:
The Society of Antiquaries of London	*Antiquaries Journal, Archaeologia.*
The Prehistoric Society	*Proceedings of the Prehistoric Society*
The Royal Archaeological Institute	*Archaeological Journal*
The Cambrian Association	*Archaeologia Cambrensis*
The Society of Antiquaries of Scotland	*Proceedings of the Society of Antiquaries of Scotland*

The major contribution of these societies to archaeology is probably their publications, which provide vehicles for large reports of field surveys and excavations which may be of more than local interest and significance. The lectures and conferences also provide an opportunity for professionals and amateurs to meet and hear about recent advances in knowledge and techniques. All of the societies except the Prehistoric Society have excellent libraries available to their members.

Other publications Most commercial publishers in Britain now produce archaeological books; some of these are aimed at the amateur market, others are highly specialized research reports unlikely to attract any market except the libraries of universities and museums. Regional guides to archaeology are available in several series, and other series are concerned with major research projects in British or other fields of prehistory and archaeology. Journals of archaeology, independent of any society, also exist, and their popularity is a reflection of the serious interest taken by the public in both specialized and general aspects of archaeology. *Antiquity* and *World Archaeology* cover all aspects of archaeology on a world-wide basis, whereas *Current Archaeology* is generally limited to the British scene. *Archaeometry* is an important journal concerned with the development of archaeological techniques.

Museums

The variety of museums in Britain is great. National museums (the British Museum, the National Museum of Wales, and the National Museum of Antiquities of Scotland) have a wide range of activities, research and rescue excavations, all aspects of conservation, storage and display of collections, and study facilities for museum staff and others. These three museums are controlled by their respective trustees who are in the main appointed by Ministers of the Crown. The permanent staff are legally employed by the Trustees, but in almost all respects they come within the orbit of the Civil Service.

Some of the regional museums, controlled by local authorities or by societies, also provide facilities for conservation and study of materials, and they act as focal points for all regional activities. On the other hand, the opportunities for research and excavation from much smaller museums, generally controlled by a town council or similar body, are sparse, and in some cases the staff of such institutions may consist of a single full- or part-time curator; in these circumstances, display and conservation are unlikely to reach adequate standards, and research carried out from the museum is impossible. There are a few notable exceptions to this, however, where interesting museum activities have been conducted almost single-handed; interested amateurs can often help. The size of a museum does not reflect the quality of its collections, and most museums, however small, possess objects of importance either for their beauty and rarity, or for their significant association and distribution. There exist in Britain a number of extremely small museums, no longer functioning as anything but holding museums, where material tends to disappear or lose records of its provenance; the importance of amateur archaeologists in recording local collections (p. 50) should not be restricted to private holdings while such public assemblages still exist.

The number of museums in Britain approaches one thousand, and many of these possess prehistoric or early historic material. An annual list, *Museums and Galleries in Great Britain and*

Northern Ireland, provides details of collections and visiting hours.

Other government offices

Apart from national and other museums supported by public funds, there are four widely separated bodies that act for archaeology under direct government finance.

Department of the Environment The Ancient Monuments Acts require the Department of the Environment to make a list of monuments, the preservation of which is desirable. The scheduling of an ancient monument does not give permanent protection, but only provides a period (three months at the moment) for negotiation and rescue excavation if the monument is threatened with damage. Permanent protection of a site can only be provided by 'guardianship', where the Inspectorate takes over the complete control of the site; an example is Stonehenge. The Inspectorate of Ancient Monuments constantly revises and publishes lists of scheduled sites, and in some cases where destruction is inevitable, due to road-building, forestry or ploughing operations, natural erosion, and so on, the threatened sites are excavated by experienced archaeologists from the Inspectorate, or others appointed by the Inspectorate. In 1969, for instance, the Department of the Environment sponsored over 150 excavations on threatened sites, and is probably the largest single employer of archaeological students, graduates and others in Britain. Other excavations by the Department are designed to allow the sites to be 'reassembled' for display purposes; an example is the West Kennet Long Barrow, Wiltshire, and another is the Croft Moraig circle in Perthshire (fig. 59). Some excavations are published by the Department as research monographs.

In Northern Ireland, the Ancient Monuments Branch of the Ministry of Finance is concerned with both protection and recording of sites, thus combining the functions of the Ancient Monuments Inspectorate and the Royal Commissions in England, Wales and Scotland.

Only a small proportion of ancient sites in Britain are protected in any way, and this is a matter of some concern to all archaeologists. Destruction of sites is inevitable, and archaeologists are aware of this (p. 251), but unnecessary damage to sites through lack of interest or knowledge should be prevented. Sites that are not listed are not necessarily of less importance than listed ones; they may not have been recognized on the ground, or may remain unlisted for a variety of reasons. They should not be treated as were some monuments in the past: 'In a western parish of Cornwall, some labourers were employed in enclosing waste land, when they came across a stone circle, and suspecting it to be akin to others popularly held in veneration, they hesitated to destroy it, and appealed for advice to a mine captain, who decided that if noticed in Borlase (a local antiquarian who published lists of archaeological sites) it should be preserved, if not, it should be demolished. The doctor's "Antiquities" being referred to, and no mention of the circle, it was at once cleared away.' (*The Gentleman's Magazine*, 1865.)

The Royal Commissions   There are three such commissions who are entrusted with the task of recording all, or most, of the ancient monuments in the counties of the United Kingdom. For England, the Royal Commission on Historical Monuments has prepared and published about twenty-five volumes on the visible remains of monuments erected before 1700; many prehistoric sites are recorded in these monographs, which also present in some cases lists and distributions of portable antiquities and discussions of prehistoric and early historic occupations. For Wales, the Royal Commission on the Ancient and Historical Monuments of Wales and Monmouthshire has published eleven volumes, and for Scotland, the Royal Commission on the Ancient and Historical Monuments of Scotland has published seventeen volumes on similar monumental remains.

The objective of the Commissions is the definitive description of every visible monument, county by county. Recently, the Commissions have been entrusted with the National Monuments Records, which relate mainly to buildings. Some excavation is carried out by the Commissions to elucidate key sites or features of sites. All of the Commissions have participated in archaeological work other than the county by county undertaking, particularly where areas are under threat of destruction. The publication of 'A Matter of Time' by the R.C.H.M.(England), describing the need for archaeological work in the gravels of England, is a good example of this recent trend.

A similar massive undertaking is the Victoria County History, started about 1900, the aim of which was to present the early history of man. Most counties in England have appeared as a volume or volumes in the V.C.H., but many of these were produced long ago and the discussions are now outdated. Others have recently appeared and have been prepared by archaeologists active in research and compilation of data.

The Ordnance Survey   The preparation and publication of maps by the Ordnance Survey represents one of the most valuable aids to archaeology that any government service provides. The Archaeology Division of the Ordnance Survey records all major visible antiquities on the maps, by constant search and revision, and by using local information and fieldwork. The range of maps for archaeological use has been noted (p. 52).

The Council for British Archaeology The Council for British Archaeology was formed in 1945, and represents national and regional archaeological interests in conservation of monuments, and co-ordination of activities. Its membership includes local societies, universities and museums, and these are combined into a number of Regional Groups which act independently within their own territories but can follow overall C.B.A. guidance. The Council also provides funds to help societies publish papers of national importance, and itself publishes various handbooks on British archaeology. Of considerable value is the Council's *Newsletter and Calendar* which advertises many field projects undertaken in Britain that require volunteer assistance; this is available for £3.00 per year from the C.B.A., 112 Kennington Road, London, SE11 6RE. The Calendar is the best source of information about work in an excavation.

Universities
Prehistoric archaeology is taught in about twenty universities in Britain, but not all of these courses of instruction lead to a primary degree (B.A. or B.Sc.) in archaeology. Some universities provide Diploma courses, or combined Honours courses where

archaeology and a related subject such as history or geography are both studied. Regulations for admission to the various departments of archaeology in Britain are themselves varied; the school subjects most relevant to university archaeological courses in prehistory are probably geography, ancient history, biology and French and German, but opinions and regulations vary, and pure scientists often adapt easily to the less-precise discipline of archaeology. The courses of instruction given in prehistoric archaeology generally provide an outline of the development of man from his earliest recognizable appearance as a hunter–gatherer, through his acquisition of the knowledge of food-production, and metallurgy, to his confrontation with literate societies of the Classical World, or of eighteenth- and nineteenth-century explorers in other parts of the world. Most courses also provide instruction in the procedures of archaeology, fieldwork, excavation, conservation and so on.

University departments of archaeology also attempt to provide facilities and time for research by members of staff, and a number of field projects and excavations are initiated by these departments, often with the collaboration of departments of geography, botany and zoology.

Instruction and careers

Formal instruction in archaeology is provided in Britain by university departments of archaeology and departments of extra-mural studies. The former generally lead to the B.A. degree, the latter sometimes leads to a Diploma in Archaeology. There are also non-Diploma courses conducted from most extra-mural departments, and these may be completed in a weekend of lectures and visits to sites, or may extend over six months. The C.B.A. *Calendar of Excavations* (p. 249) provides details of many of these courses, which may be entirely introductory in their approach to archaeology, or may be extremely specialized; the range of interests provided is very great, and includes excavation techniques, conservation, recording and photography. Some courses include instruction on archaeological sites. Details of B.A. or Diploma courses are obtainable from the University departments concerned.

Careers in prehistoric archaeology are not abundant in Britain, but there is no reason why a first-class archaeologist should not obtain a post after the completion of some research. The possible jobs for a professional include university teaching, museums and the Civil Service.

University teaching positions are not abundant, but increases in the staff of departments, and the creation of new departments provide some hope for future jobs in departments of archaeology and in extra-mural studies. The training for such positions generally involves a primary degree in archaeology (B.A.) followed by research leading to a doctorate; this takes at least six years in all. Often, however, archaeological experience and research publications weigh as heavily as a doctorate in assessing candidates for a position.

Museum jobs are extremely varied in the demands they put upon the holders; some posts are wholly technical, concerned with conservation or photography, others may be almost entirely research and display. A primary degree in archaeology is a useful start, but is not essential, and various museums' diploma courses can be taken before or during the museum work. The variation in scope for archaeological work in museums is indescribable.

Archaeological positions within the Civil Service include the Inspectorate of Ancient Monuments, the Ordnance Survey, and the various Royal Commissions. The range of work again is varied, and can include rescue and research excavations for both the Inspectorate and the Royal Commissions, maintenance of protected monuments, recording of visible antiquities, aerial photographic work, drawing and describing for publication. There are also positions as borough and county archaeologists now. The qualifications required for the work are varied.

Rescue and motorway archaeology
The increasing destruction of archaeological sites of all periods by the development of road systems, urban redevelopment and spread, gravel digging, forestry operations, and deep ploughing, has recently reached what can only be described as epidemic proportions. The full implications of this, that Britain will lose a majority of its ancient sites within the next thirty years, have only recently been publicized by archaeologists (p. 132). An organization

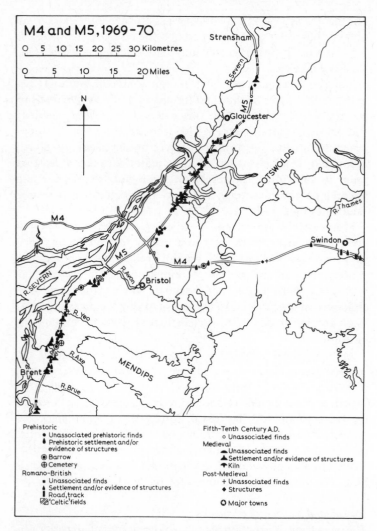

Fig. 78 Map of discoveries made by rescue fieldwork and excavation on the route of the M4 and M5 motorways in the Cotswold–Mendip region (from Archaeological Review 5, 1970, published by Department of Extra-Mural Studies, University of Bristol).

called *Rescue* has been established in the hope of raising enough funds, and support, to preserve or record as much of Britain's prehistoric and historic evidence as possible. *Rescue* has gained the moral support of most established archaeological interests in this country, and requires financial assistance to pursue its aims. The minimum subscription is £1, and the address for funds is: The National Westminster Bank Ltd, 3 The Cross, Worcester.

Motorway archaeology is a part of the whole aspect of rescue operations, and is probably the most dramatic in its recovery of sites from the very teeth of earth-moving machines. Motorways that cross many hundreds of miles, cutting through county and local territorial boundaries, call for more than unrelated salvage operations by local groups of varying energies. In many areas of Britain, the danger of wholesale destruction of sites has been averted through Motorway Research Committees set up to guide local bodies into a co-operative effort to record sites in advance of their inevitable destruction. Not all areas have been aware of the dangers, and various motorways in Scotland and in England have been constructed with virtually no archaeological interest evinced. The loss of evidence from these is not comparable to the loss from the construction of Britain's railways in the last century, but is nonetheless serious.

The land to be covered by or removed for motorways is about 50–100 m wide, and most Research Committees now divide the length of the proposed road into suitable stretches, each one of which is the responsibility of a local museum, society or other group. The areas are searched by fieldwork, by aerial observation and photography, by checking locations of known finds and sites on or near the land. This produces some estimates of the number and type of sites to be destroyed. Field survey and excavation then takes place on selected sites in advance of the motorway work. There follows the task of watching the removal of earth during the actual motorway operations, and recording suspected or hitherto unknown sites literally as they disappear. Co-operation with motorway authorities, and aid from the Department of the Environment, is essential for this activity, but the bulk of the work is done by local amateurs. The results beggar the imagination; on a stretch of the M 5, the recorded sites rose from two to about 150 (fig. 78). An average of two sites per mile of motorway seems established for the M 5 in an area within Somerset, observed by about thirty separate organizations, including flying clubs, museums, societies, schools, and aided by the engineering companies concerned.

It is perhaps here that amateur archaeology should play its greatest part in the acquisition of knowledge about past human behaviour. The days of the wealthy amateur, who could spend his time excavating on his own, or on his friends' lands, are firmly past, and research excavations do not have sufficient finance to allow full amateur participation. Rescue excavations need not be hurried salvage operations, and they may be highly organized motorway-type undertakings, or entirely local attempts to extract evidence from a small threatened site. In all of this the amateur can and must play a leading role, in the acquisition of information about man's past history in these islands.

General books on archaeological procedures and guides to types of field monuments and finds

M. AITKEN, 'Magnetic Location', in Brothwell and Higgs, 1969, 681–94.

J. ALEXANDER, *The Directing of Archaeological Excavations*. John Baker, London, 1970.

J. ARNOLD, *The Shell Book of Country Crafts,*. John Baker, London, 1968.

R. J. C. ATKINSON, *Field Archaeology*. 2nd edition, Methuen, London, 1953.

R. J. C. ATKINSON, 'Resistivity Surveying in Archaeology', in Pyddoke, 1963, 1–30.

D. BROTHWELL, *Digging up Bones*. British Museum, London, 1963.

D. BROTHWELL and E. S. HIGGS (ed), *Science in Archaeology*. 2nd edition, Thames and Hudson, London, 1969.

G. CLARK, *Archaeology and Society*. 3rd edition, Methuen, London, 1957.

M. B. COOKSON, *Photography for Archaeologists*. Parrish, London, 1954.

J. X. W. P. CORCORAN, *The Young Field Archaeologist's Guide*. Bell, London, 1966.

I. W. CORNWALL, *Soils for the Archaeologist*. Phoenix, London, 1958.

Council for British Archaeology, *Handbook of Scientific Aids and Evidence for Archaeologists*. C.B.A., London, 1970.

O. G. S. CRAWFORD, *Archaeology in the Field*. Phoenix, London, 1953.

S. J. DE LAET, *Archaeology and its Problems*. Phoenix, London, 1957.

L. DE PAOR, *Archaeology. An illustrated introduction*. Penguin, London, 1967.

E. A. DOWMAN, *Conservation in Field Archaeology*. Methuen, London, 1970.

R. FEACHEM, *A Guide to Prehistoric Scotland*. Batsford, London, 1963.

D. H. FRYER, *Surveying for Archaeologists*. 4th edition, University of Durham, 1971.

F. H. GOODYEAR, *Archaeological Site Science*. Heinemann, London, 1971.

L. GRINSELL, P. RAHTZ, A. WARHURST, *The Preparation of Archaeological Reports*. John Baker, London, 1966.

R. F. HEIZER and J. A. GRAHAM, *A Guide to Field Methods in Archaeology*. National Press, Palo Alto, California, 1967.

H. HODGES, *Artifacts*. John Baker, London, 1964.

F. HOLE and R. F. HEIZER, *An Introduction to Prehistoric Archaeology*. 2nd edition, Holt, Rinehart and Winston, New York, 1969.

K. M. KENYON, *Beginning in Archaeology*. Dent, London, 1964.

K. P. OAKLEY, *Man the Tool-maker*. British Museum, London, 1952.

Ordnance Survey, *Field Archaeology*. *Some Notes for Beginners*. 4th edition, H.M.S.O., London, 1963 (5th edition in preparation).

S. PIGGOTT, *Approach to Archaeology*. Adam and Black, London, 1959.

H. A. POLACH and J. GOLSON, *Collection of Specimens for Radiocarbon Dating and Interpretation of Results*. Australian Institute of Aboriginal Studies, Canberra, 1966.

E. PYDDOKE (ed), *The Scientist and Archaeology*. Phoenix, London, 1963.

Royal Commission on Historical Monuments (England), *A Matter of Time*. H.M.S.O., London, 1960.

M. L. RYDER, *Animal Bones in Archaeology*. Blackwell, Oxford, 1969.

J. K. S. ST JOSEPH (ed), *The Uses of Air Photography*. John Baker, London, 1966.

N. THOMAS, *A Guide to Prehistoric England*. Batsford, London, 1960.

W. WATSON, *Flint Implements*. British Museum, London, 1950.

G. WEBSTER, *Practical Archaeology*. Adam and Black, London, 1963.

M. WHEELER, *Archaeology from the Earth*. Penguin, London, 1956.

E. S. WOOD, *Collins Field Guide to Archaeology*. Collins, London, 1963.

Excavations and field survey reports

A list of archaeological excavations and field surveys, chosen mainly from recent issues of national journals in England, Wales and Scotland, to indicate different approaches to sites and areas. The excavation reports describe the methods of excavation, all have plans of sites with details of the structures recovered, and some attempt to reconstruct and interpret the remains. The field surveys indicate the reasons for the work undertaken, the methods used, and some attempt to explain the results.

L. ALCOCK, Castell Odo: an embanked settlement on Mynydd Ystum, near Aberdaron, Caernarvonshire. *Arch. Camb.* 109. 1960, 78–135.
(excavation by trench and square mainly vertical to obtain sequence of occupation).

L. ALCOCK, Excavations at South Cadbury Castle, 1967. A summary report. *Ant. J.* 48, 1968, 6–17.
(suggestions made by geophysical survey tested by excavation, see fig. 12 in this book).

L. ALCOCK, Excavations at South Cadbury Castle, 1970. Summary report. *Ant. J.* 51, 1971, 1–7.
(short report on season's work, with illustration of area excavations on large hill-fort, and entire area geophysically surveyed as guide to excavation and test of equipment).

J. ALEXANDER, P. and A. OZANNE, Report on the investigation of a round barrow on Arreton Down, Isle of Wight. *Proc. Prehist. Soc.* 26, 1960, 263–302.
(excavation of a barrow disturbed 1237, early 19th century, early 20th century, 1942).

P. ASHBEE, The great barrow at Bishop's Waltham, Hampshire. *Proc. Prehist. Soc.* 23, 1957, 137–66.
(rescue excavation of barrow by narrow trenches, central area expanded to reveal wooden coffin and soil silhouette of body; attempt to relate structure to society of the time).

P. ASHBEE, *The Bronze Age Round Barrow in Britain*. Phoenix House, London, 1960.
(description of barrow features with many examples of excavation).

P. ASHBEE, The Fussell's Lodge long barrow. Excavations 1957. *Archaeologia* 100, 1966, 1–80.
(extensive box and trench excavation, full description of methods, reconstruction of social and economic implications).

R. J. C. ATKINSON, *Stonehenge*. Hamish Hamilton, London, 1956.
(meticulous excavation of part of monument to solve certain problems; display–reconstruction of monument).

G. P. BURSTOW and G. HOLLEYMAN, Late Bronze Age settlement on Itford Hill, Sussex. *Proc. Prehist. Soc.* 23, 1957, 167–212.
(box system excavation with trenches on periphery, informative photographs, interpretation and reconstruction of huts and settlement with associated fields; evidence of agricultural practices).

M. CAMPBELL and M. L. S. SANDEMAN, Mid-Argyll: a field survey of the historic and prehistoric monuments. *Proc. Soc. Ant. Scot.* 95, 1961–2, 1–125.
(catalogue of ancient monuments over *circa* 300 square miles, survey 1954–63, with descriptions and N.G.R.).

P. M. CHRISTIE, A barrow-cemetery of the second millennium B.C. in Wiltshire, England. *Proc. Prehist. Soc.* 33, 1967, 336–66.
(radial baulks necessary for demonstration and determination of multiple-period monument).

J. G. D. CLARK, *Excavations at Star Carr*. C.U.P., Cambridge, 1954.
(open excavation of water-logged settlement; use of environmental data and economic evidence for reconstructions of conditions; recovery of organic material for conservation).

J. G. D. CLARK, Excavations at the Neolithic site at Hurst Fen, Mildenhall, Suffolk. *Proc. Prehist. Soc.* 26, 1960, 202–45.
(open excavation with description of procedures, recognition of hollows and scoops but no reconstruction possible and admitted).

J. M. COLES, The early settlement of Scotland: excavations at Morton, Fife. *Proc. Prehist. Soc.* 37, 1971, 284–366.
(open excavation over period of years, environmental data extensively used, reconstruction of local conditions).

J. M. COLES, F. A. HIBBERT and C. F. CLEMENTS, Prehistoric Roads and Tracks in Somerset, England: 2, Neolithic. *Proc. Prehist. Soc.* 36, 1970, 125–51.
(fieldwork by local archaeologist, excavation of selected sites in peat, field survey of Neolithic activity in area).

J. M. COLES and D. D. A. SIMPSON, The excavation of a Neolithic round barrow at Pitnacree, Perthshire, Scotland. *Proc. Prehist. Soc.* 31, 1965, 34–57.
(box and trench system altered to open excavation where possible; field survey of related monuments).

H. COUTTS, *Ancient Monuments of Tayside.* Dundee Museum and Art Gallery, 1970.
(description and distribution of monuments from literature and field-work).

B. CUNLIFFE, A Bronze Age settlement at Chalton, Hants (site 78). *Ant. J.* 50, 1970, 1–13.
(rescue excavation of three days' duration).

G. EOGAN, The excavation of a stone alignment and circle at Cholwich-town, Lee Moor, Devonshire, England. *Proc. Prehist. Soc.* 30, 1964, 25–38.
(open excavation over 200 m to expose entire row and circle).

R. W. FEACHEM, The palisaded settlements at Harehope, Peeblesshire. Excavations 1960. *Proc. Soc. Ant. Scot.* 93, 1959–60, 174–91.
(small open excavation within site and box system at entrance allows reconstruction of palisaded homestead; sequence of buildings elucidated by horizontal observations).

A. FLEMING, Territorial patterns in Bronze Age Wessex. *Proc. Prehist. Soc.* 37, 1971, 138–66.
(using field surveys of others, distributional and spacing evidence to reconstruct societies).

J. FORDE-JOHNSTON, The hill-forts of the Clwyds. *Arch. Camb.* 114, 1965, 146–78.
(survey of surface features of hill-forts in local area).

A. FOX. Celtic fields and farms on Dartmoor, in the light of recent excavations at Kestor. *Proc. Prehist. Soc.* 20, 1954, 87–102.
(survey of field systems and huts, excavations and reconstructions).

W. E. GRIFFITHS, The excavation of stone circles near Penmaenmawr, North Wales. *Proc. Prehist. Soc.* 26, 1960, 303–39.
(radial and peripheral trenches to expose structural features of circle, with central area expanded; distribution of sites in local area, and attempt to relate site to region).

L. V. GRINSELL, *The Archaeology of Exmoor.* David and Charles, Newton Abbot, 1970.
(survey based on fieldwork and aerial photographs, with maps and lists of sites including N.G.R.).

B. R. HARTLEY, The Wandlebury Iron Age hill-fort, excavations of 1955–6. *Proc. Camb. Ant. Soc.* 50, 1956, 1–27.
(small box excavation within embankments, and trench through ditch and bank system).

A. S. HENSHALL, A dagger-grave and other cist burials at Ashgrove, Methilhill, Fife. *Proc. Soc. Ant. Scot.* 97, 1963–4, 166–79.
(rescue excavation of cist burials in housing estate, with local vandalism upon discovery; need for guard upon such sites).

A. S. HENSHALL and J. C. WALLACE, A Bronze Age cist burial at Masterton, Pitreavie, Fife. *Proc. Soc. Ant. Scot.* 96, 1962–3, 145–54.
(excavation of cist with detailed recording of jet necklace).

C. H. HOULDER, The excavation of a Neolithic stone implement factory on Mynydd Rhiw in Caernarvonshire. *Proc. Prehist. Soc.* 27, 1961, 108–43.
(area excavation plus stratigraphical details of site; character of site explained in economic terms).

A. D. LACAILLE and W. F. GRIMES, The prehistory of Caldey. *Arch. Camb.* 104, 1955, 85–165, and 110, 1961, 30–70.
(geological and archaeological investigation of earliest human occupation, plus survey of later prehistoric finds on island).

I. H. LONGWORTH, A massive cist with multiple burials of the Iron Age at Lochend, Dunbar. *Proc. Soc. Ant. Scot.* 98, 1964–6, 173–98.
(excavation procedure for rescue examination of cist filled with human remains).

A. MACE, An upper Palaeolithic open-site at Hengistbury Head, Christchurch, Hants. *Proc. Prehist. Soc.* 25, 1959, 233–59.
(open site excavated by box system opening from exploratory trench; boxes progressively filled-in as excavation proceeded).

E. W. MACKIE, A dwelling site of the earlier Iron Age at Ballevulin, Tiree, excavated in 1912 by A. Henderson Bishop. *Proc. Soc. Ant. Scot.* 96, 1962–3, 155–83.
(publication of site excavated fifty years before, based on excavator's notes and finds).

G. S. MAXWELL, Excavations at Drumcarrow, Fife; an Iron Age unenclosed settlement. *Proc. Soc. Ant. Scot.* 100, 1967–8, 100–8.
(open excavation of small collapsed house with reconstruction).

C. B. M. MCBURNEY, Report on the first season's fieldwork on British upper Palaeolithic cave deposits. *Proc. Prehist. Soc.* 25, 1959, 260–9.
(excavation at cave entrance by box system for stratigraphy and dating).

F. DE M. MORGAN, The excavation of a long barrow at Nutbane, Hants. *Proc. Prehist. Soc.* 25, 1959, 15–51.
(hitherto unrecognized barrow; open excavation with trenches across mound and ditches, reconstruction of mortuary enclosure).

S. PIGGOTT, *The West Kennet Long Barrow. Excavations 1955–56.* Ministry of Works Archaeological Reports, 4. H.M.S.O., 1962.
(excavation for research into burial practices and for display reconstruction of monument; single trench across part of mound, burial chambers examined and restored).

S. PIGGOTT and D. D. A. SIMPSON, Excavation of a stone circle at Croft Moraig, Perthshire, Scotland. *Proc. Prehist. Soc.* 37, 1971, 1–15.
(box system for open excavation plus sections; photogrammetric record).

J. RADLEY and P. MELLARS, A Mesolithic structure at Deepcar, Yorkshire, England, and the affinities of its associated flint industries. *Proc. Prehist. Soc.* 30, 1964, 1–24.
(open excavation with densities of finds used to reconstruct activities; mainly typological discussion).

P. RAHTZ, Excavations at Shearplace Hill, Sydling St Nicholas, Dorset, England. *Proc. Prehist. Soc.* 28, 1962, 289–328.
(open excavation of settlement, relation with field system and roads).

C. A. RALEGH RADFORD, Prehistoric settlements on Dartmoor and the Cornish Moors. *Proc. Prehist. Soc.* 18, 1952, 55–84.
(fieldwork on hut-circles and associated fields).

I. F. SMITH and D. D. A. SIMPSON, Excavation of a round barrow on Overton Hill, North Wiltshire. *Proc. Prehist. Soc.* 32, 1966, 122–55.
(open excavation following drawing of transverse sections; children's graves leading to suggestions about nature of family tomb).

I. M. STEAD, An Iron Age hill-fort at Grimthorpe, Yorkshire, England. *Proc. Prehist. Soc.* 34, 1968, 148–90.
(area excavation plus trenches to examine embanked areas, see fig. 64 in this book).

M. E. C. STEWART, The excavation of two circular enclosures at Dalnaglar, Perthshire. *Proc. Soc. Ant. Scot.* 95, 1961–2, 134–58.
(field survey of enclosures and excavation: see fig. 1 in this book for field survey results, fig. 17, 41, 42, 43 for site).

F. DE M. VATCHER, The excavation of the long mortuary enclosure on Normanton Down, Wilts. *Proc. Prehist. Soc.* 27, 1961, 160–73.
(box system over most of enclosure, compact report).

G. J. WAINWRIGHT, The excavation of a Durotrigian farmstead near Tollard Royal in Cranbourne Chase, southern England. *Proc. Prehist. Soc.* 34, 1968, 102–47.
(box plan for open excavation, total settlement excavated, sectioning of pits and post-holes).

G. J. WAINWRIGHT and I. H. LONGWORTH, *Durrington Walls: Excavations 1966–1968.* *Rep. Res. Comm. Soc. Ant. London* 29, 1971.
(open excavation, use of machinery on enormous site, followed by careful excavation allowing detailed publication with reconstructions).

R. E. M. WHEELER, *Maiden Castle, Dorset. Rep. Res. Comm. Soc. Ant. London* 12, 1943.
(selective excavation by box and trench of features of hill-fort, across ramparts, at gateway, and within fort; extremely complex sequence, full publication).

J. WYMER, Excavations at the Maglemosian sites at Thatcham, Berkshire, England. *Proc. Prehist. Soc.* 28, 1962, 329–61.
(extended box system over wide area linking sites, coffer dam for waterlogged sites, environmental data for reconstruction of conditions).

Index